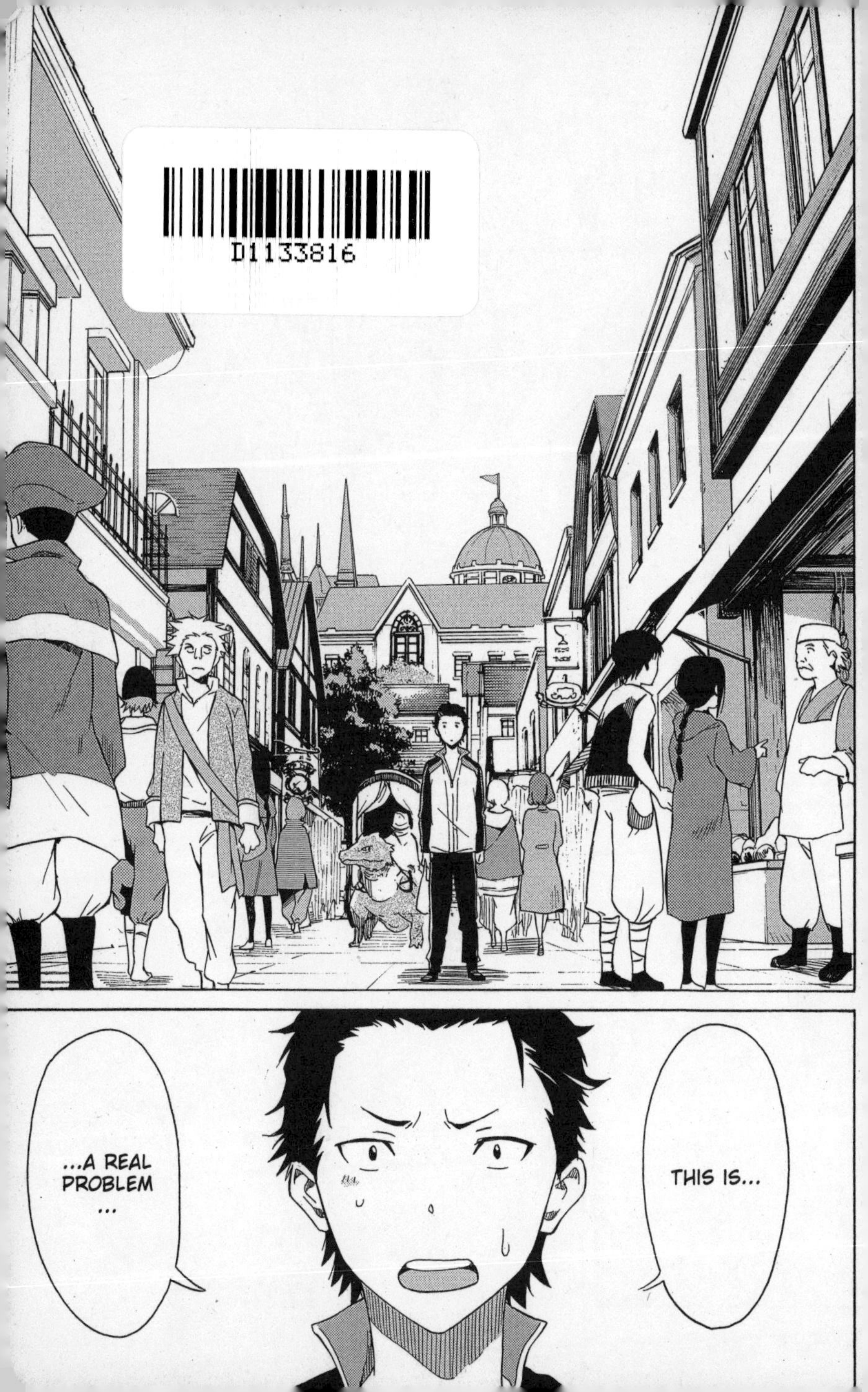
THIS IS...
...A REAL PROBLEM ...

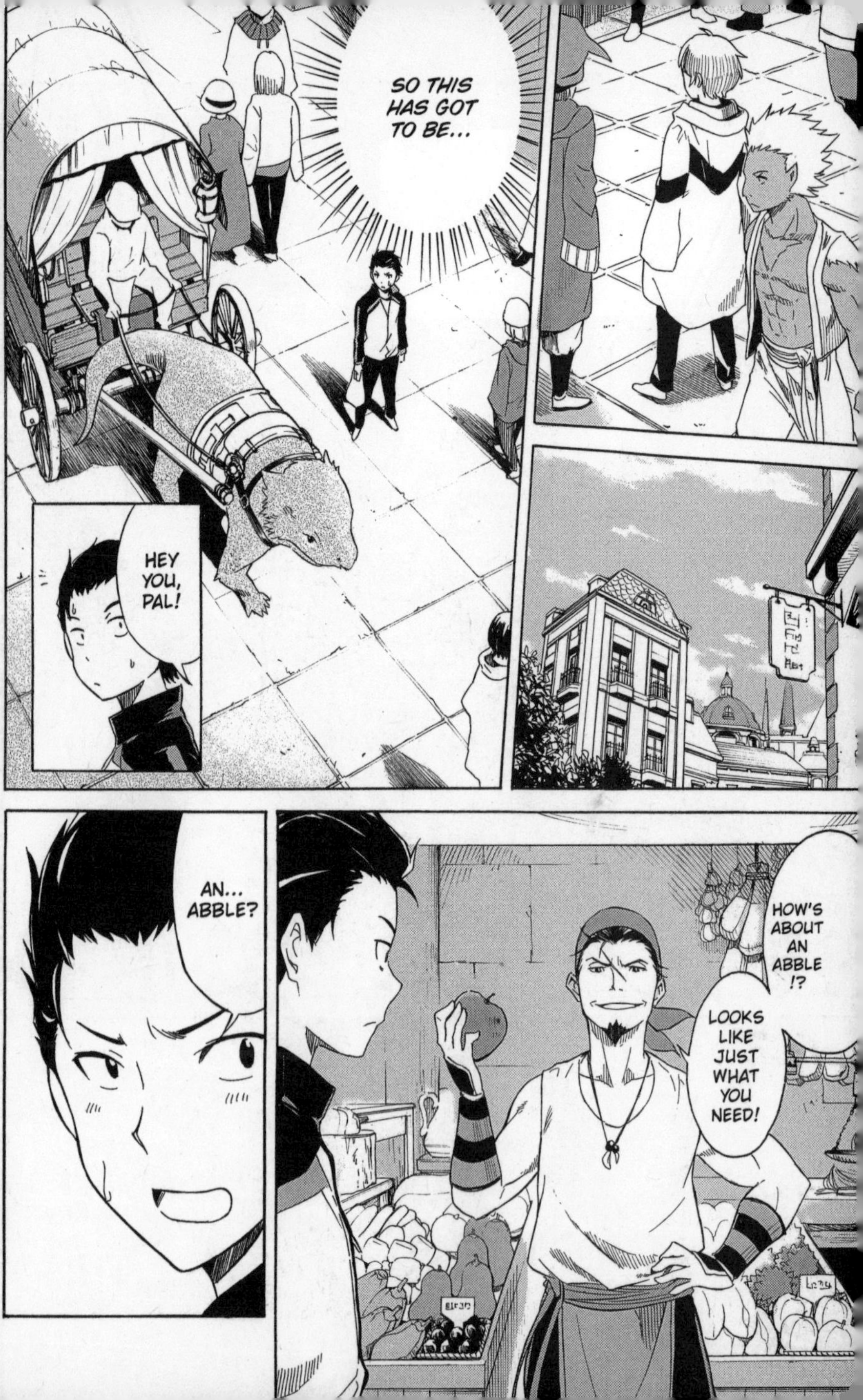
SO THIS HAS GOT TO BE...
HEY YOU, PAL!
HOW'S ABOUT AN ABBLE !?
LOOKS LIKE JUST WHAT YOU NEED!
AN... ABBLE?

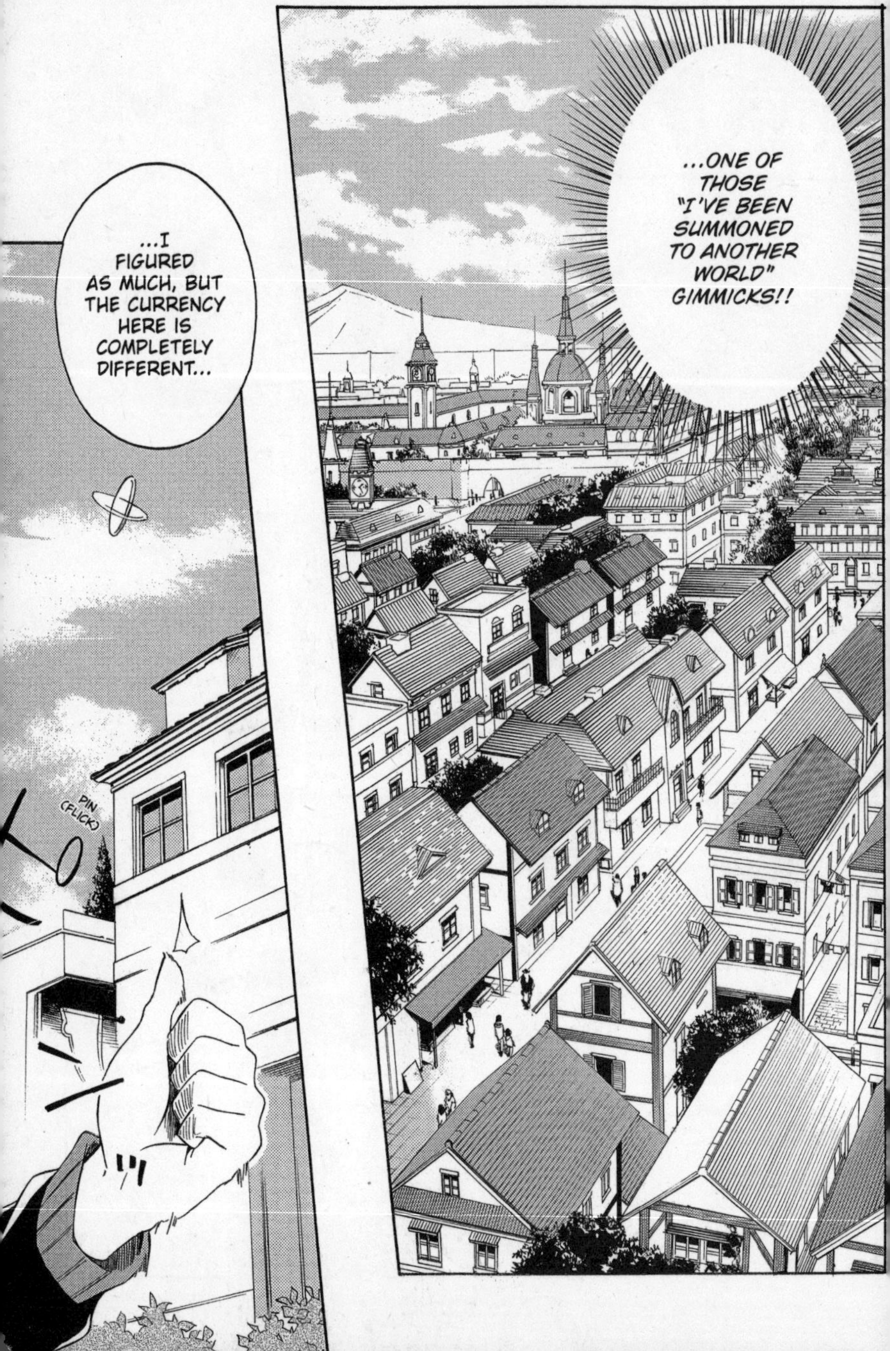
...ONE OF THOSE "I'VE BEEN SUMMONED TO ANOTHER WORLD" GIMMICKS!!
...I FIGURED AS MUCH, BUT THE CURRENCY HERE IS COMPLETELY DIFFERENT...
PIN (FLICK)

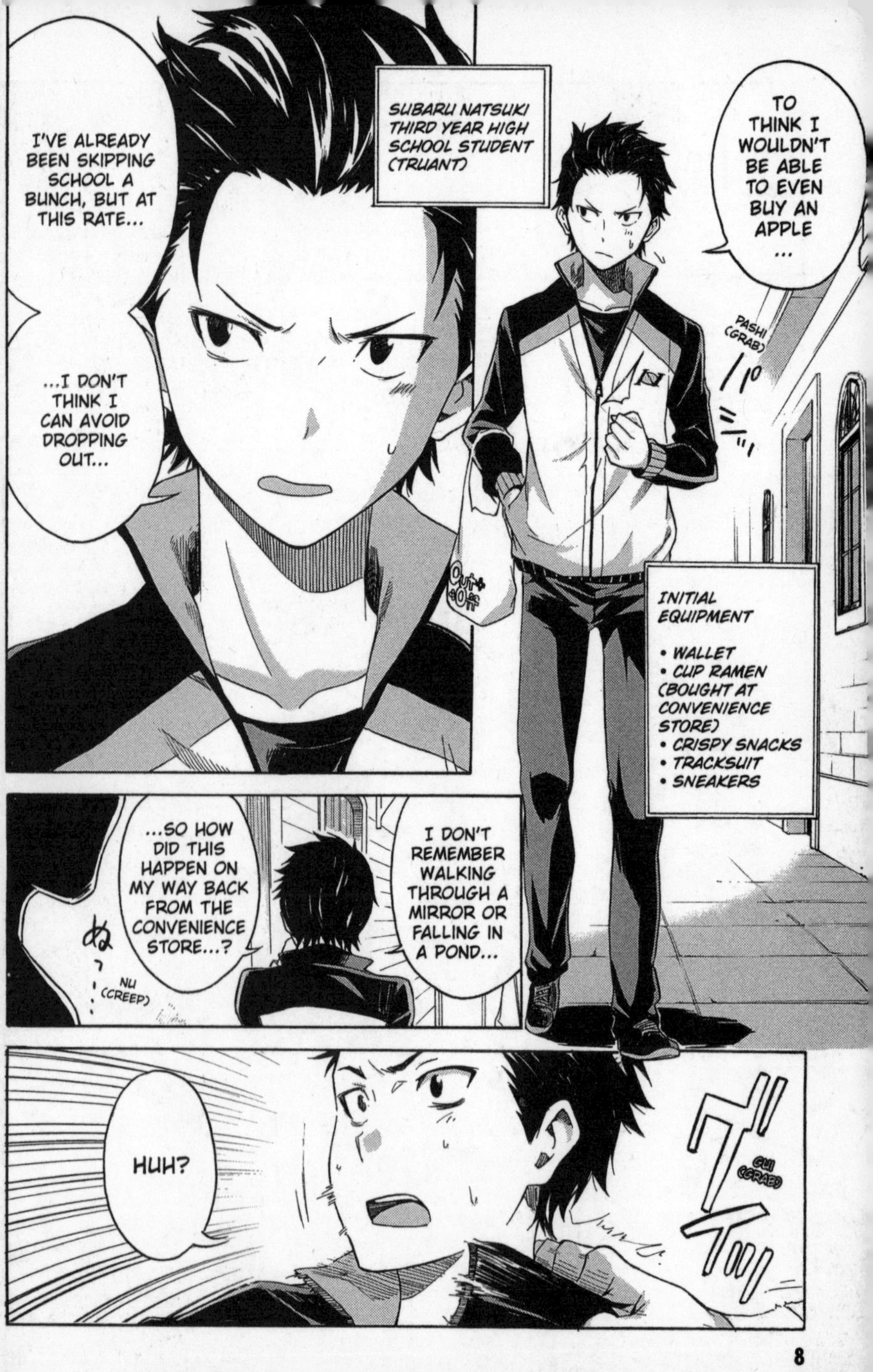
TO THINK I WOULDN'T BE ABLE TO EVEN BUY AN APPLE ...
SUBARU NATSUKI THIRD YEAR HIGH SCHOOL STUDENT (TRUANT)
PASHI (GRAB)
INITIAL EQUIPMENT
• WALLET
• CUP RAMEN (BOUGHT AT CONVENIENCE STORE)
• CRISPY SNACKS
• TRACKSUIT
• SNEAKERS
I'VE ALREADY BEEN SKIPPING SCHOOL A BUNCH, BUT AT THIS RATE...
...I DON'T THINK I CAN AVOID DROPPING OUT...
I DON'T REMEMBER WALKING THROUGH A MIRROR OR FALLING IN A POND...
...SO HOW DID THIS HAPPEN ON MY WAY BACK FROM THE CONVENIENCE STORE...?
ぬ
NU (CREEP)
グイ
GUI (GRAB)
HUH?

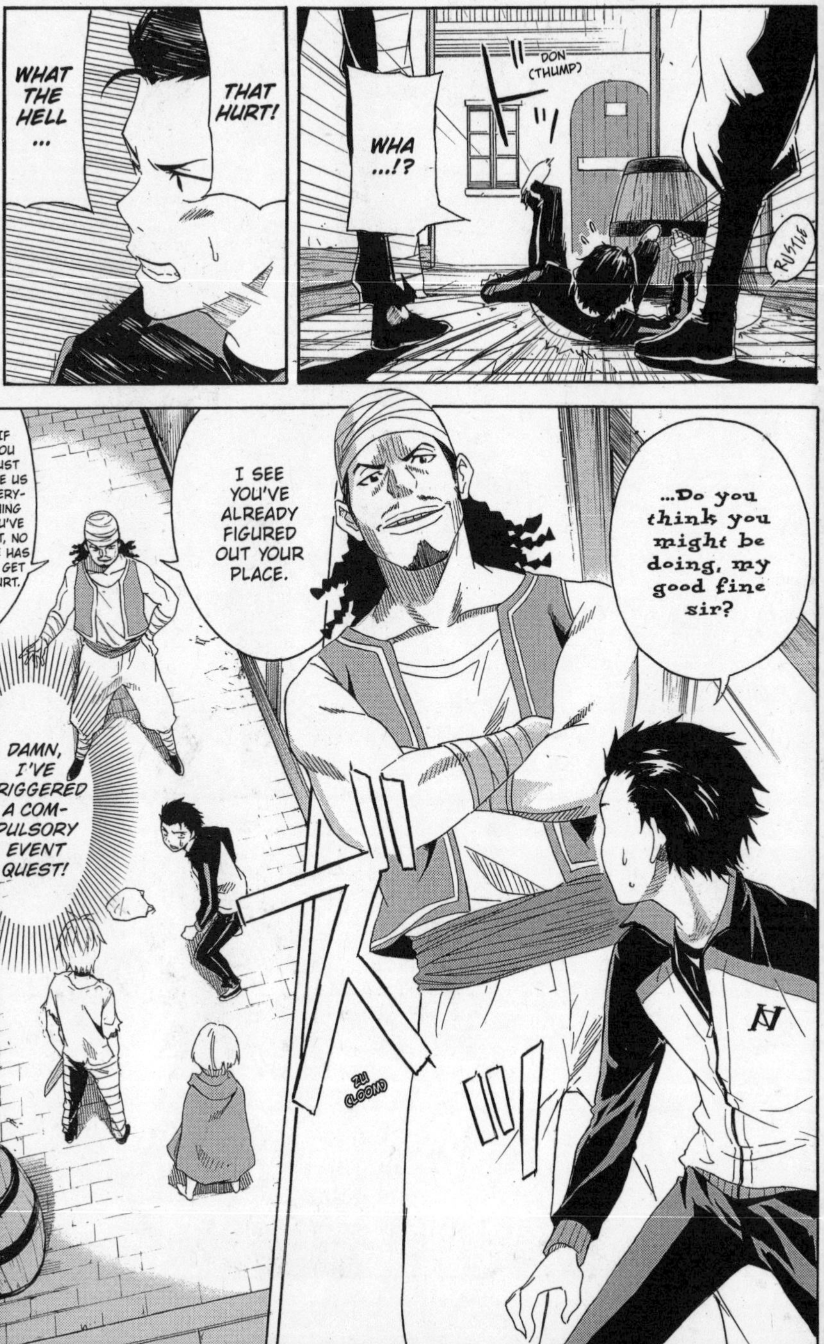
DON (THUMP)
WHA ...!?
RUSTLE
THAT HURT!
WHAT THE HELL ...
...Do you think you might be doing, my good fine sir?
I SEE YOU'VE ALREADY FIGURED OUT YOUR PLACE.
IF YOU JUST GIVE US EVERY-THING YOU'VE GOT, NO ONE HAS TO GET HURT.
DAMN, I'VE TRIGGERED A COM-PULSORY EVENT QUEST!
ZU (GLOOM)

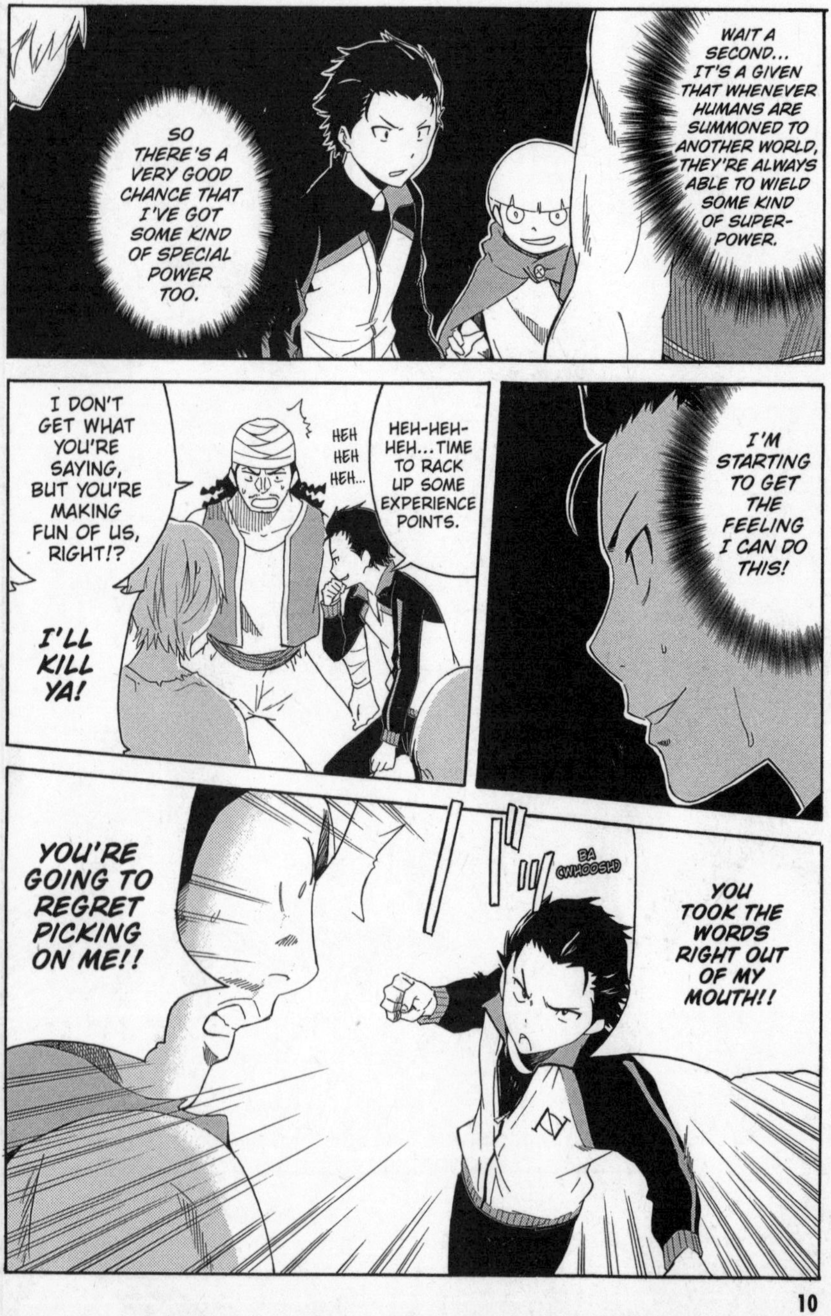
WAIT A SECOND... IT'S A GIVEN THAT WHENEVER HUMANS ARE SUMMONED TO ANOTHER WORLD, THEY'RE ALWAYS ABLE TO WIELD SOME KIND OF SUPER-POWER.
SO THERE'S A VERY GOOD CHANCE THAT I'VE GOT SOME KIND OF SPECIAL POWER TOO.
I'M STARTING TO GET THE FEELING I CAN DO THIS!
HEH-HEH-HEH...TIME TO RACK UP SOME EXPERIENCE POINTS.
HEH HEH HEH...
I DON'T GET WHAT YOU'RE SAYING, BUT YOU'RE MAKING FUN OF US, RIGHT!?
I'LL KILL YA!
BA (WHOOSH)
YOU TOOK THE WORDS RIGHT OUT OF MY MOUTH!!
YOU'RE GOING TO REGRET PICKING ON ME!!

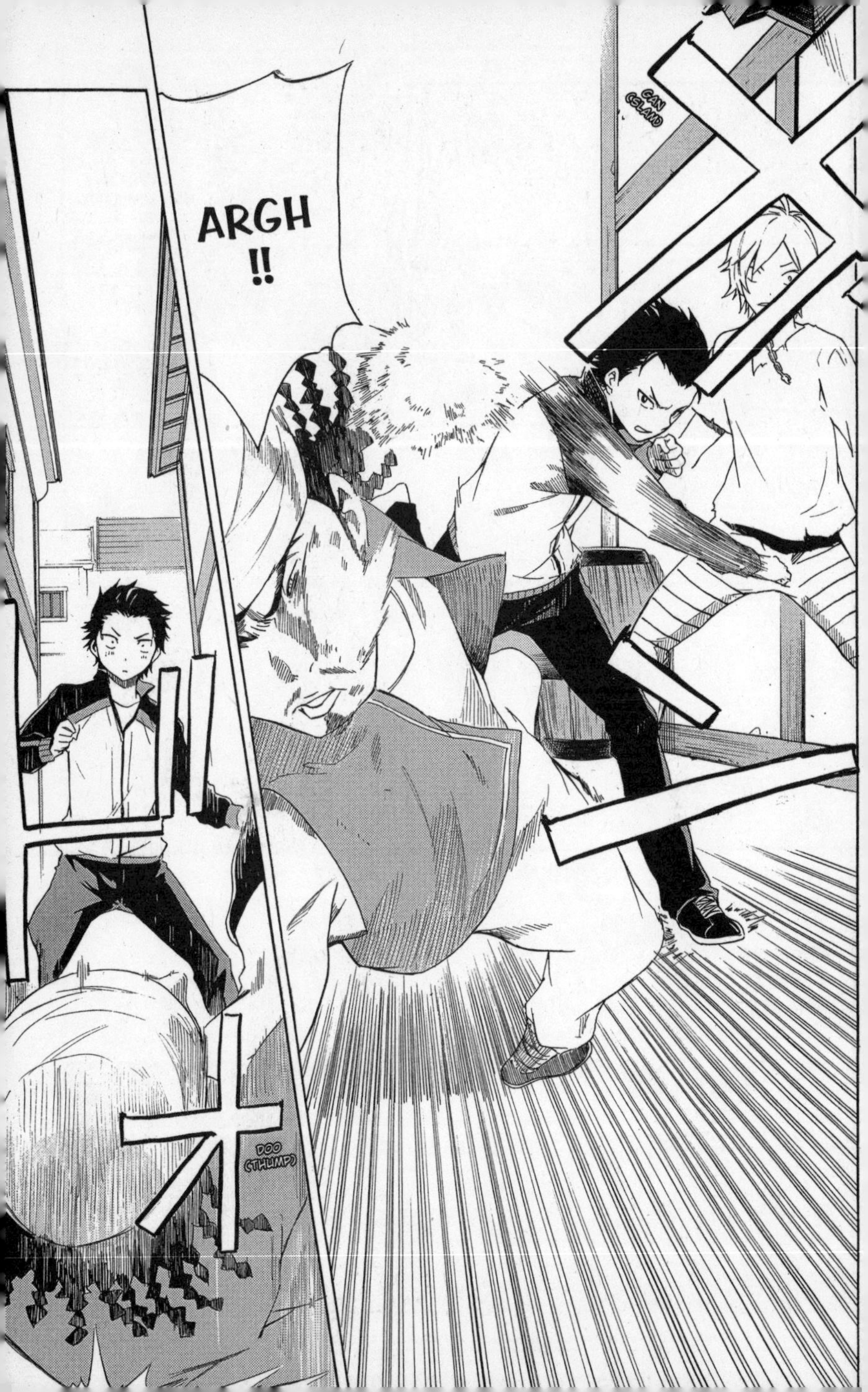
GAN (SLAM)
ARGH !!
DOO (THUMP)

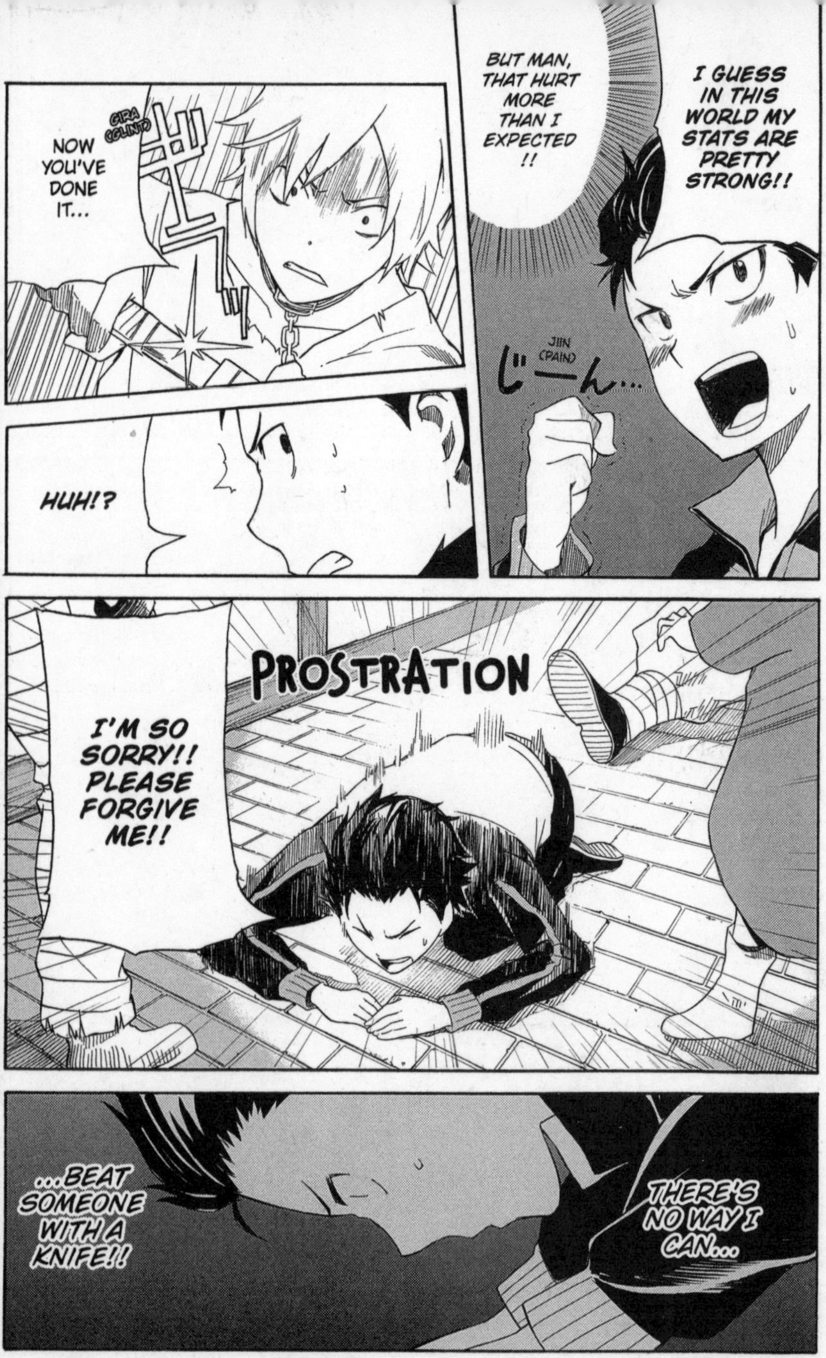
I GUESS IN THIS WORLD MY STATS ARE PRETTY STRONG!!
BUT MAN, THAT HURT MORE THAN I EXPECTED!!
JIIN (PAIN)
じーん…
GIRA (GLINT)
NOW YOU'VE DONE IT...
HUH!?
PROSTRATION
I'M SO SORRY!! PLEASE FORGIVE ME!!
THERE'S NO WAY I CAN...
...BEAT SOMEONE WITH A KNIFE!!

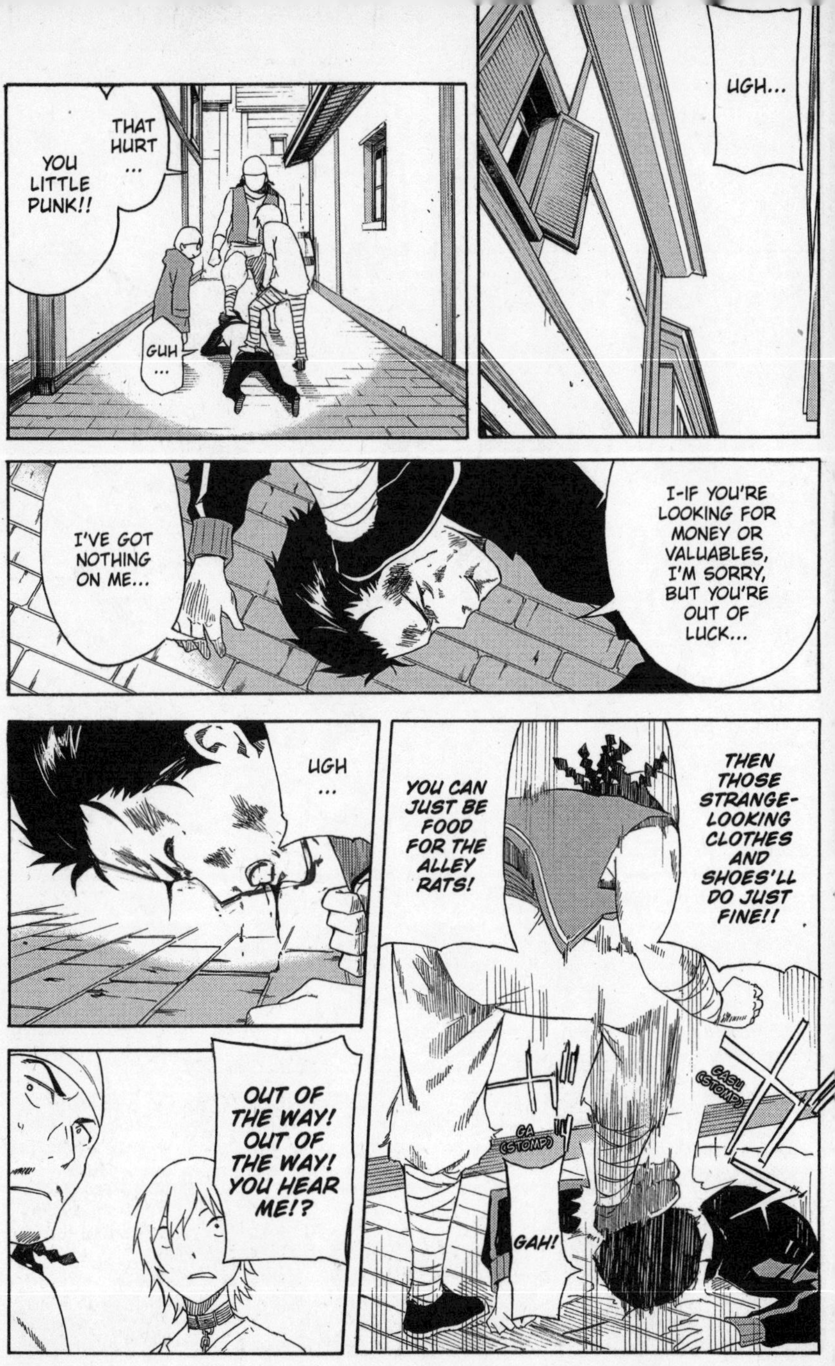
UGH...
THAT HURT...
YOU LITTLE PUNK!!
GUH...
I-IF YOU'RE LOOKING FOR MONEY OR VALUABLES, I'M SORRY, BUT YOU'RE OUT OF LUCK...
I'VE GOT NOTHING ON ME...
THEN THOSE STRANGE-LOOKING CLOTHES AND SHOES'LL DO JUST FINE!!
YOU CAN JUST BE FOOD FOR THE ALLEY RATS!
GASU (STOMP)
GA (STOMP)
GAH!
UGH...
OUT OF THE WAY! OUT OF THE WAY! YOU HEAR ME!?

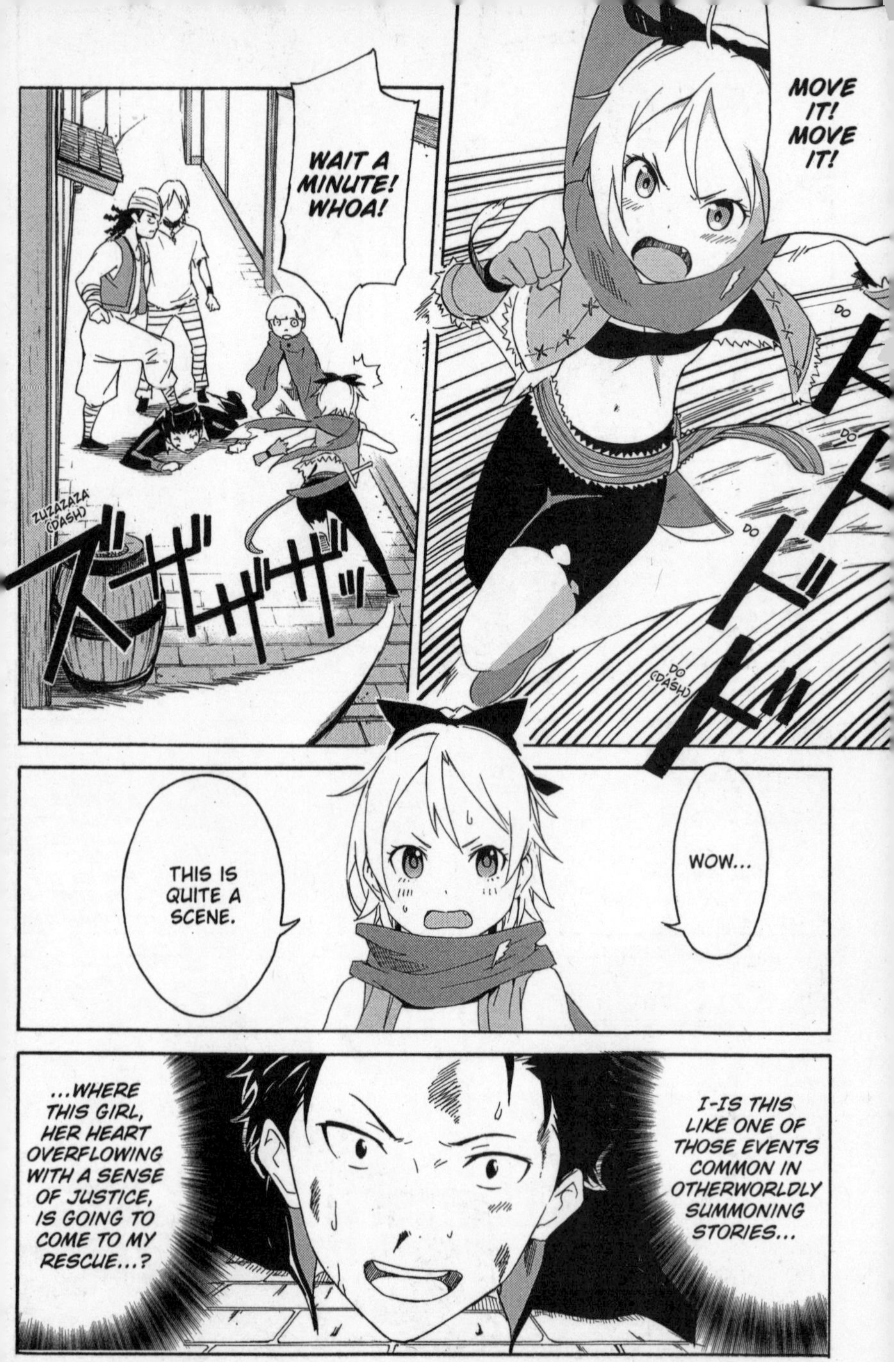
MOVE IT! MOVE IT!
DO
DO
DO
DO (DASH)
WAIT A MINUTE! WHOA!
ZUZAZAZA (DASH)
WOW...
THIS IS QUITE A SCENE.
I-IS THIS LIKE ONE OF THOSE EVENTS COMMON IN OTHERWORLDLY SUMMONING STORIES...
...WHERE THIS GIRL, HER HEART OVERFLOWING WITH A SENSE OF JUSTICE, IS GOING TO COME TO MY RESCUE...?

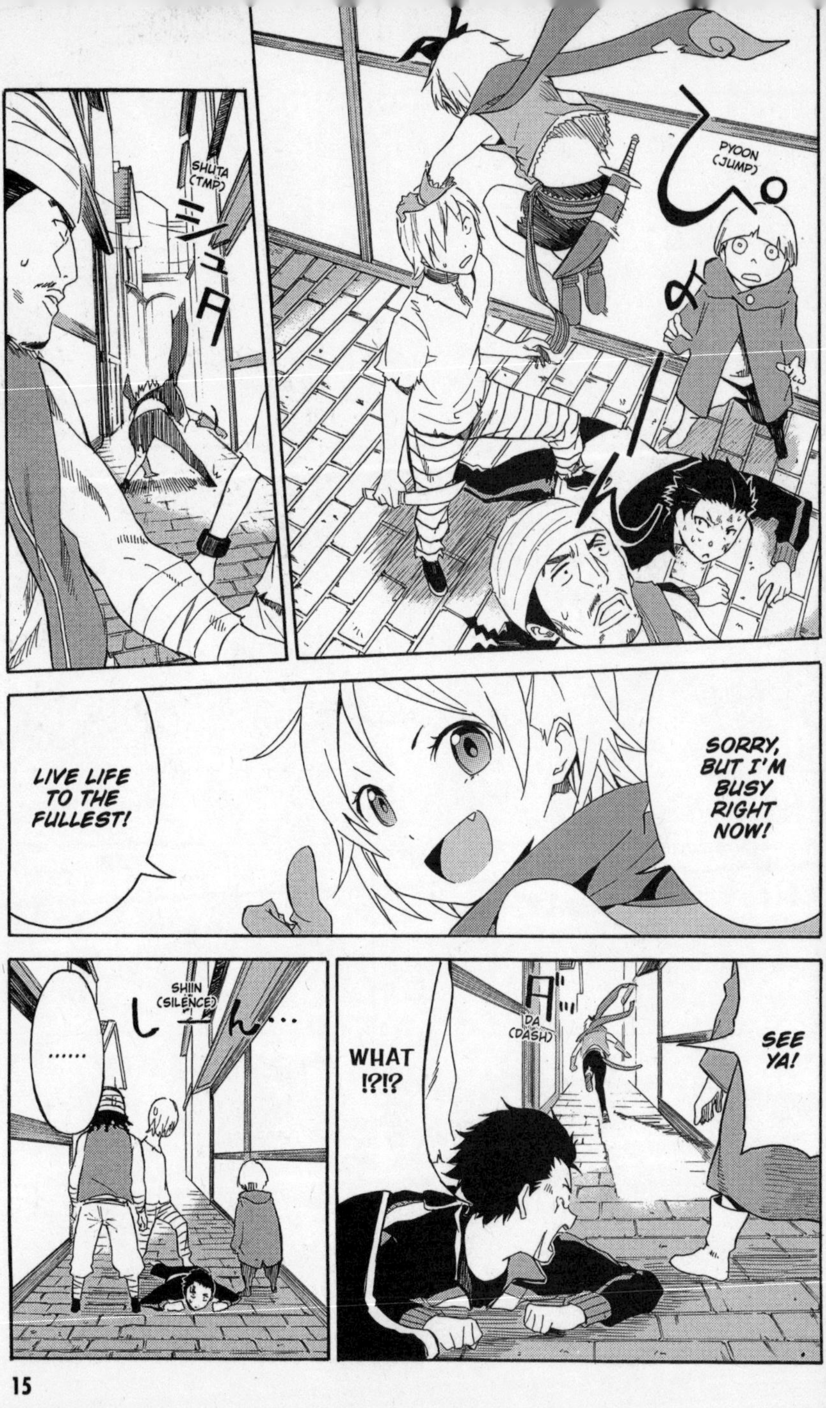
PYOON (JUMP)
ぴょーん
SHUTA (TMP)
シュタ
SORRY, BUT I'M BUSY RIGHT NOW!
LIVE LIFE TO THE FULLEST!
SEE YA!
DA (DASH)
ダッ
WHAT !?!?
SHIIN (SILENCE)
しーん…
......

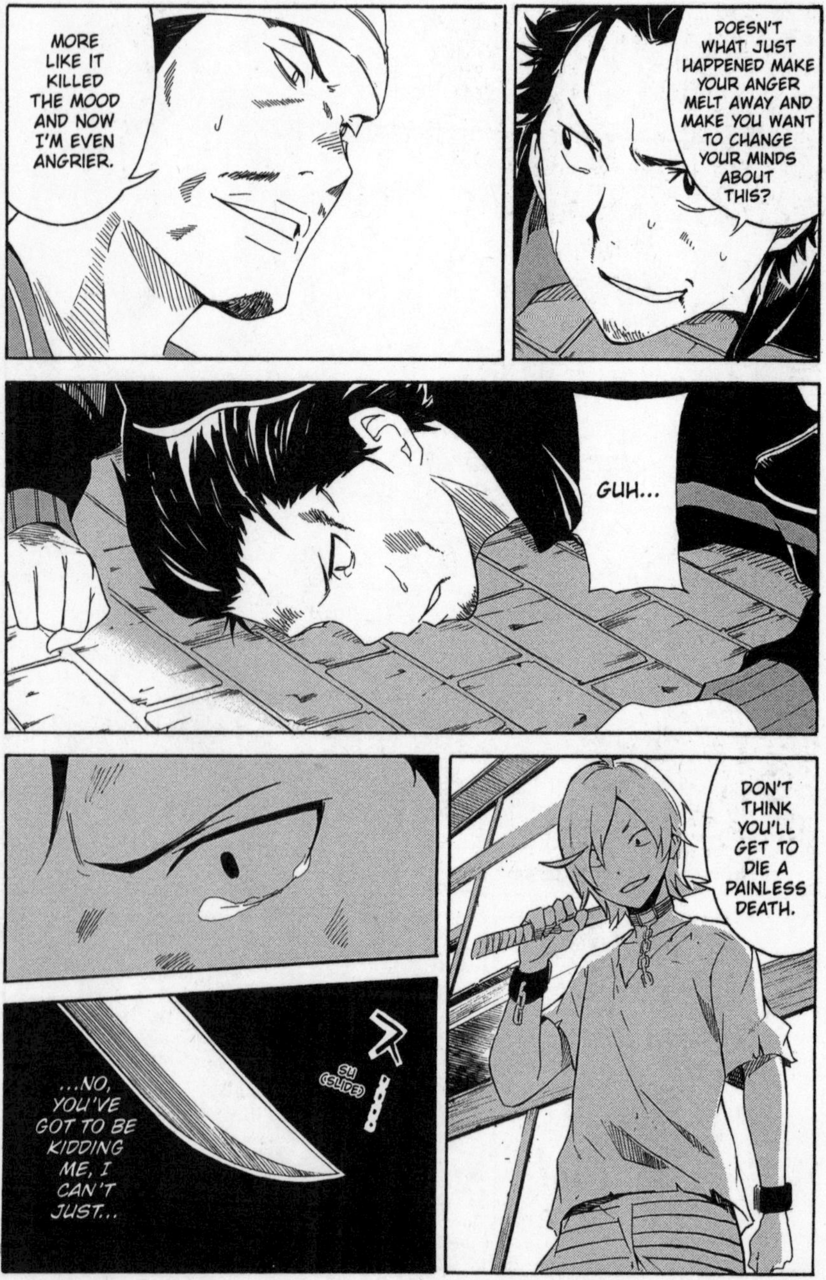
DOESN'T WHAT JUST HAPPENED MAKE YOUR ANGER MELT AWAY AND MAKE YOU WANT TO CHANGE YOUR MINDS ABOUT THIS?
MORE LIKE IT KILLED THE MOOD AND NOW I'M EVEN ANGRIER.
GUH...
DON'T THINK YOU'LL GET TO DIE A PAINLESS DEATH.
SU (SLIDE)
...NO, YOU'VE GOT TO BE KIDDING ME, I CAN'T JUST...

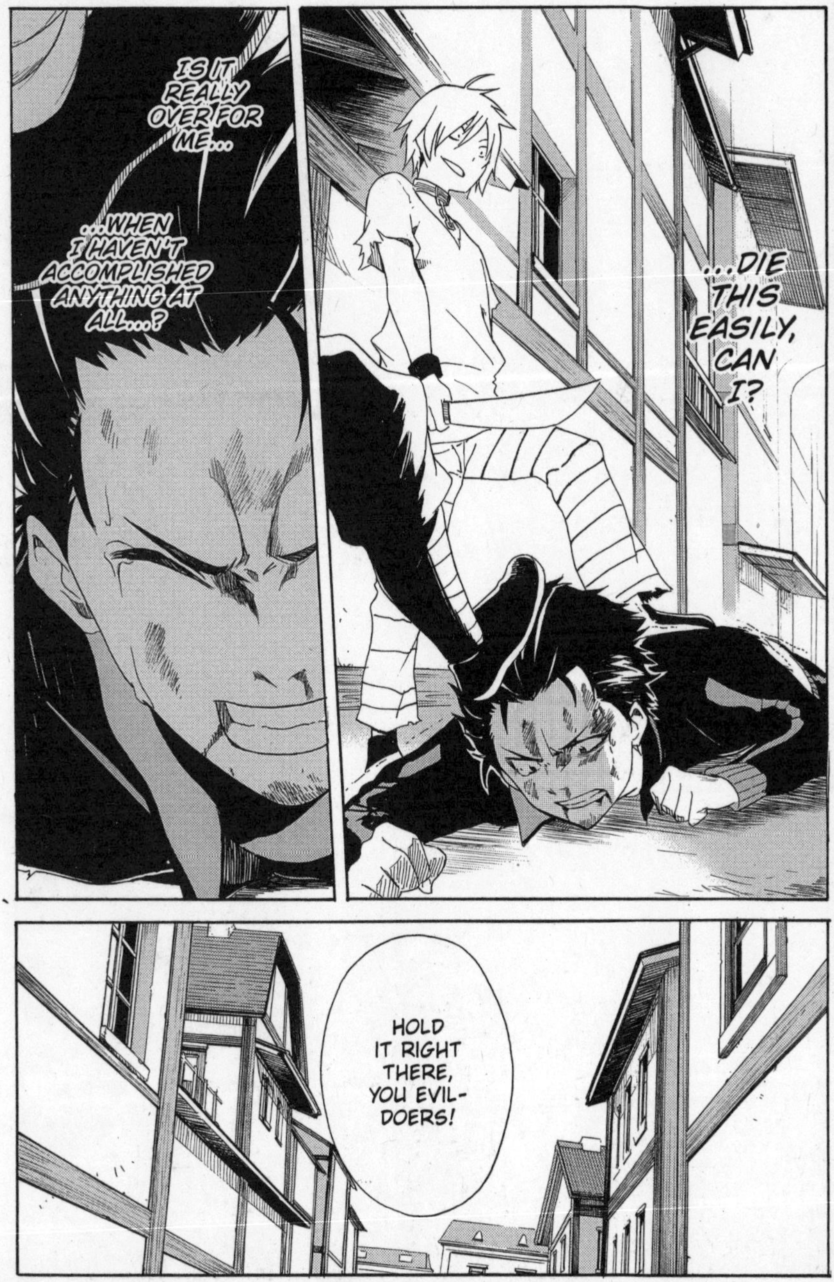
...DIE THIS EASILY, CAN I?
IS IT REALLY OVER FOR ME...
...WHEN I HAVEN'T ACCOMPLISHED ANYTHING AT ALL...?
HOLD IT RIGHT THERE, YOU EVIL-DOERS!

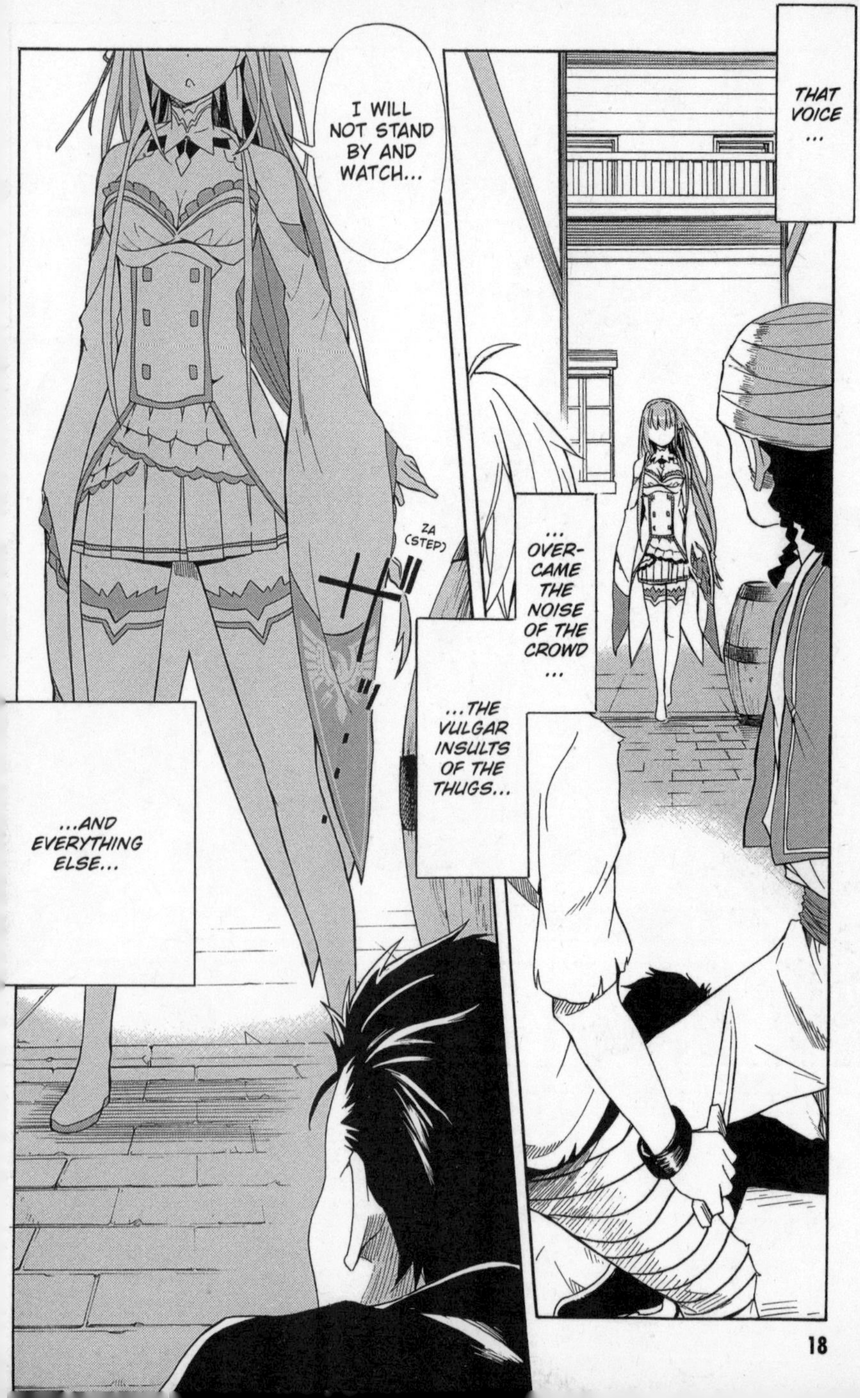
THAT VOICE ...
... OVER-CAME THE NOISE OF THE CROWD ...
...THE VULGAR INSULTS OF THE THUGS...
I WILL NOT STAND BY AND WATCH...
ZA (STEP)
...AND EVERYTHING ELSE...

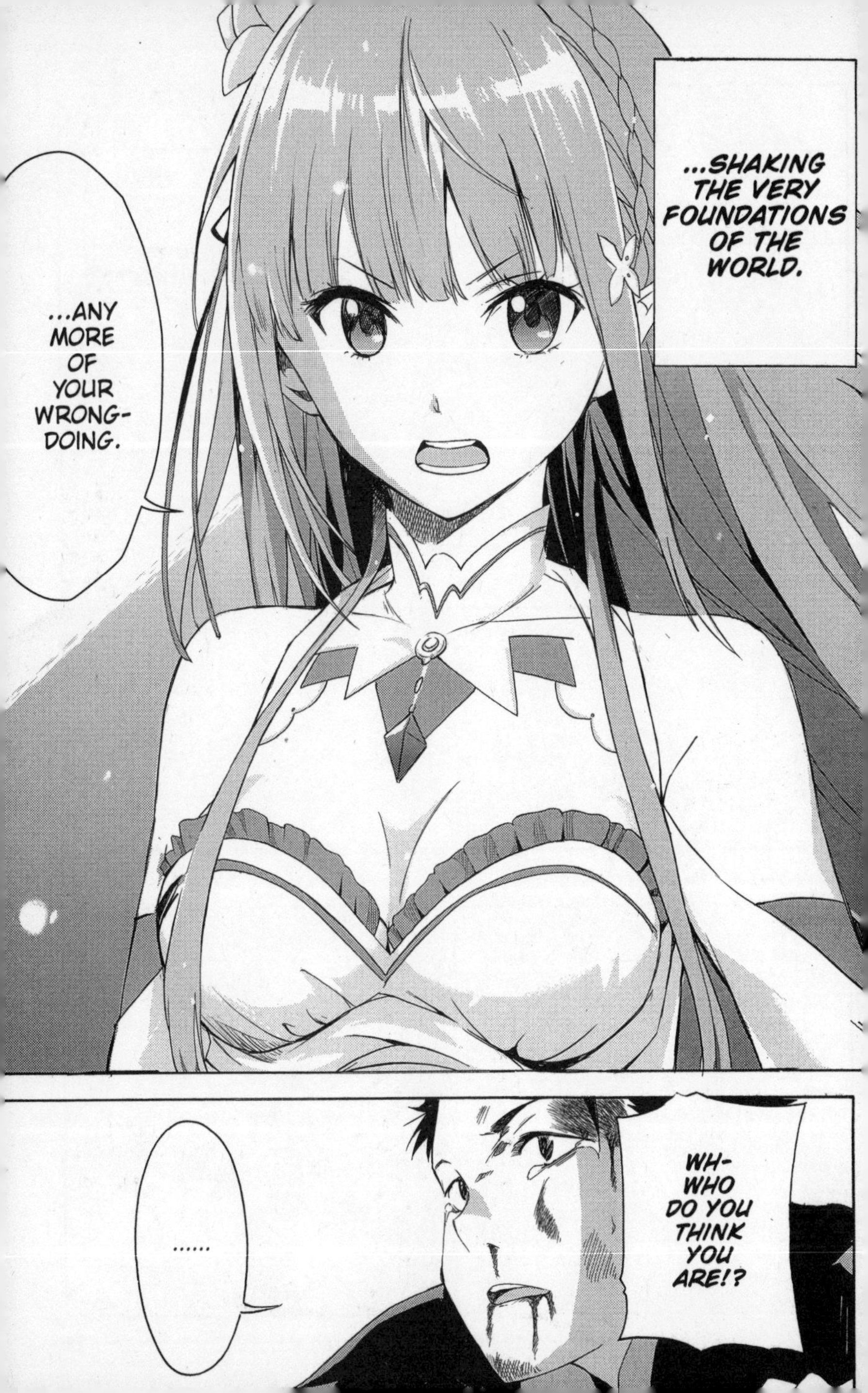
...SHAKING THE VERY FOUNDATIONS OF THE WORLD.
...ANY MORE OF YOUR WRONG-DOING.
WH-WHO DO YOU THINK YOU ARE!?
......

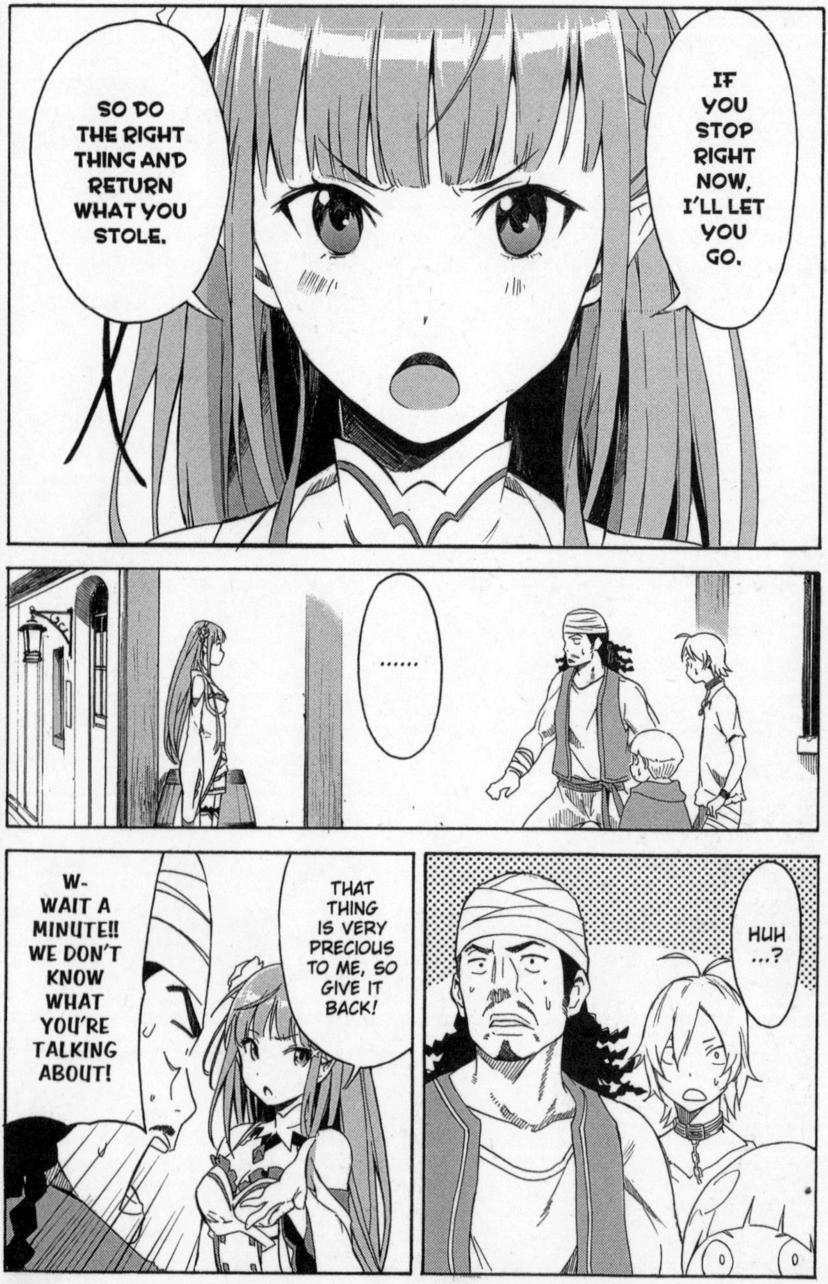
IF YOU STOP RIGHT NOW, I'LL LET YOU GO.
SO DO THE RIGHT THING AND RETURN WHAT YOU STOLE.
......
HUH ...?
THAT THING IS VERY PRECIOUS TO ME, SO GIVE IT BACK!
W- WAIT A MINUTE!! WE DON'T KNOW WHAT YOU'RE TALKING ABOUT!

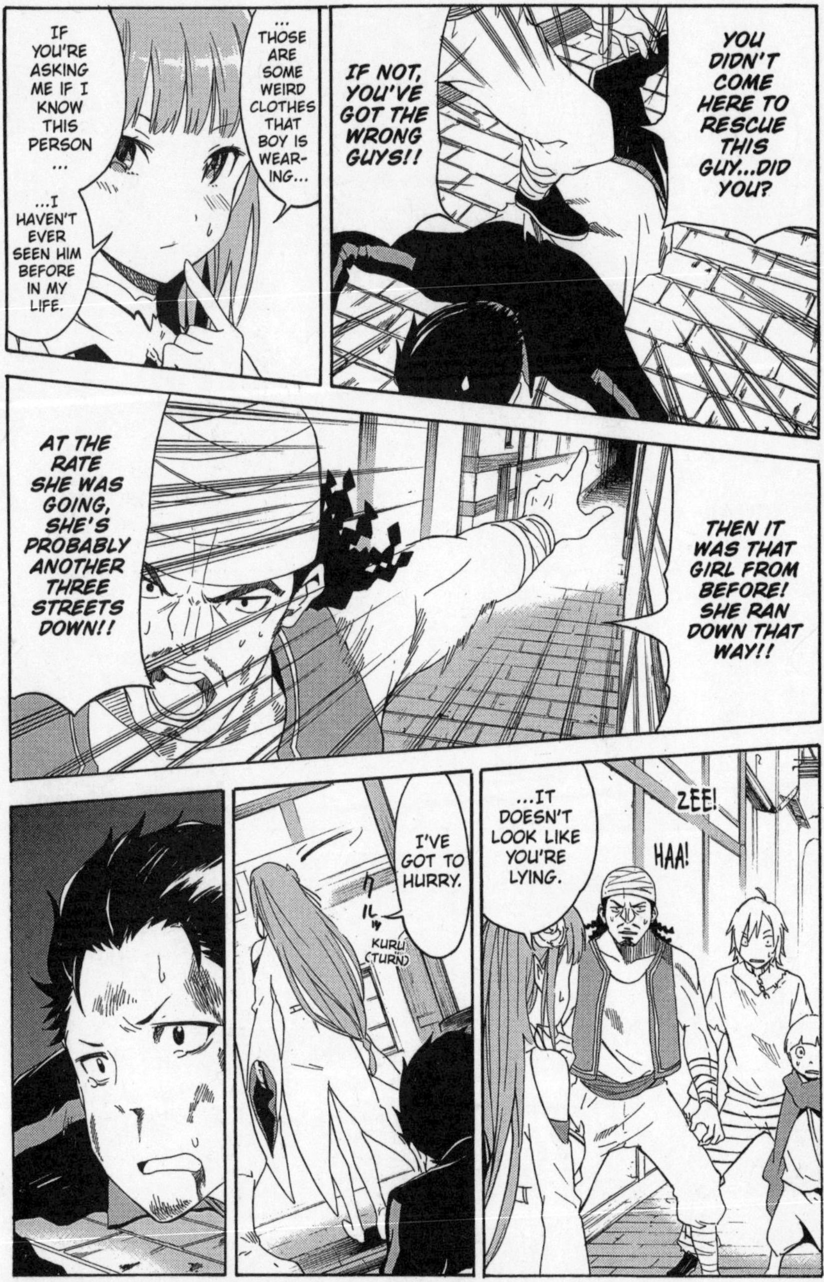
YOU DIDN'T COME HERE TO RESCUE THIS GUY...DID YOU?
IF NOT, YOU'VE GOT THE WRONG GUYS!!
...THOSE ARE SOME WEIRD CLOTHES THAT BOY IS WEAR-ING...
IF YOU'RE ASKING ME IF I KNOW THIS PERSON...
...I HAVEN'T EVER SEEN HIM BEFORE IN MY LIFE.
THEN IT WAS THAT GIRL FROM BEFORE! SHE RAN DOWN THAT WAY!!
AT THE RATE SHE WAS GOING, SHE'S PROBABLY ANOTHER THREE STREETS DOWN!!
ZEE!
HAA!
...IT DOESN'T LOOK LIKE YOU'RE LYING.
I'VE GOT TO HURRY.
クルッ
KURU (TURN)

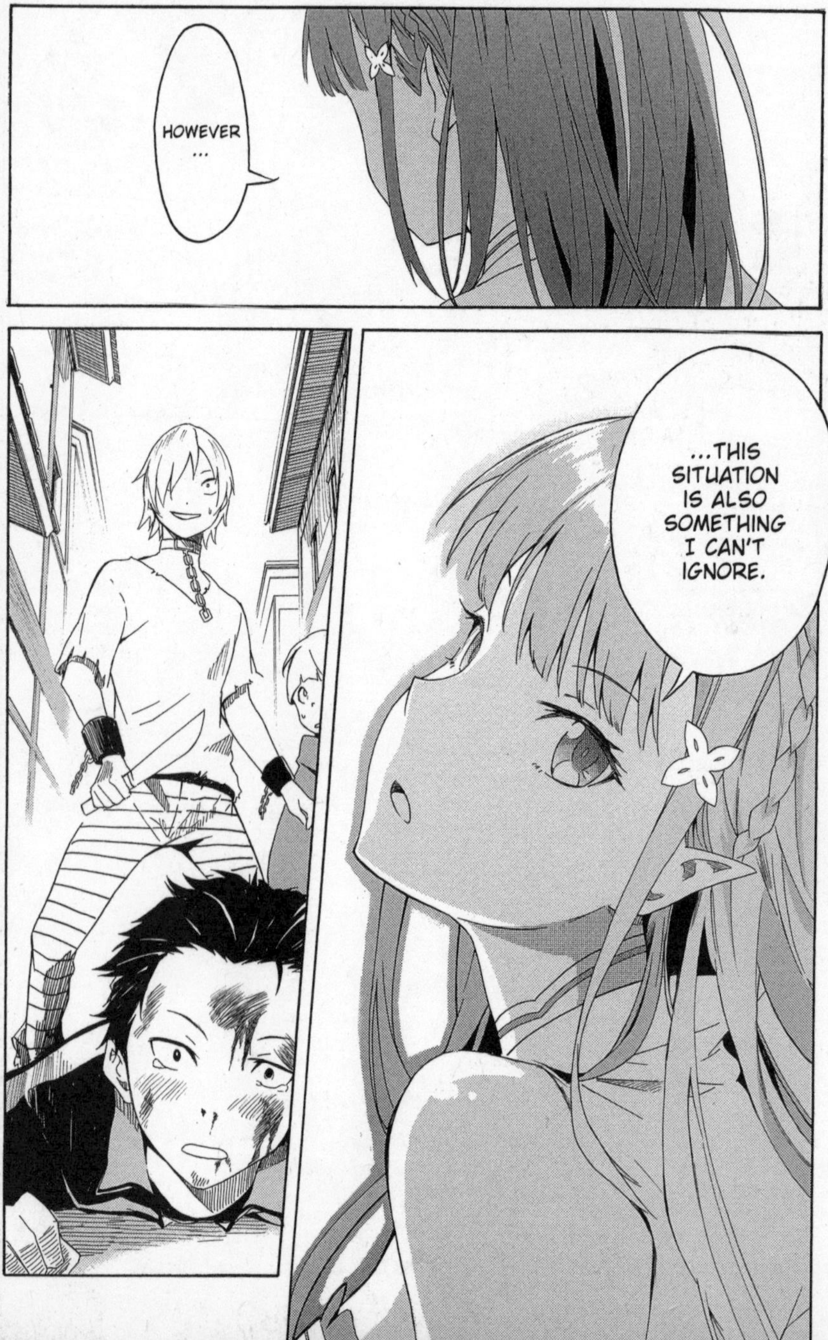
HOWEVER ...
...THIS SITUATION IS ALSO SOMETHING I CAN'T IGNORE.

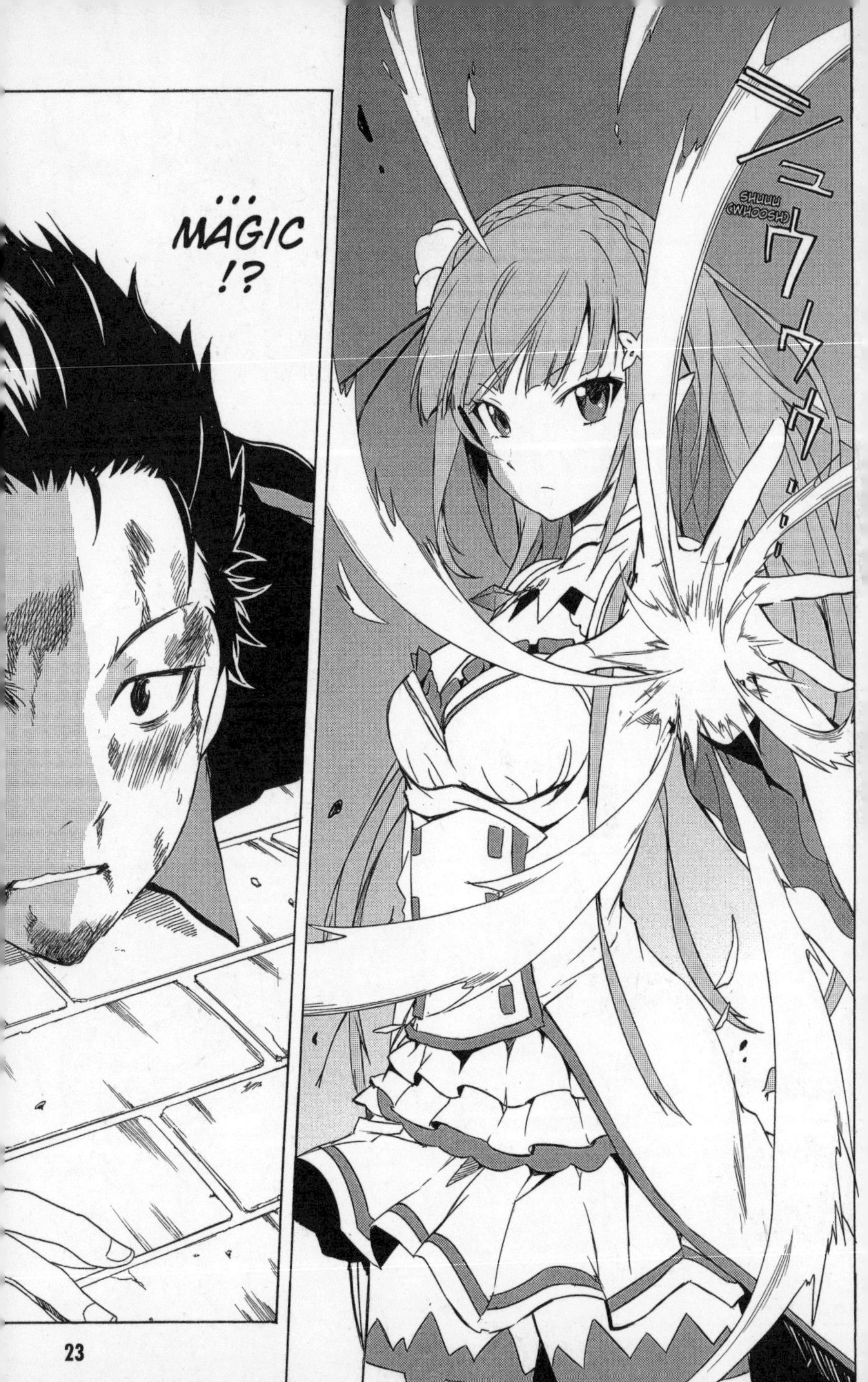
シュウゥゥ…
SHUUU (WHOOSH)
...MAGIC!?

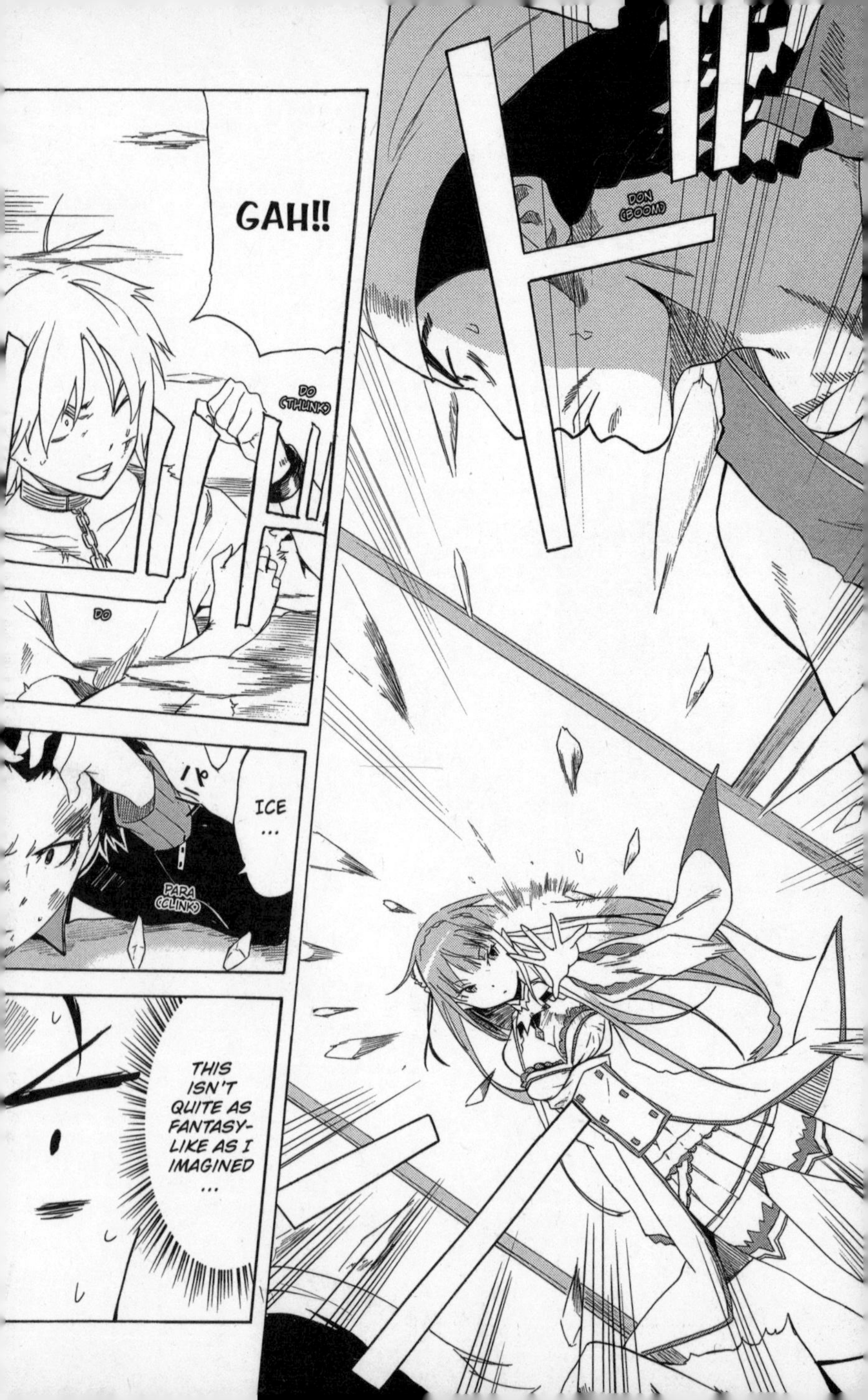
DON (BOOM)
GAH!!
DO (THUNK)
DO
ICE ...
PARA (CLINK)
THIS ISN'T QUITE AS FANTASY-LIKE AS I IMAGINED ...

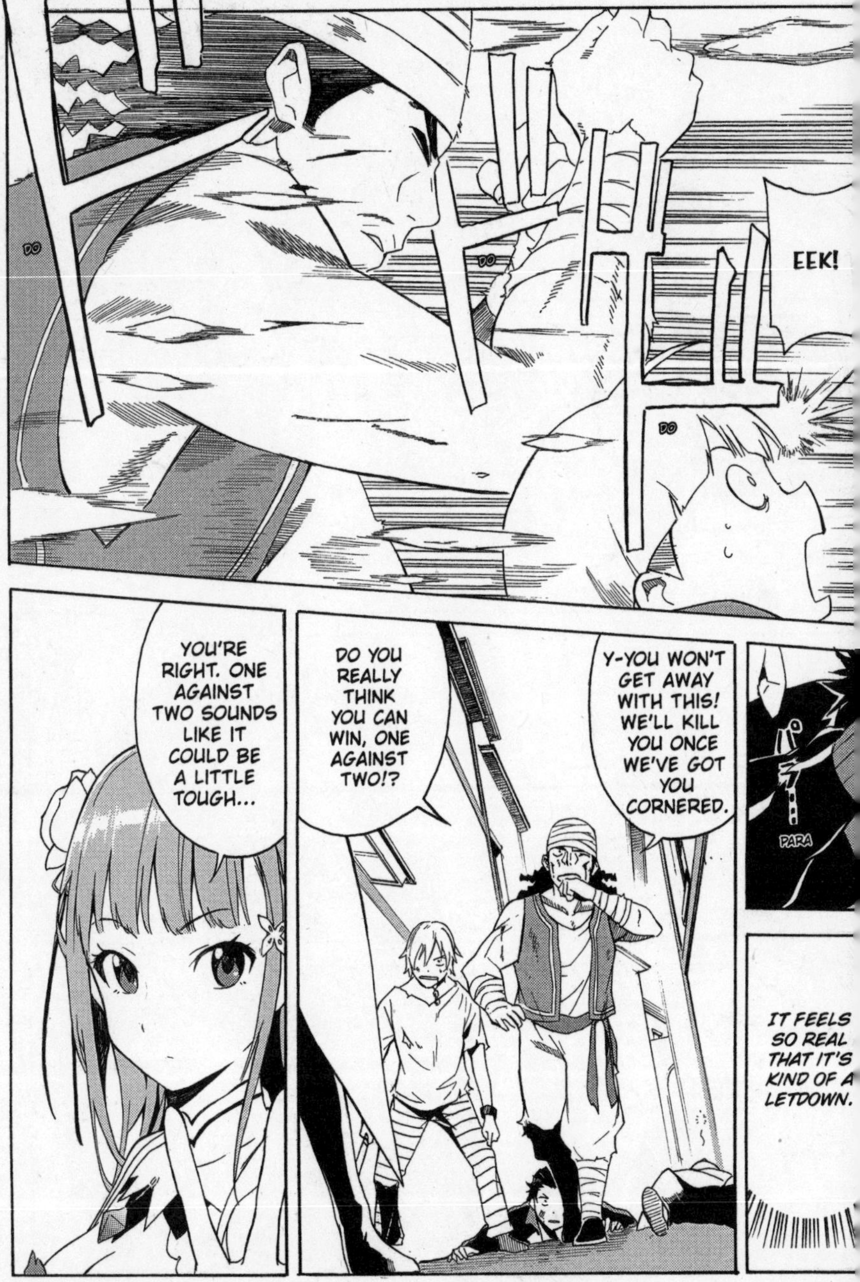
EEK!
DO
DO
DO
PARA
IT FEELS SO REAL THAT IT'S KIND OF A LETDOWN.
Y-YOU WON'T GET AWAY WITH THIS! WE'LL KILL YOU ONCE WE'VE GOT YOU CORNERED.
DO YOU REALLY THINK YOU CAN WIN, ONE AGAINST TWO!?
YOU'RE RIGHT. ONE AGAINST TWO SOUNDS LIKE IT COULD BE A LITTLE TOUGH...

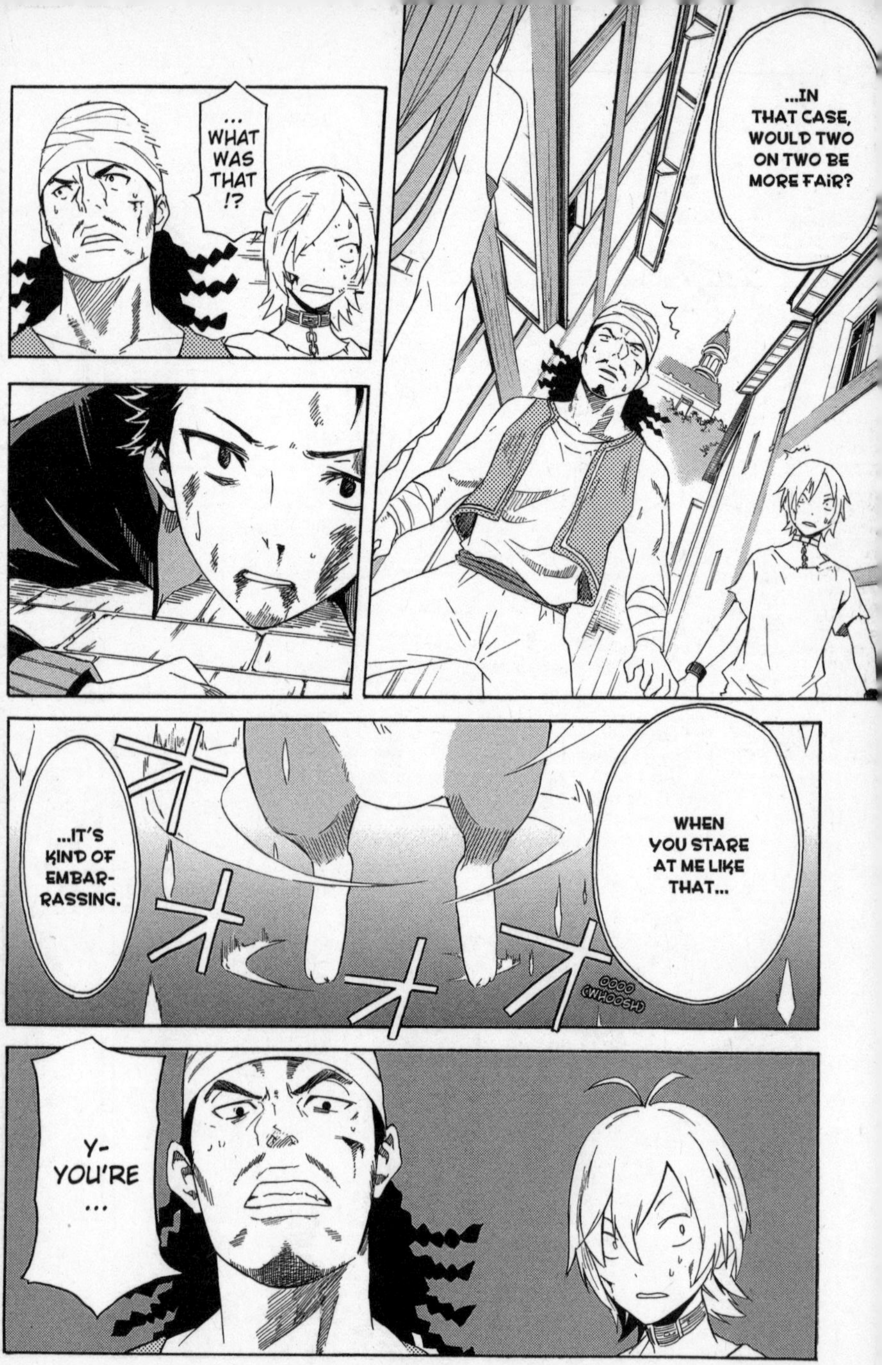
...IN THAT CASE, WOULD TWO ON TWO BE MORE FAIR?
...WHAT WAS THAT!?
WHEN YOU STARE AT ME LIKE THAT...
...IT'S KIND OF EMBARRASSING.
OOOO OOO (WHOOSH)
Y-YOU'RE...

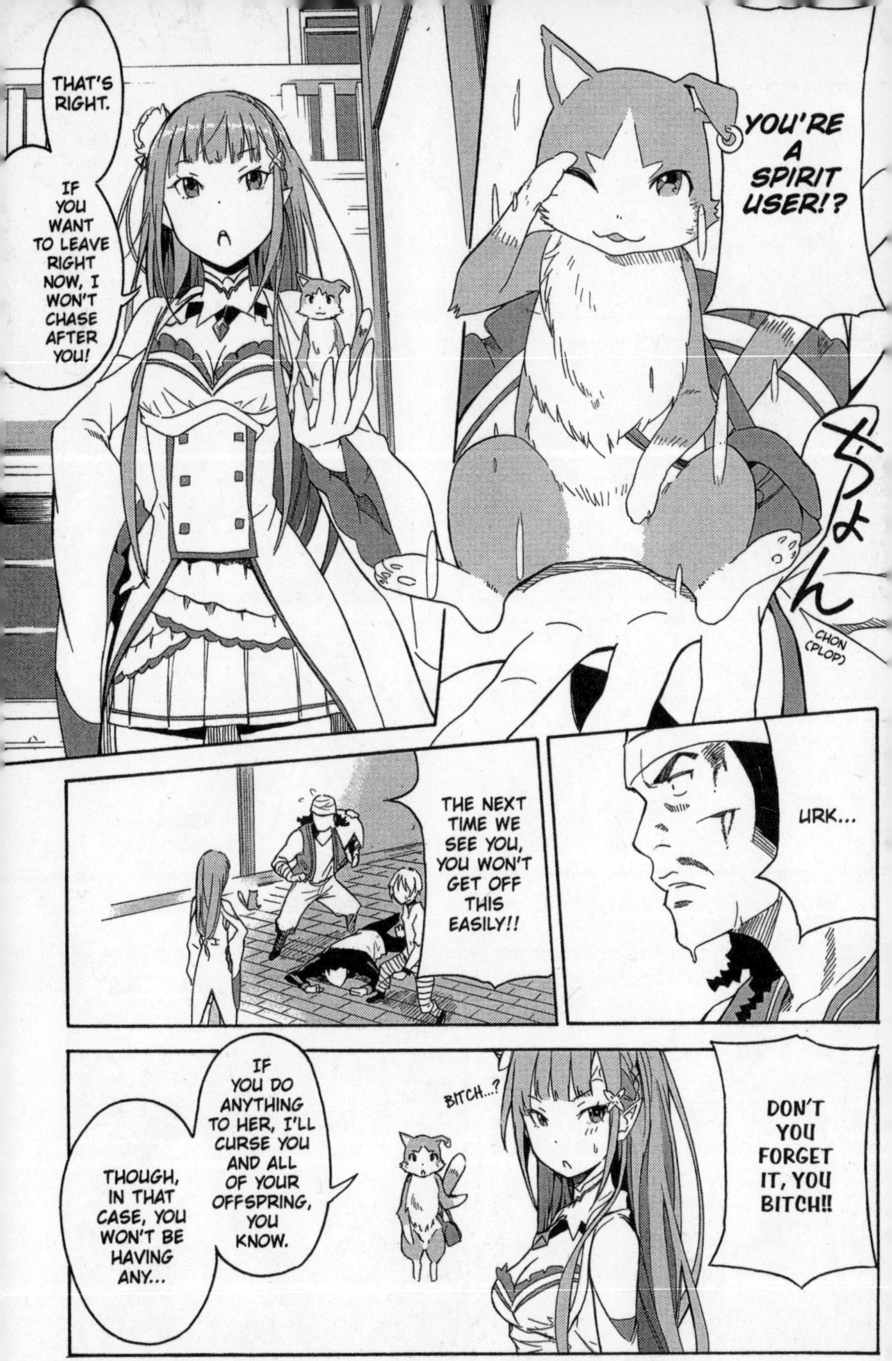
YOU'RE A SPIRIT USER!?
ちょん
CHON (PLOP)
THAT'S RIGHT.
IF YOU WANT TO LEAVE RIGHT NOW, I WON'T CHASE AFTER YOU!
URK...
THE NEXT TIME WE SEE YOU, YOU WON'T GET OFF THIS EASILY!!
DON'T YOU FORGET IT, YOU BITCH!!
BITCH...?
IF YOU DO ANYTHING TO HER, I'LL CURSE YOU AND ALL OF YOUR OFFSPRING, YOU KNOW.
THOUGH, IN THAT CASE, YOU WON'T BE HAVING ANY...

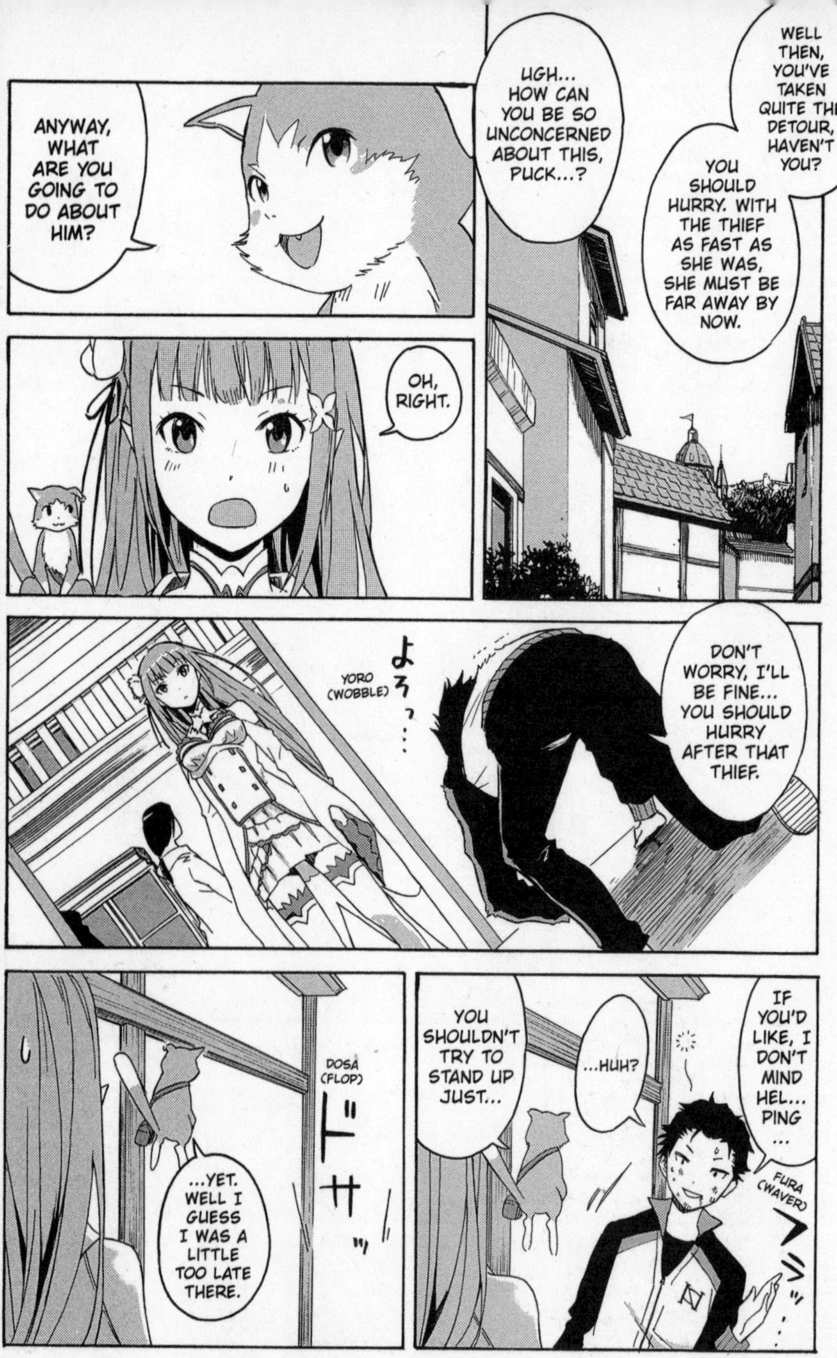
WELL THEN, YOU'VE TAKEN QUITE THE DETOUR, HAVEN'T YOU?
YOU SHOULD HURRY. WITH THE THIEF AS FAST AS SHE WAS, SHE MUST BE FAR AWAY BY NOW.
UGH... HOW CAN YOU BE SO UNCONCERNED ABOUT THIS, PUCK...?
ANYWAY, WHAT ARE YOU GOING TO DO ABOUT HIM?
OH, RIGHT.
DON'T WORRY, I'LL BE FINE... YOU SHOULD HURRY AFTER THAT THIEF.
YORO (WOBBLE)
よろっ...
IF YOU'D LIKE, I DON'T MIND HEL... PING...
FURA (WAVER)
...HUH?
YOU SHOULDN'T TRY TO STAND UP JUST...
DOSA (FLOP)
ドサッ
...YET. WELL I GUESS I WAS A LITTLE TOO LATE THERE.

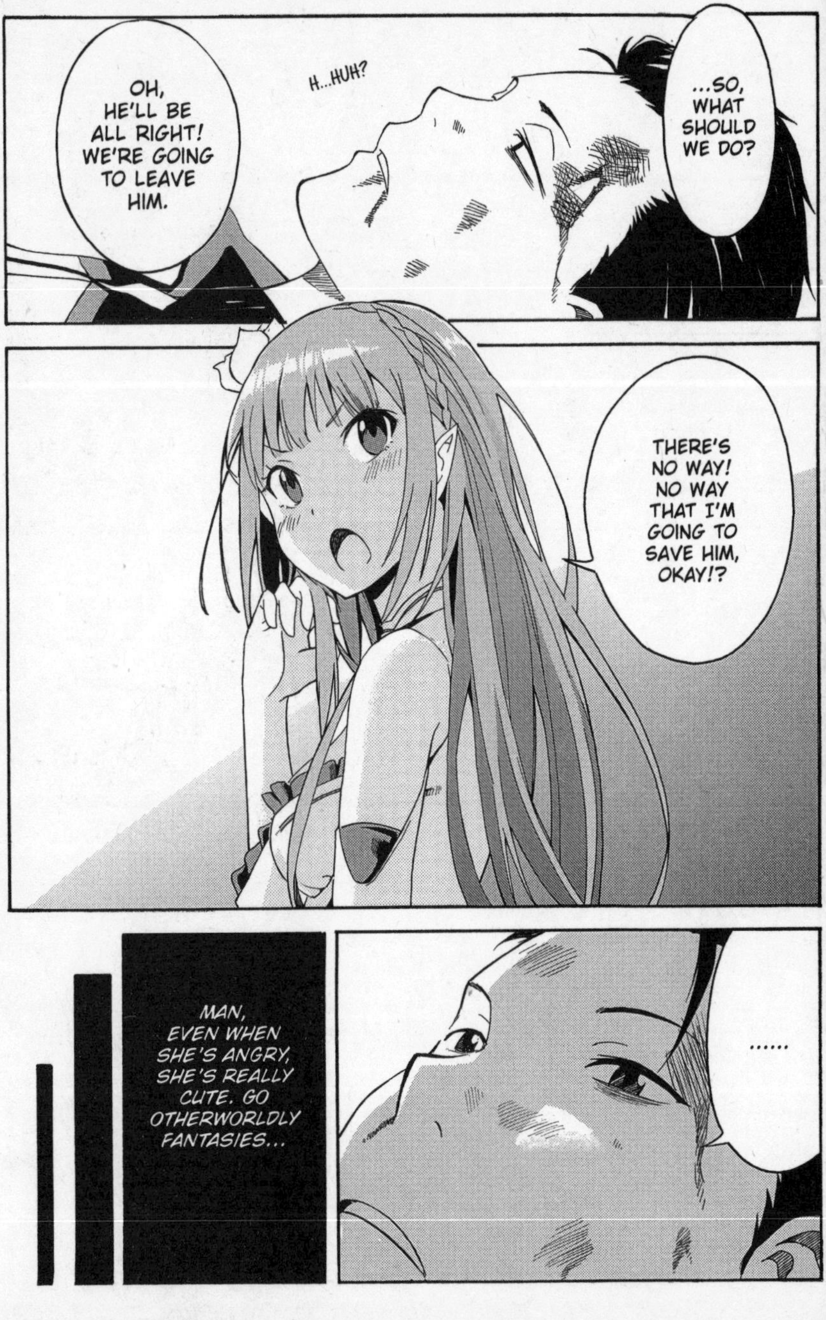
...SO, WHAT SHOULD WE DO?
H...HUH?
OH, HE'LL BE ALL RIGHT! WE'RE GOING TO LEAVE HIM.
THERE'S NO WAY! NO WAY THAT I'M GOING TO SAVE HIM, OKAY!?
......
MAN, EVEN WHEN SHE'S ANGRY, SHE'S REALLY CUTE. GO OTHERWORLDLY FANTASIES...

Re:ZeRo

-Starting Life in Another World-

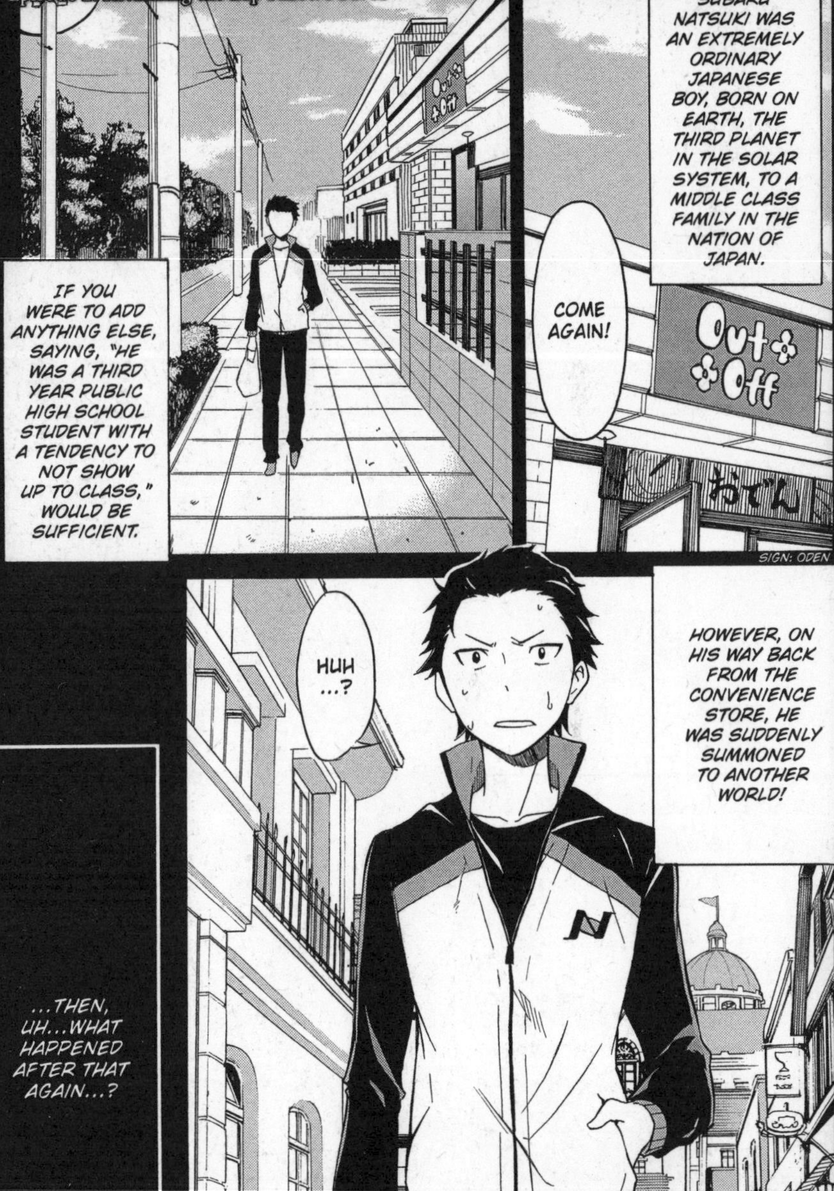
SUBARU NATSUKI WAS AN EXTREMELY ORDINARY JAPANESE BOY, BORN ON EARTH, THE THIRD PLANET IN THE SOLAR SYSTEM, TO A MIDDLE CLASS FAMILY IN THE NATION OF JAPAN.
COME AGAIN!
Out Off
おでん
SIGN: ODEN
IF YOU WERE TO ADD ANYTHING ELSE, SAYING, "HE WAS A THIRD YEAR PUBLIC HIGH SCHOOL STUDENT WITH A TENDENCY TO NOT SHOW UP TO CLASS," WOULD BE SUFFICIENT.
HOWEVER, ON HIS WAY BACK FROM THE CONVENIENCE STORE, HE WAS SUDDENLY SUMMONED TO ANOTHER WORLD!
HUH ...?
...THEN, UH...WHAT HAPPENED AFTER THAT AGAIN...?

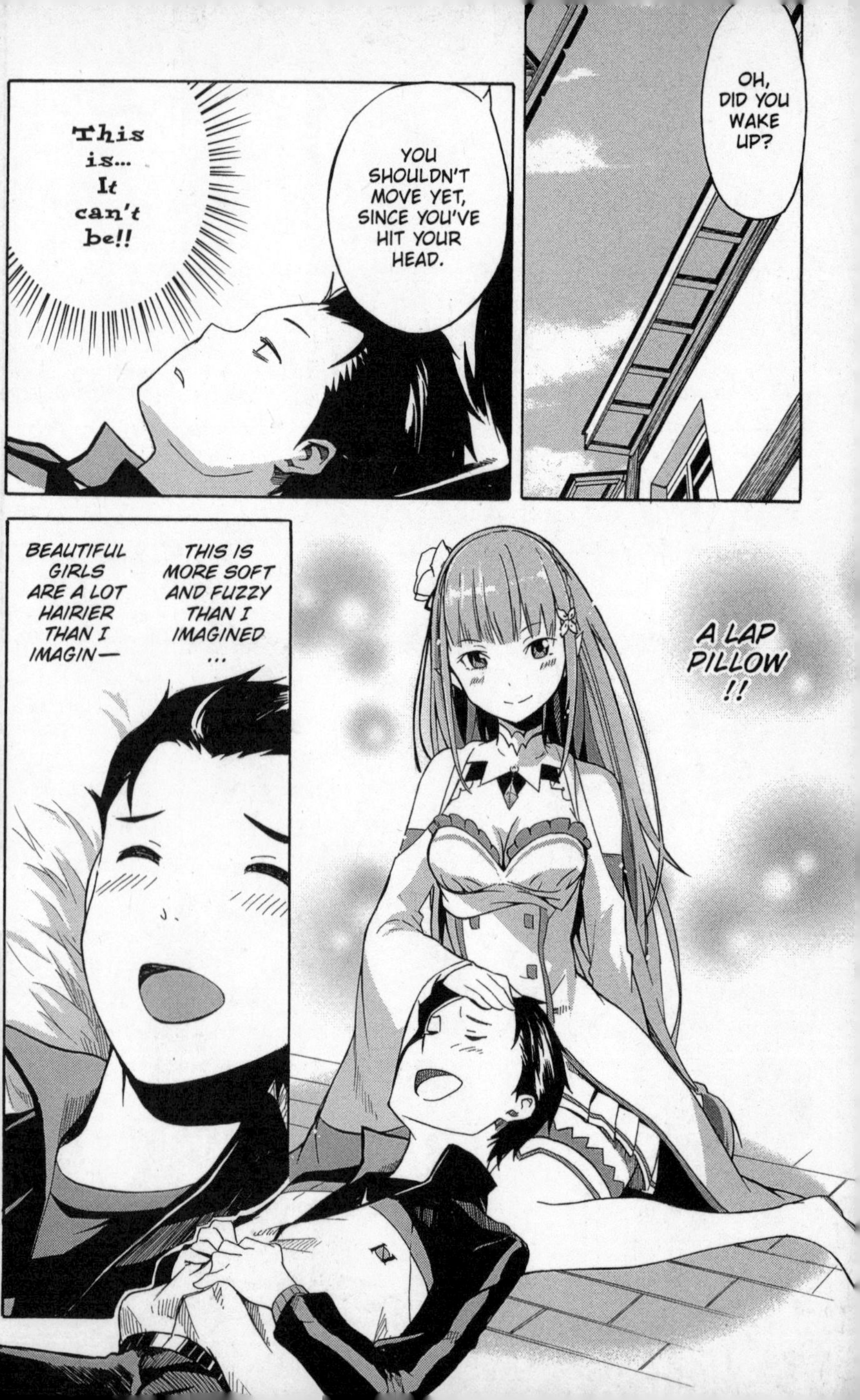
OH, DID YOU WAKE UP?
YOU SHOULDN'T MOVE YET, SINCE YOU'VE HIT YOUR HEAD.
This is... It can't be!!
A LAP PILLOW!!
THIS IS MORE SOFT AND FUZZY THAN I IMAGINED...
BEAUTIFUL GIRLS ARE A LOT HAIRIER THAN I IMAGIN—

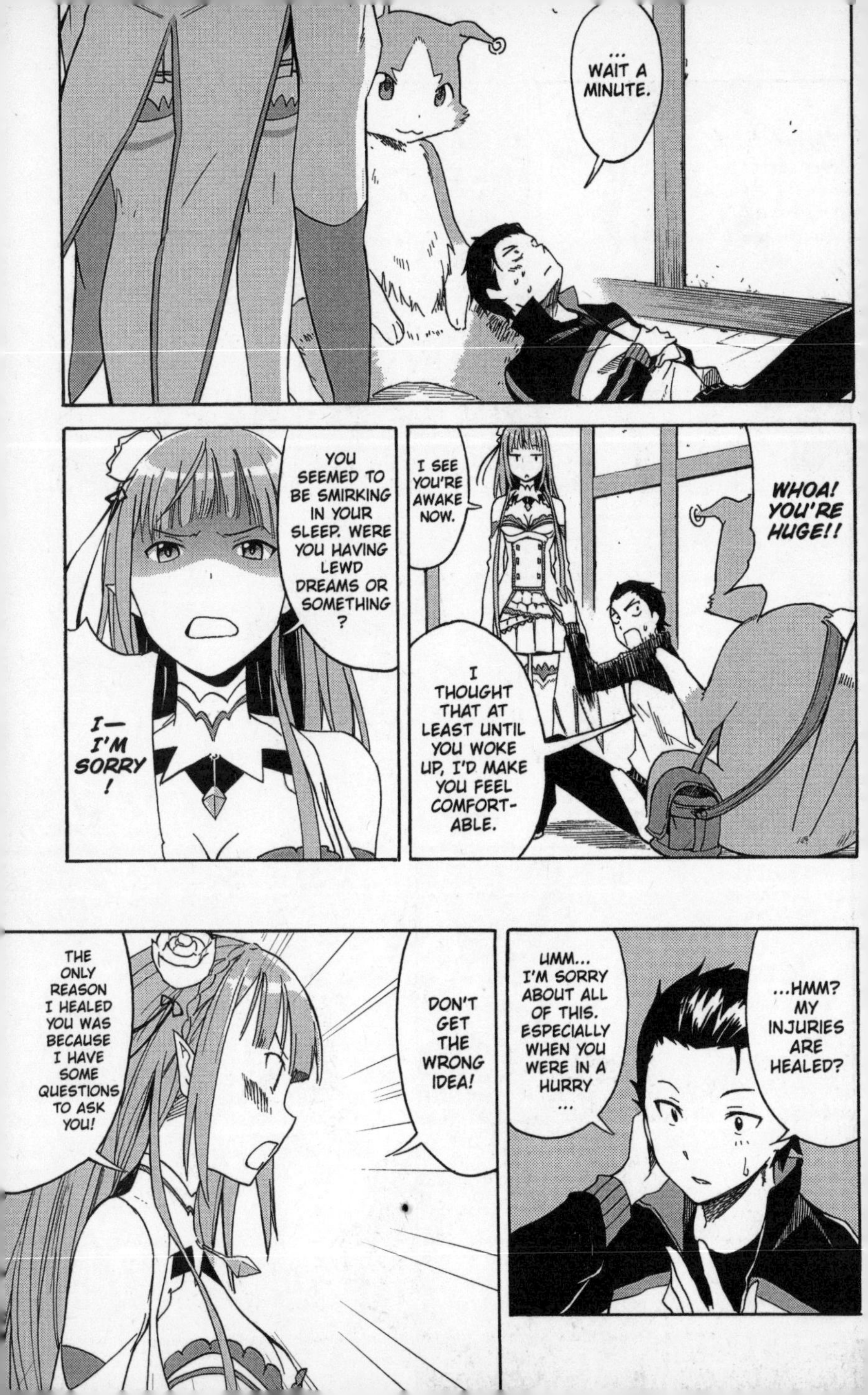

... WAIT A MINUTE.
WHOA! YOU'RE HUGE!!
I SEE YOU'RE AWAKE NOW.
I THOUGHT THAT AT LEAST UNTIL YOU WOKE UP, I'D MAKE YOU FEEL COMFORT-ABLE.
YOU SEEMED TO BE SMIRKING IN YOUR SLEEP. WERE YOU HAVING LEWD DREAMS OR SOMETHING?
I— I'M SORRY!
...HMM? MY INJURIES ARE HEALED?
UMM... I'M SORRY ABOUT ALL OF THIS. ESPECIALLY WHEN YOU WERE IN A HURRY...
DON'T GET THE WRONG IDEA!
THE ONLY REASON I HEALED YOU WAS BECAUSE I HAVE SOME QUESTIONS TO ASK YOU!

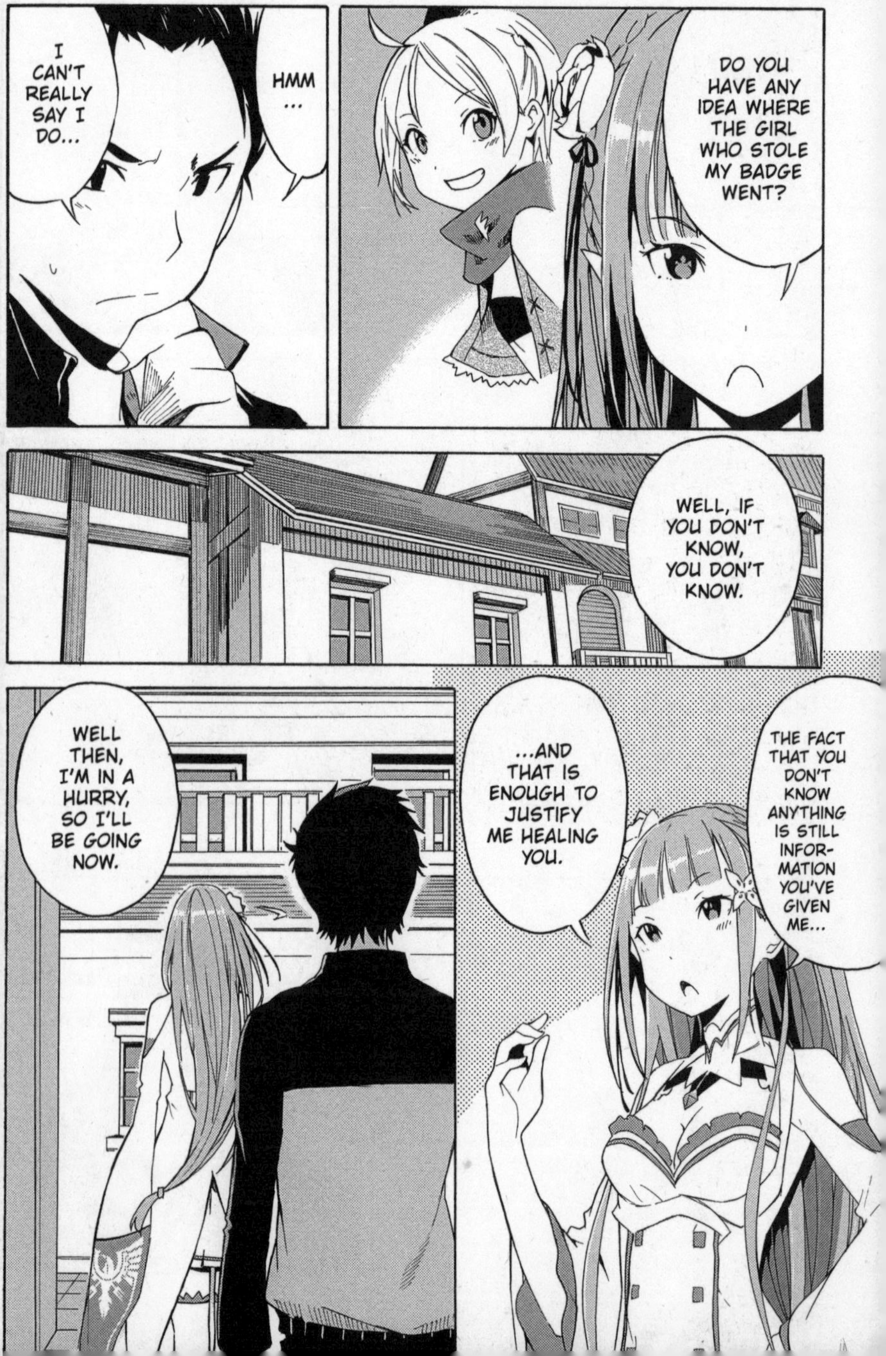
DO YOU HAVE ANY IDEA WHERE THE GIRL WHO STOLE MY BADGE WENT?
HMM ...
I CAN'T REALLY SAY I DO...
WELL, IF YOU DON'T KNOW, YOU DON'T KNOW.
THE FACT THAT YOU DON'T KNOW ANYTHING IS STILL INFOR-MATION YOU'VE GIVEN ME...
...AND THAT IS ENOUGH TO JUSTIFY ME HEALING YOU.
WELL THEN, I'M IN A HURRY, SO I'LL BE GOING NOW.

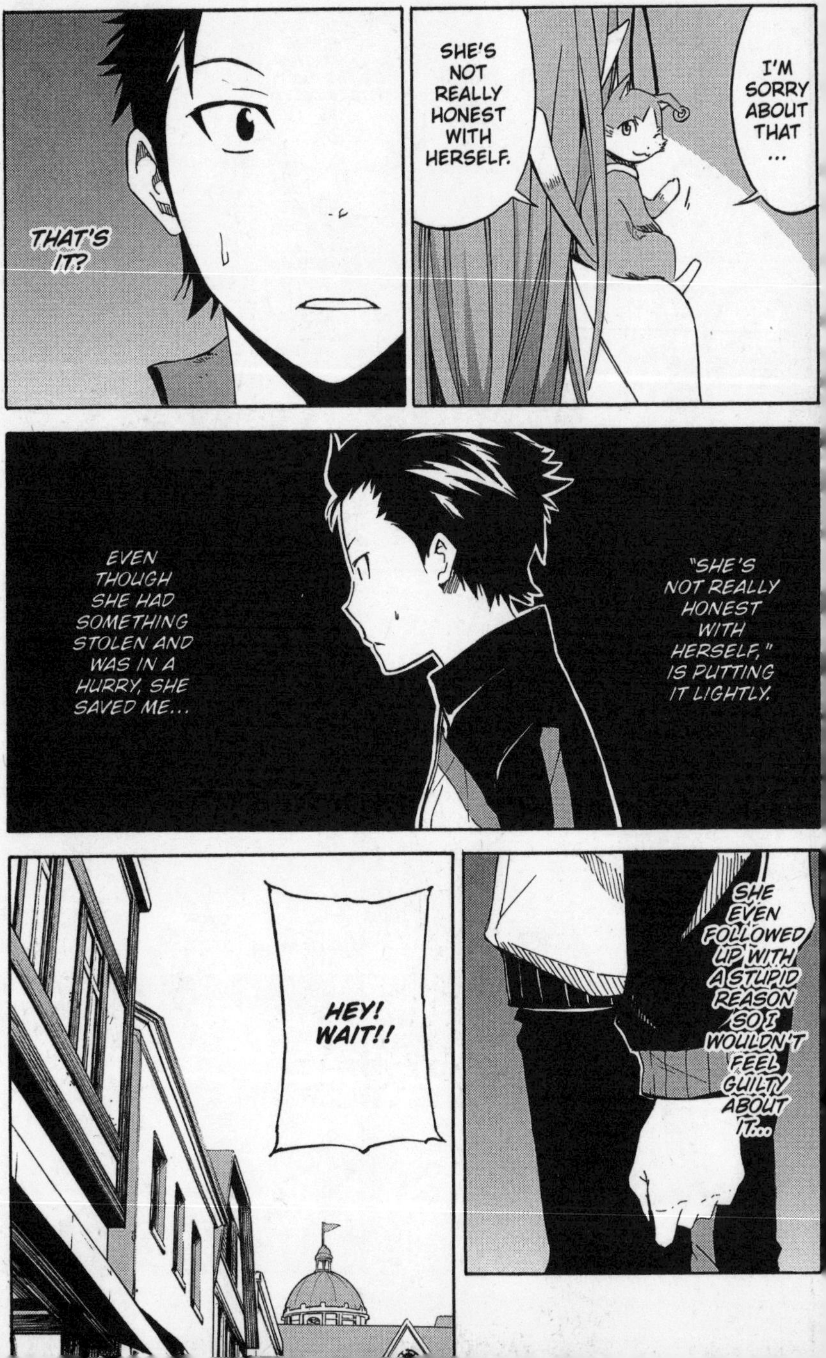
I'M SORRY ABOUT THAT ...
SHE'S NOT REALLY HONEST WITH HERSELF.
THAT'S IT?
"SHE'S NOT REALLY HONEST WITH HERSELF," IS PUTTING IT LIGHTLY.
EVEN THOUGH SHE HAD SOMETHING STOLEN AND WAS IN A HURRY, SHE SAVED ME...
SHE EVEN FOLLOWED UP WITH A STUPID REASON SO I WOULDN'T FEEL GUILTY ABOUT IT...
HEY! WAIT!!

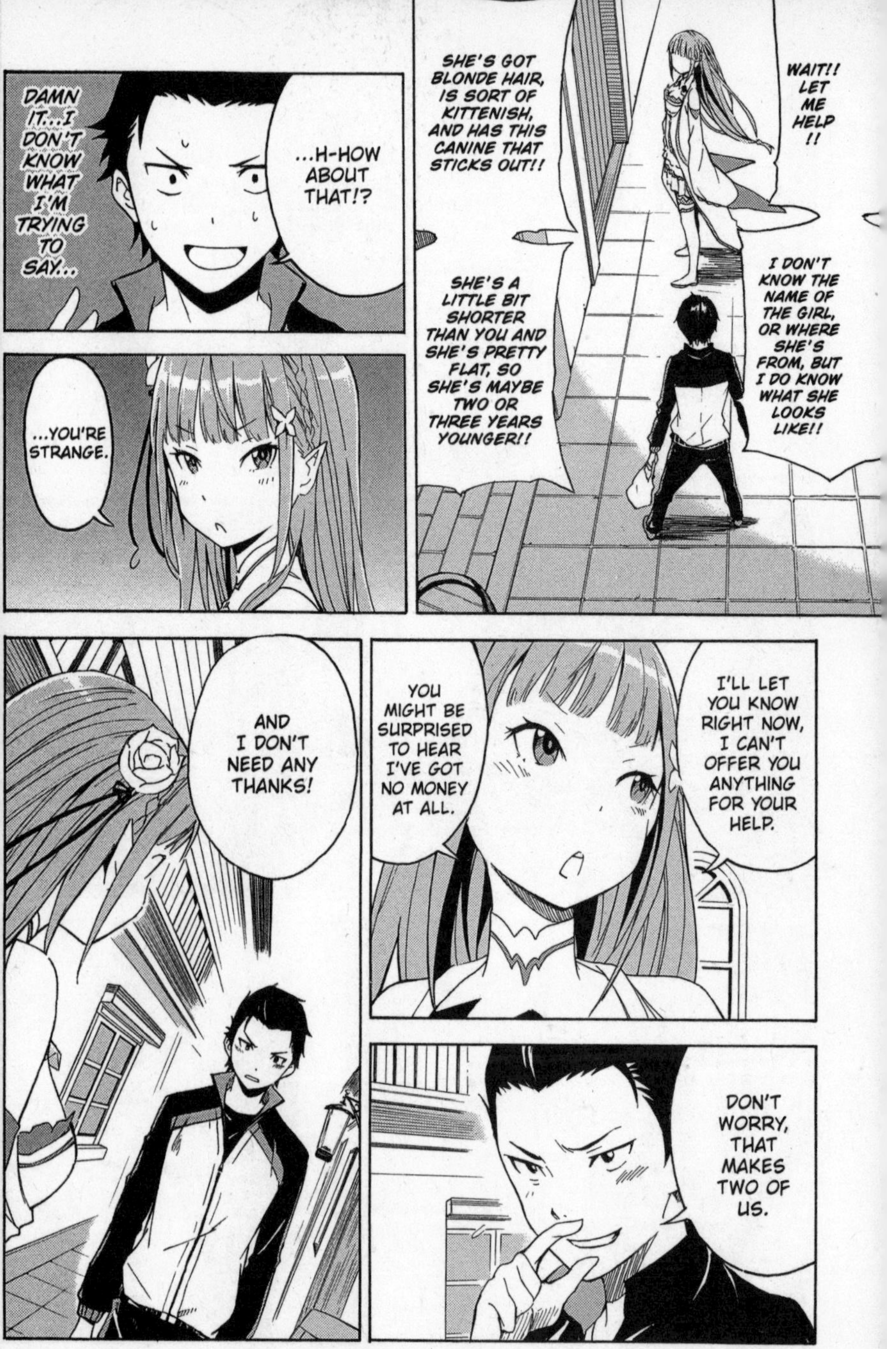
WAIT!! LET ME HELP!!
I DON'T KNOW THE NAME OF THE GIRL, OR WHERE SHE'S FROM, BUT I DO KNOW WHAT SHE LOOKS LIKE!!
SHE'S GOT BLONDE HAIR, IS SORT OF KITTENISH, AND HAS THIS CANINE THAT STICKS OUT!!
SHE'S A LITTLE BIT SHORTER THAN YOU AND SHE'S PRETTY FLAT, SO SHE'S MAYBE TWO OR THREE YEARS YOUNGER!!
...H-HOW ABOUT THAT!?
DAMN IT...I DON'T KNOW WHAT I'M TRYING TO SAY...
...YOU'RE STRANGE.
I'LL LET YOU KNOW RIGHT NOW, I CAN'T OFFER YOU ANYTHING FOR YOUR HELP.
YOU MIGHT BE SURPRISED TO HEAR I'VE GOT NO MONEY AT ALL.
DON'T WORRY, THAT MAKES TWO OF US.
AND I DON'T NEED ANY THANKS!

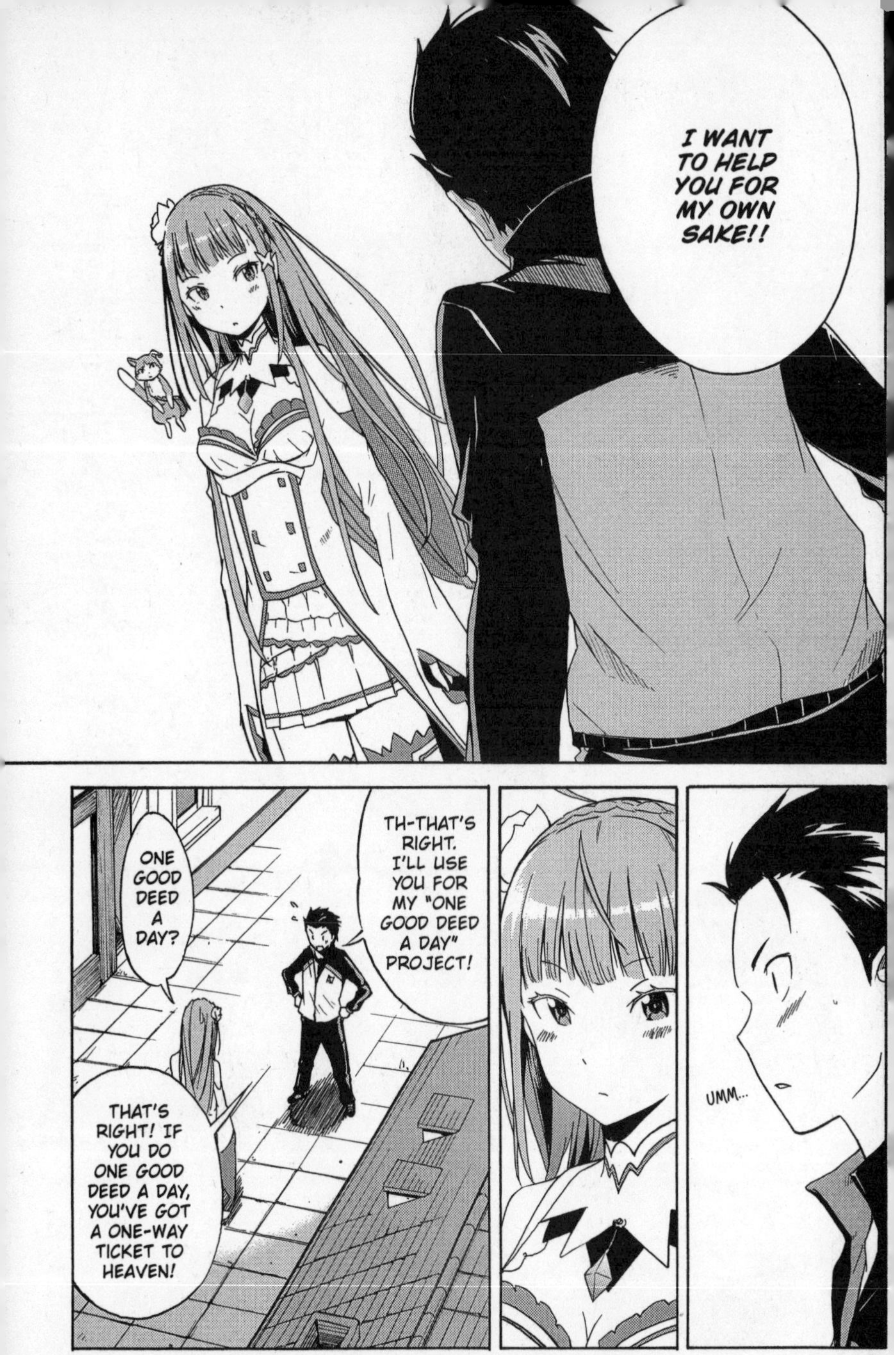
I WANT TO HELP YOU FOR MY OWN SAKE!!
UMM...
TH-THAT'S RIGHT. I'LL USE YOU FOR MY "ONE GOOD DEED A DAY" PROJECT!
ONE GOOD DEED A DAY?
THAT'S RIGHT! IF YOU DO ONE GOOD DEED A DAY, YOU'VE GOT A ONE-WAY TICKET TO HEAVEN!

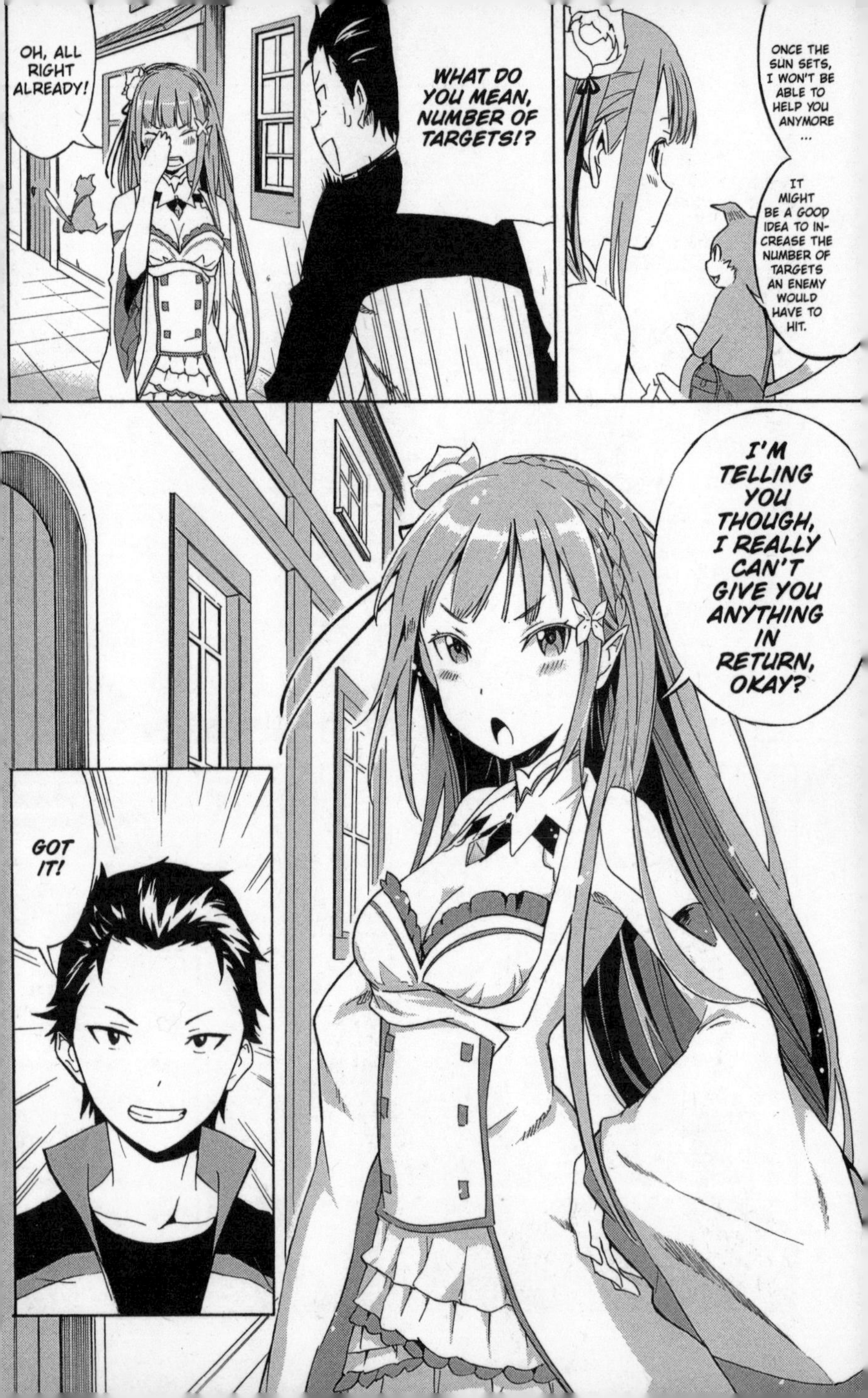
ONCE THE SUN SETS, I WON'T BE ABLE TO HELP YOU ANYMORE ...
IT MIGHT BE A GOOD IDEA TO INCREASE THE NUMBER OF TARGETS AN ENEMY WOULD HAVE TO HIT.
WHAT DO YOU MEAN, NUMBER OF TARGETS!?
OH, ALL RIGHT ALREADY!
I'M TELLING YOU THOUGH, I REALLY CAN'T GIVE YOU ANYTHING IN RETURN, OKAY?
GOT IT!

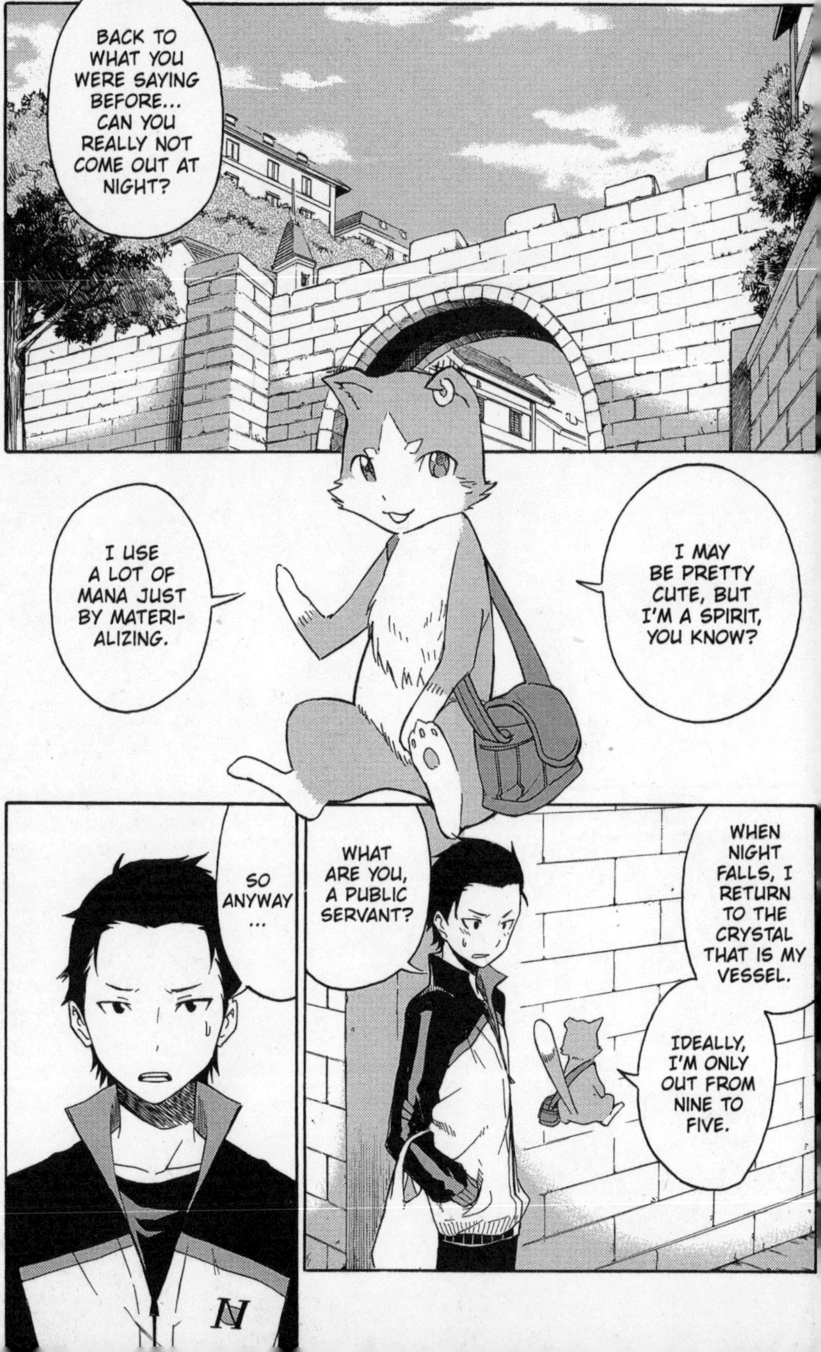
BACK TO WHAT YOU WERE SAYING BEFORE... CAN YOU REALLY NOT COME OUT AT NIGHT?
I MAY BE PRETTY CUTE, BUT I'M A SPIRIT, YOU KNOW?
I USE A LOT OF MANA JUST BY MATERI-ALIZING.
WHEN NIGHT FALLS, I RETURN TO THE CRYSTAL THAT IS MY VESSEL.
IDEALLY, I'M ONLY OUT FROM NINE TO FIVE.
WHAT ARE YOU, A PUBLIC SERVANT?
SO ANYWAY ...

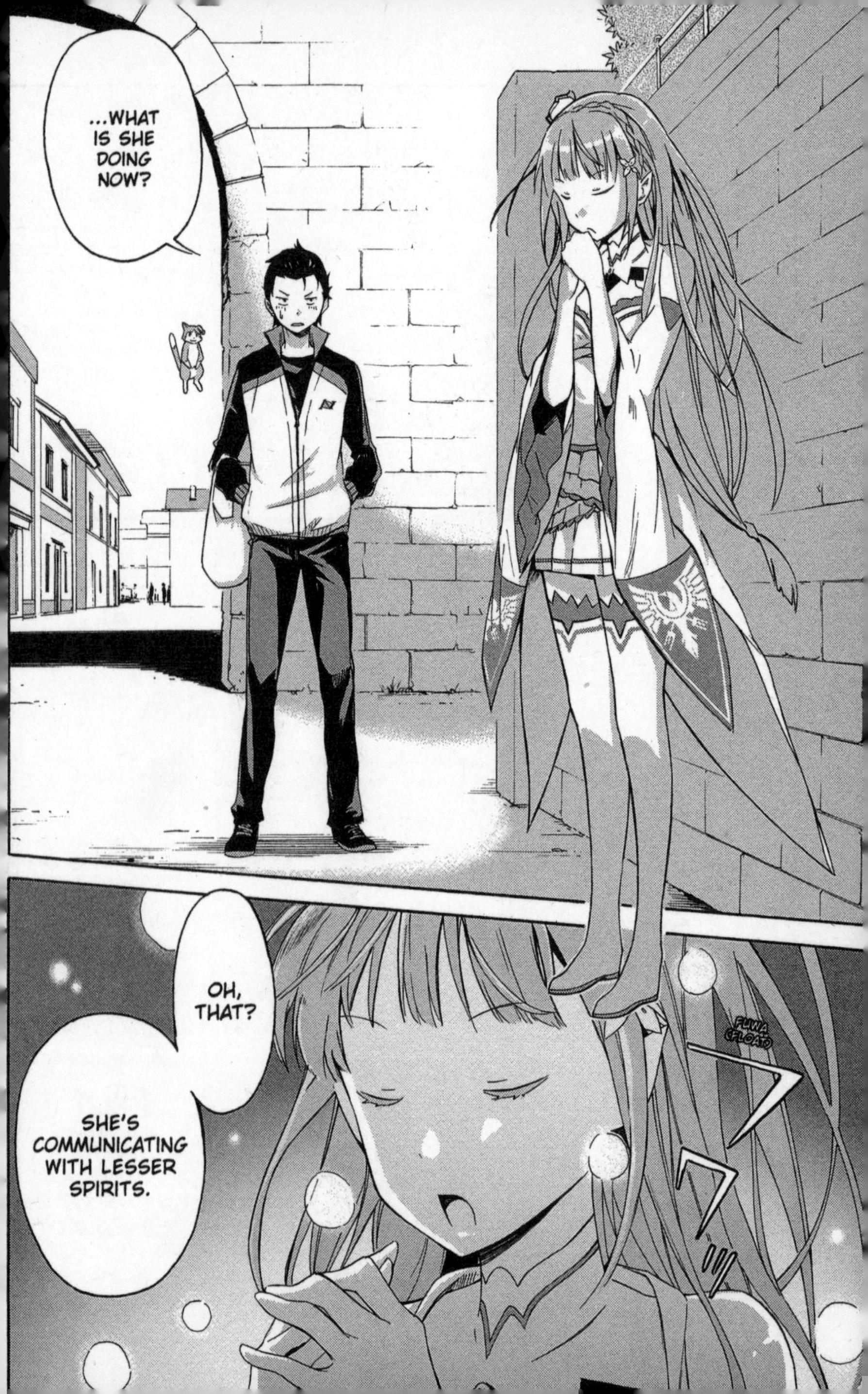
...WHAT IS SHE DOING NOW?
OH, THAT?
SHE'S COMMUNICATING WITH LESSER SPIRITS.
FUWA (FLOAT)

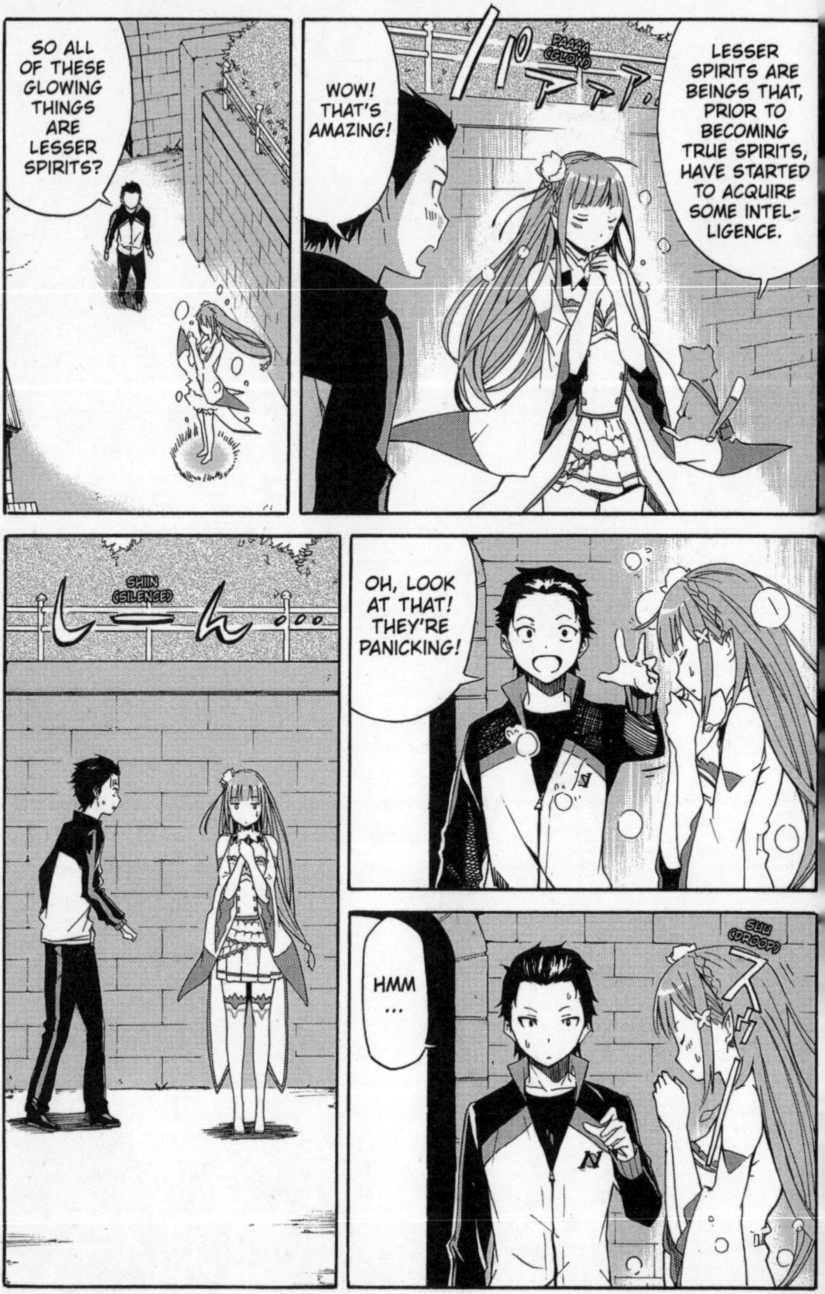
LESSER SPIRITS ARE BEINGS THAT, PRIOR TO BECOMING TRUE SPIRITS, HAVE STARTED TO ACQUIRE SOME INTEL-LIGENCE.
PAAAA (GLOW)
WOW! THAT'S AMAZING!
SO ALL OF THESE GLOWING THINGS ARE LESSER SPIRITS?
OH, LOOK AT THAT! THEY'RE PANICKING!
SUU (DROOP)
HMM ...
SHIIN (SILENCE)

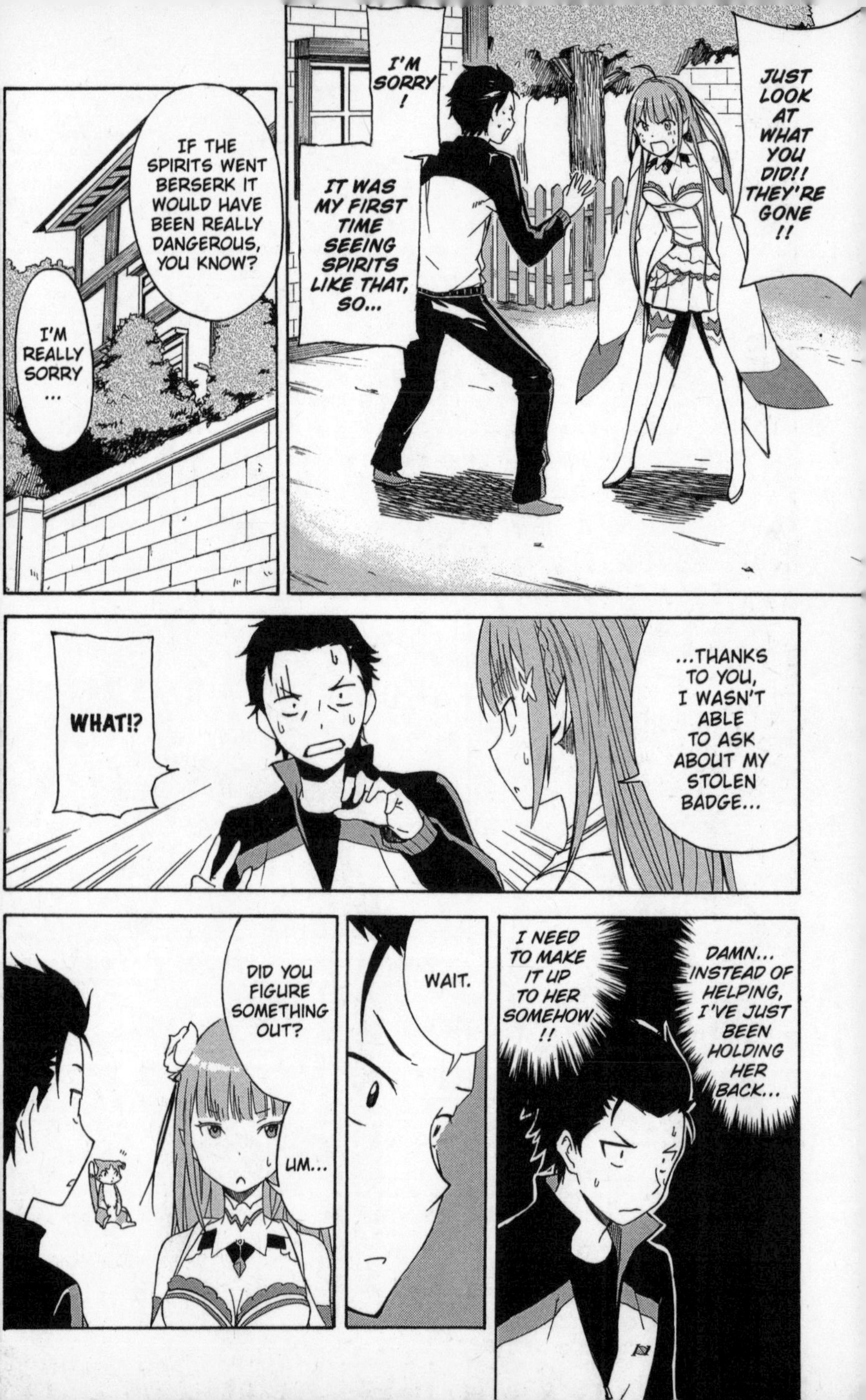
JUST LOOK AT WHAT YOU DID!! THEY'RE GONE!!
I'M SORRY!
IT WAS MY FIRST TIME SEEING SPIRITS LIKE THAT, SO...
IF THE SPIRITS WENT BERSERK IT WOULD HAVE BEEN REALLY DANGEROUS, YOU KNOW?
I'M REALLY SORRY...
...THANKS TO YOU, I WASN'T ABLE TO ASK ABOUT MY STOLEN BADGE...
WHAT!?
DAMN... INSTEAD OF HELPING, I'VE JUST BEEN HOLDING HER BACK...
I NEED TO MAKE IT UP TO HER SOMEHOW!!
WAIT.
DID YOU FIGURE SOMETHING OUT?
UM...

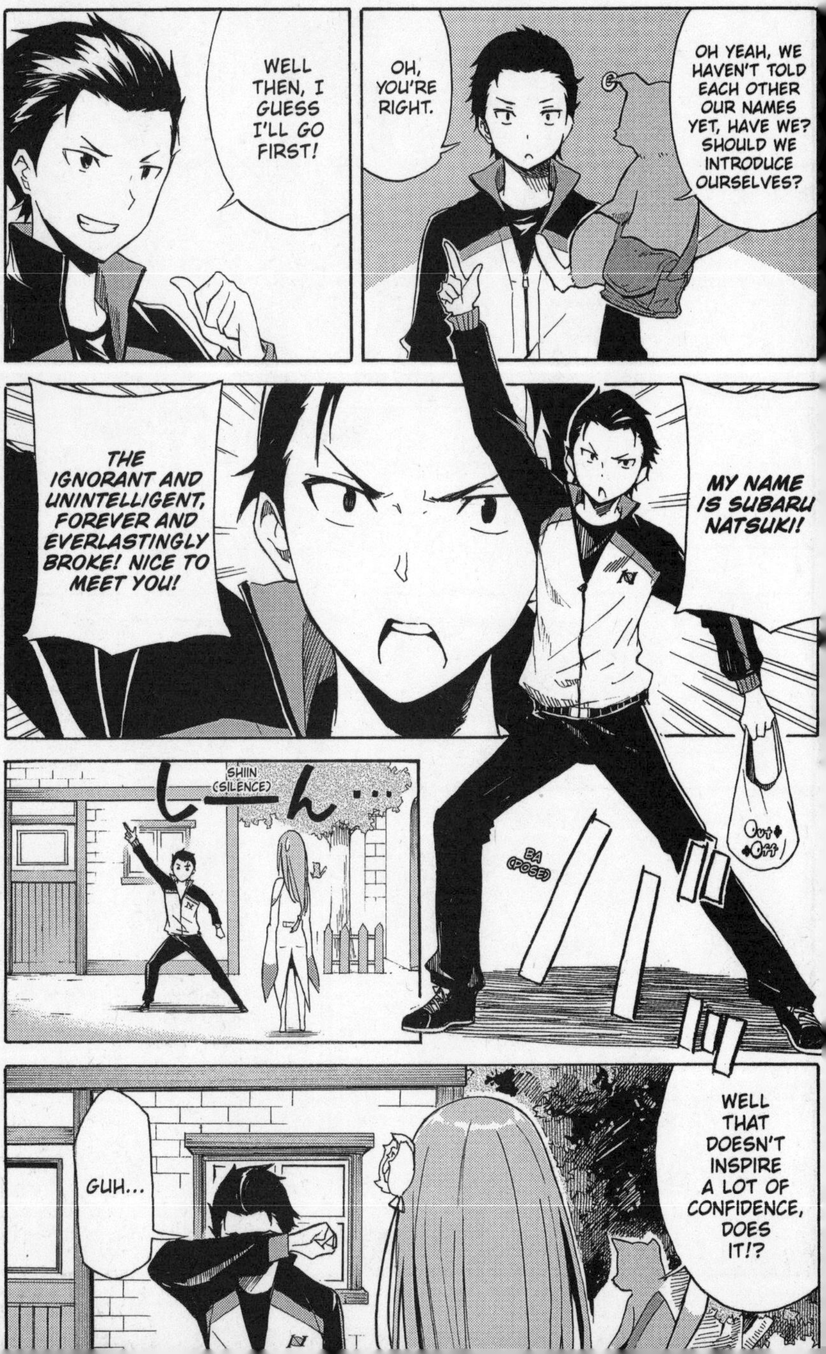
OH YEAH, WE HAVEN'T TOLD EACH OTHER OUR NAMES YET, HAVE WE? SHOULD WE INTRODUCE OURSELVES?
OH, YOU'RE RIGHT.
WELL THEN, I GUESS I'LL GO FIRST!
MY NAME IS SUBARU NATSUKI!
BA (POSE)
THE IGNORANT AND UNINTELLIGENT, FOREVER AND EVERLASTINGLY BROKE! NICE TO MEET YOU!
しーん…
SHIIN (SILENCE)
WELL THAT DOESN'T INSPIRE A LOT OF CONFIDENCE, DOES IT!?
GUH...

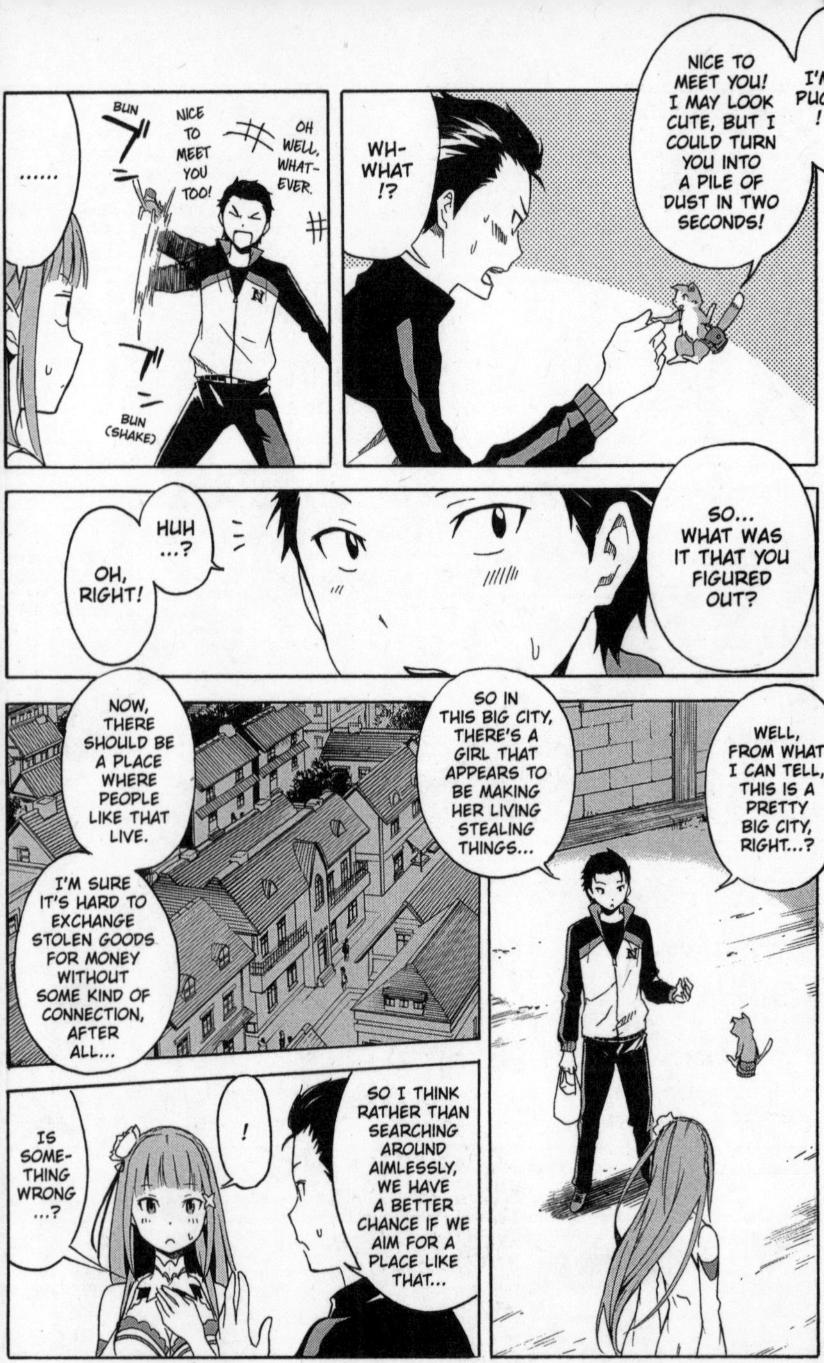
I'M PUCK!
NICE TO MEET YOU! I MAY LOOK CUTE, BUT I COULD TURN YOU INTO A PILE OF DUST IN TWO SECONDS!
WH-WHAT!?
OH WELL, WHATEVER.
NICE TO MEET YOU TOO!
BUN
BUN (SHAKE)
......
SO... WHAT WAS IT THAT YOU FIGURED OUT?
HUH...?
OH, RIGHT!
WELL, FROM WHAT I CAN TELL, THIS IS A PRETTY BIG CITY, RIGHT...?
SO IN THIS BIG CITY, THERE'S A GIRL THAT APPEARS TO BE MAKING HER LIVING STEALING THINGS...
NOW, THERE SHOULD BE A PLACE WHERE PEOPLE LIKE THAT LIVE.
I'M SURE IT'S HARD TO EXCHANGE STOLEN GOODS FOR MONEY WITHOUT SOME KIND OF CONNECTION, AFTER ALL...
SO I THINK RATHER THAN SEARCHING AROUND AIMLESSLY, WE HAVE A BETTER CHANCE IF WE AIM FOR A PLACE LIKE THAT...
!
IS SOMETHING WRONG...?

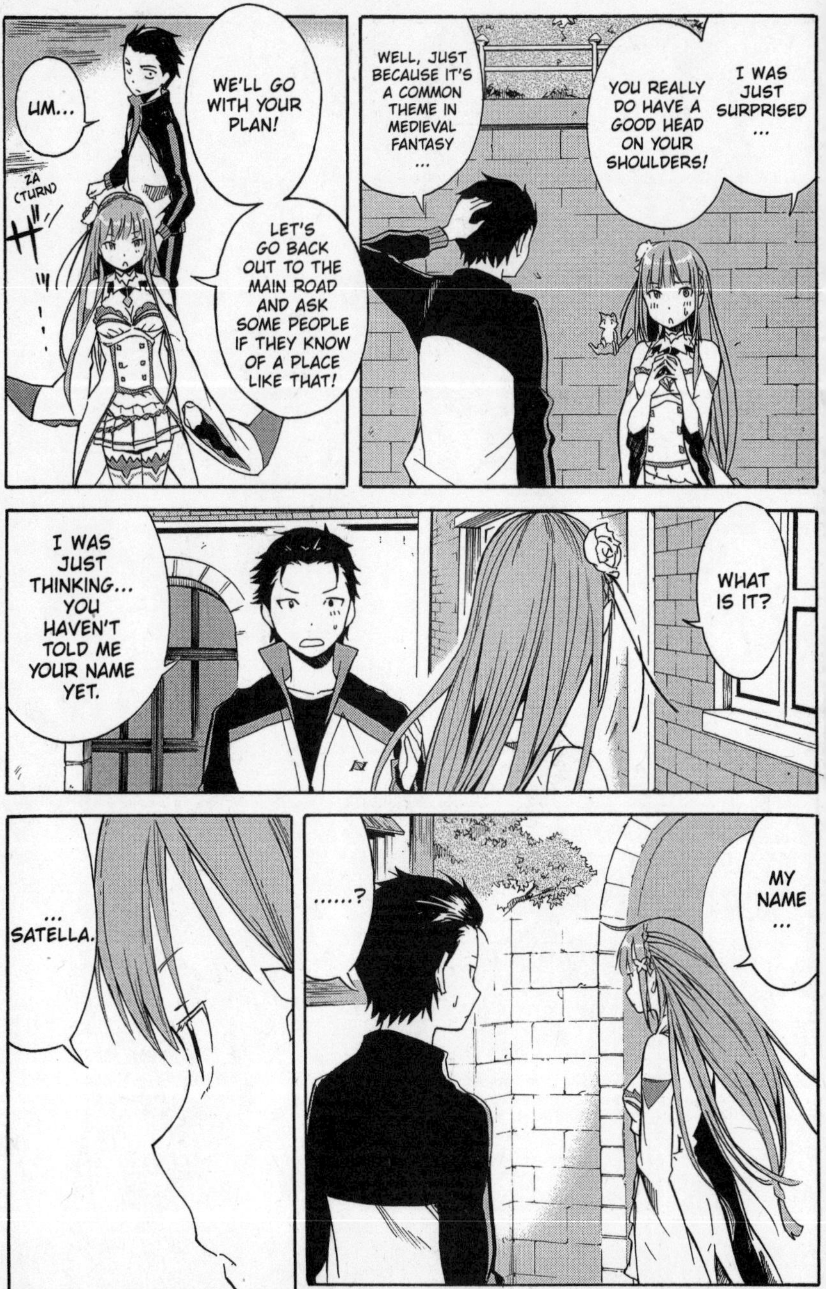
I WAS JUST SURPRISED...
YOU REALLY DO HAVE A GOOD HEAD ON YOUR SHOULDERS!
WELL, JUST BECAUSE IT'S A COMMON THEME IN MEDIEVAL FANTASY...
WE'LL GO WITH YOUR PLAN!
LET'S GO BACK OUT TO THE MAIN ROAD AND ASK SOME PEOPLE IF THEY KNOW OF A PLACE LIKE THAT!
ZA (TURN)
UM...
WHAT IS IT?
I WAS JUST THINKING... YOU HAVEN'T TOLD ME YOUR NAME YET.
MY NAME...
......?
... SATELLA.

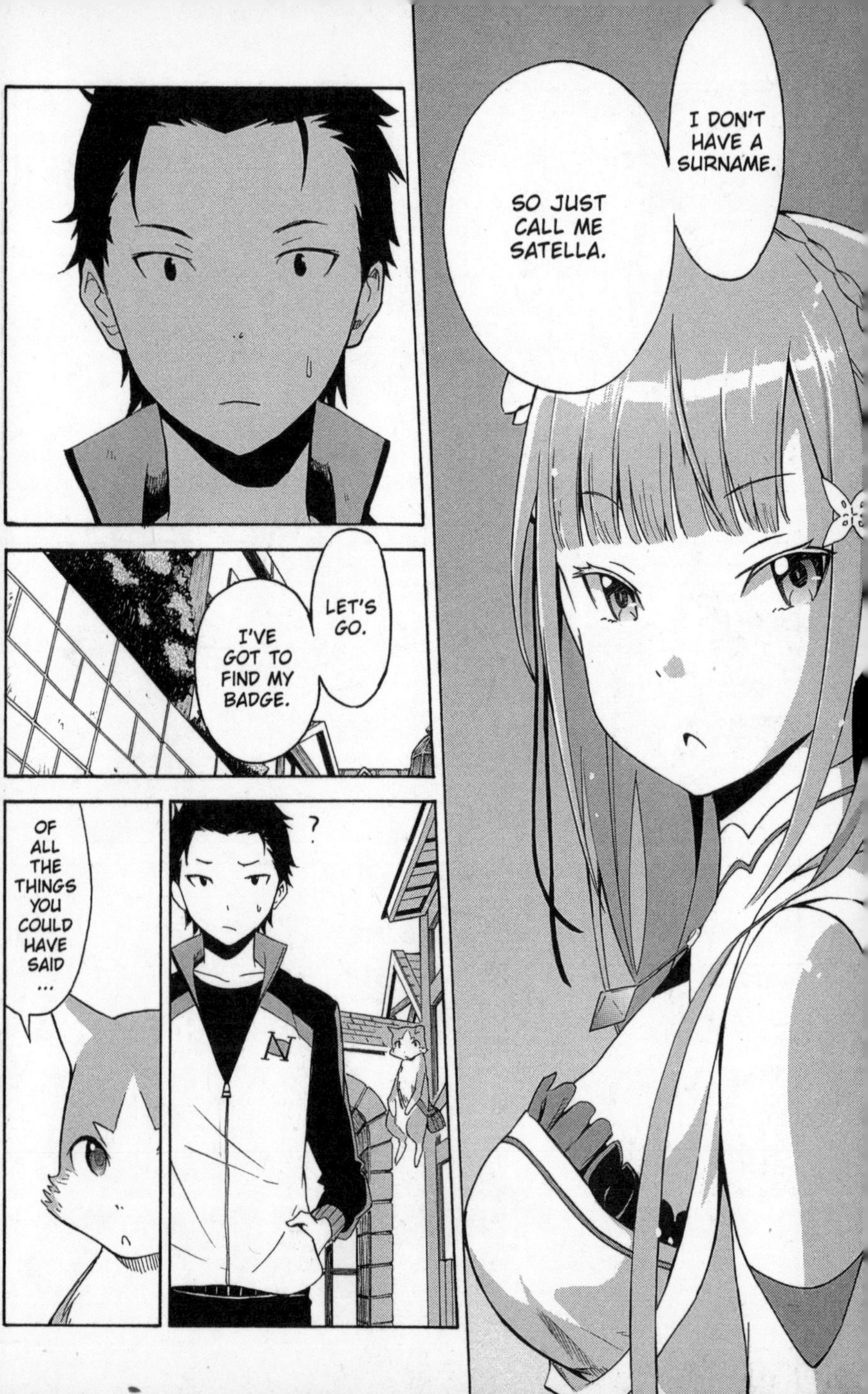
I DON'T HAVE A SURNAME.
SO JUST CALL ME SATELLA.
LET'S GO.
I'VE GOT TO FIND MY BADGE.
?
OF ALL THE THINGS YOU COULD HAVE SAID ...

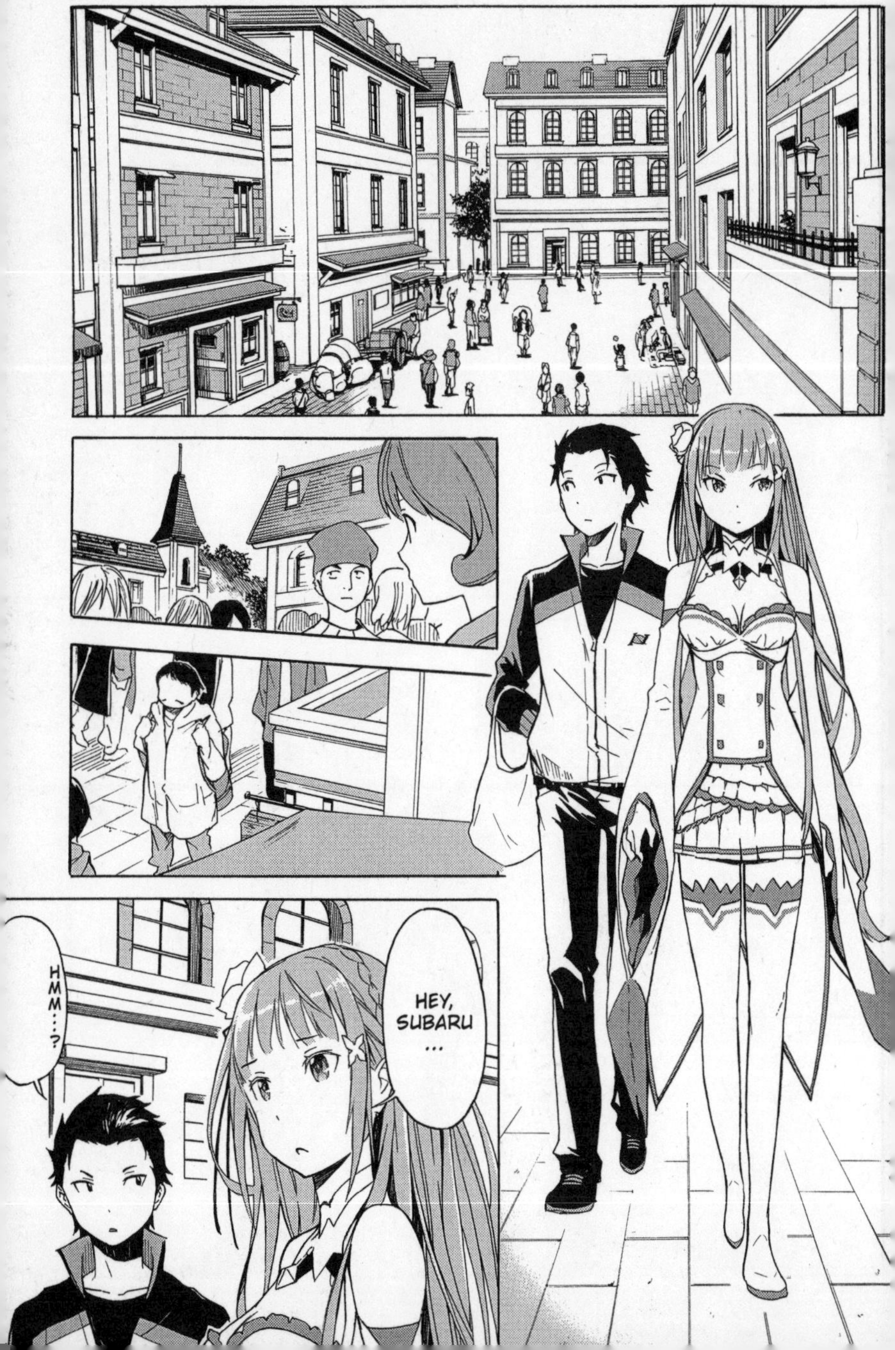
HEY, SUBARU ...
HMM...?

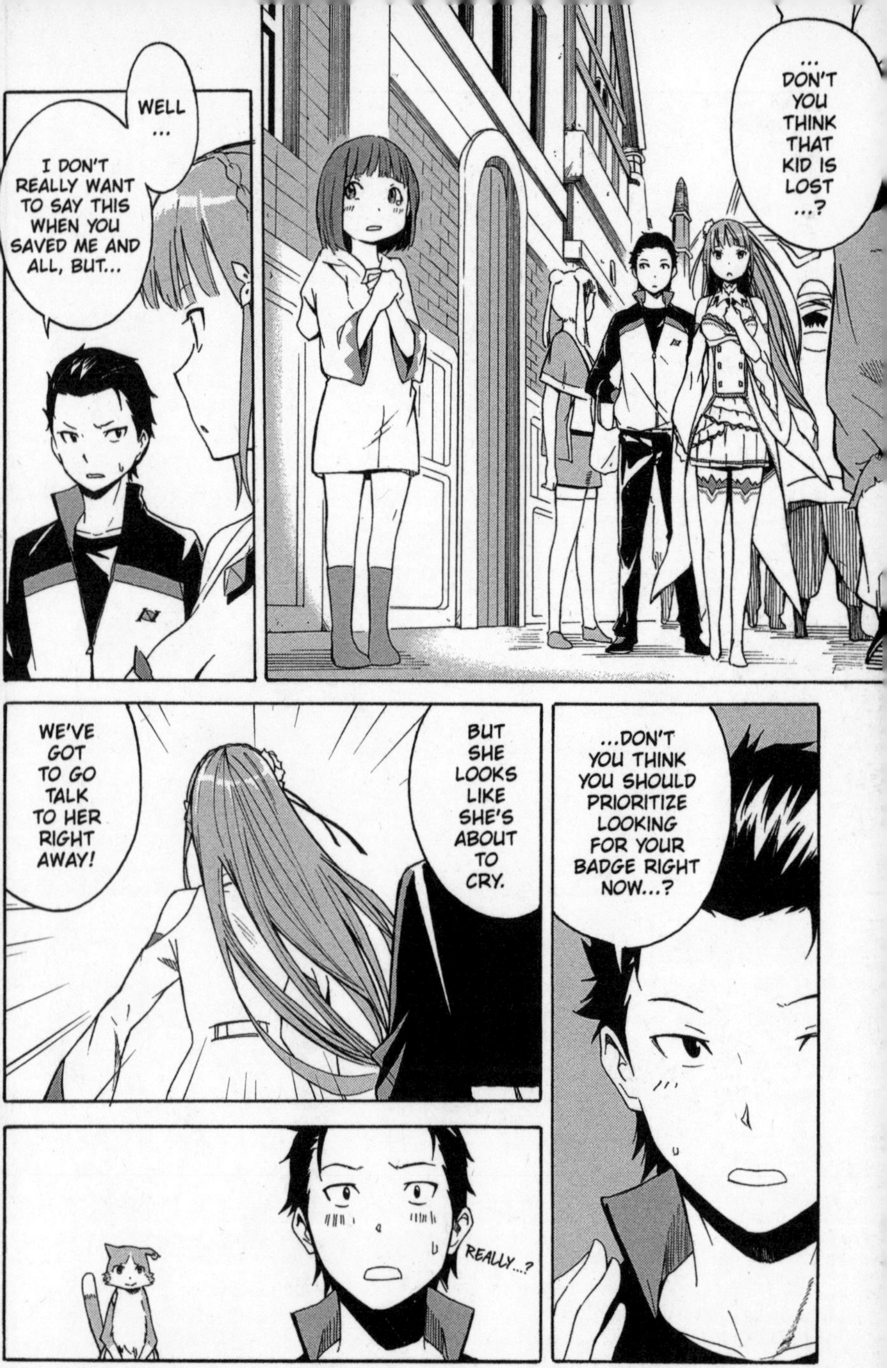
...DON'T YOU THINK THAT KID IS LOST...?
WELL...
I DON'T REALLY WANT TO SAY THIS WHEN YOU SAVED ME AND ALL, BUT...
...DON'T YOU THINK YOU SHOULD PRIORITIZE LOOKING FOR YOUR BADGE RIGHT NOW...?
BUT SHE LOOKS LIKE SHE'S ABOUT TO CRY.
WE'VE GOT TO GO TALK TO HER RIGHT AWAY!
REALLY...?

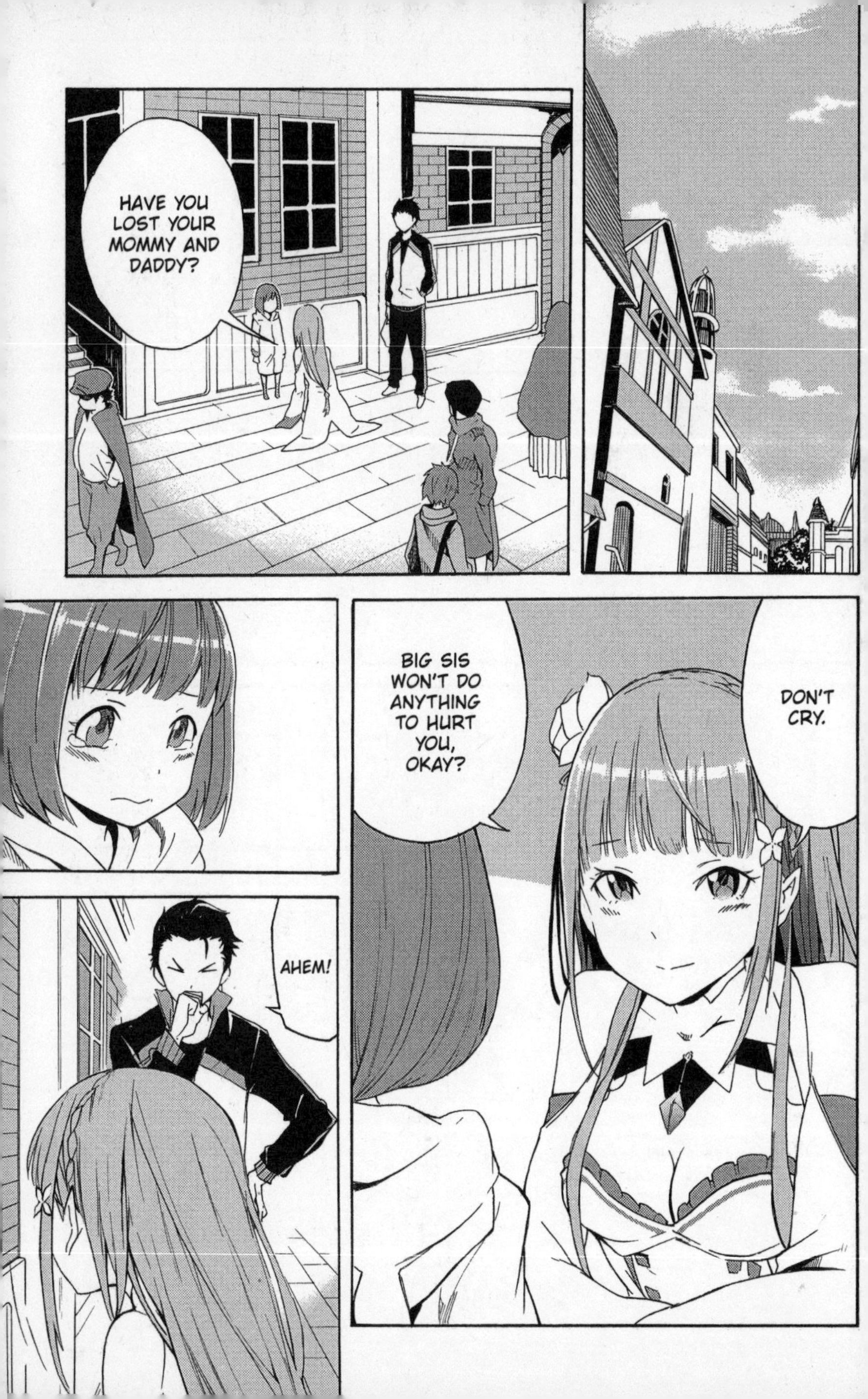
HAVE YOU LOST YOUR MOMMY AND DADDY?
DON'T CRY.
BIG SIS WON'T DO ANYTHING TO HURT YOU, OKAY?
AHEM!

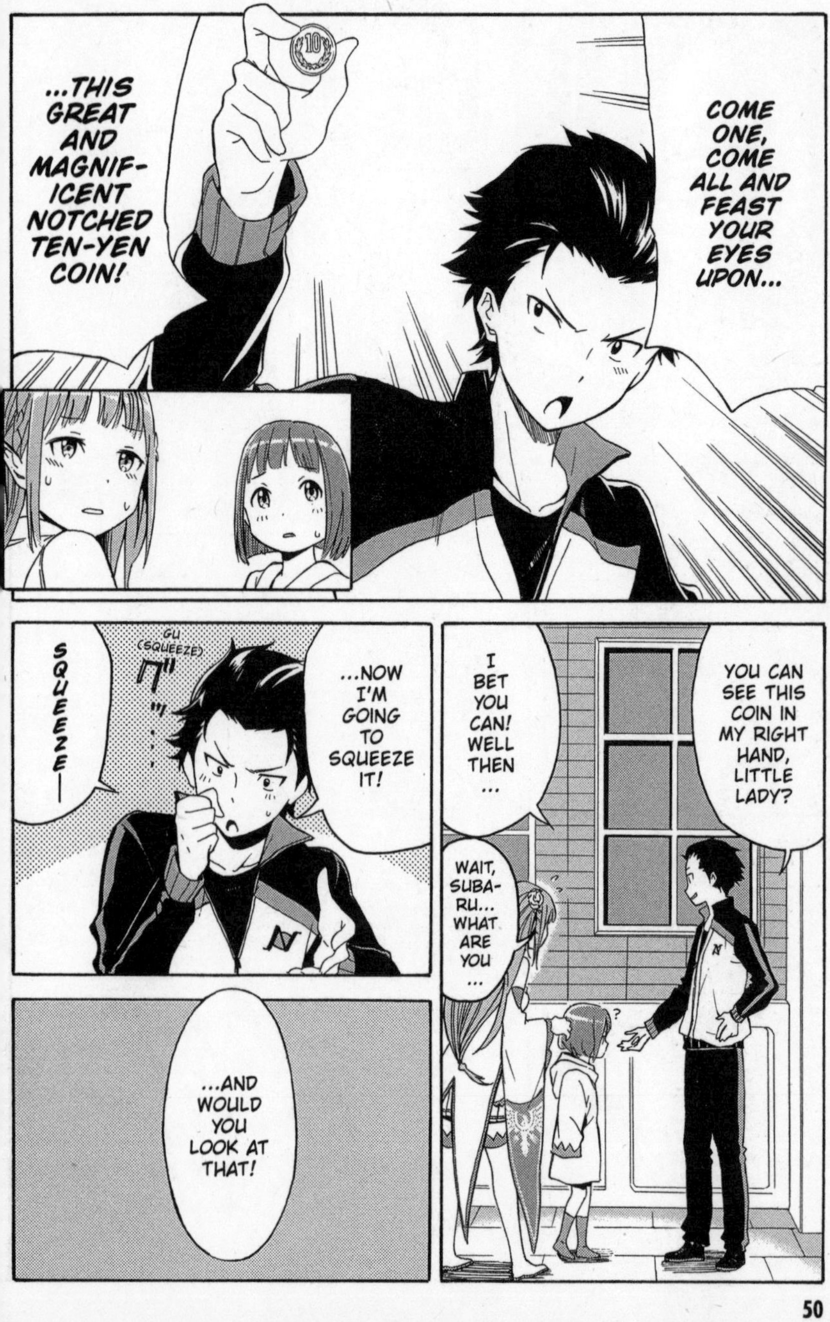
COME ONE, COME ALL AND FEAST YOUR EYES UPON...
...THIS GREAT AND MAGNIFICENT NOTCHED TEN-YEN COIN!
YOU CAN SEE THIS COIN IN MY RIGHT HAND, LITTLE LADY?
I BET YOU CAN! WELL THEN...
WAIT, SUBARU... WHAT ARE YOU...
...NOW I'M GOING TO SQUEEZE IT!
GU (SQUEEZE)
SQUEEEZE—
...AND WOULD YOU LOOK AT THAT!

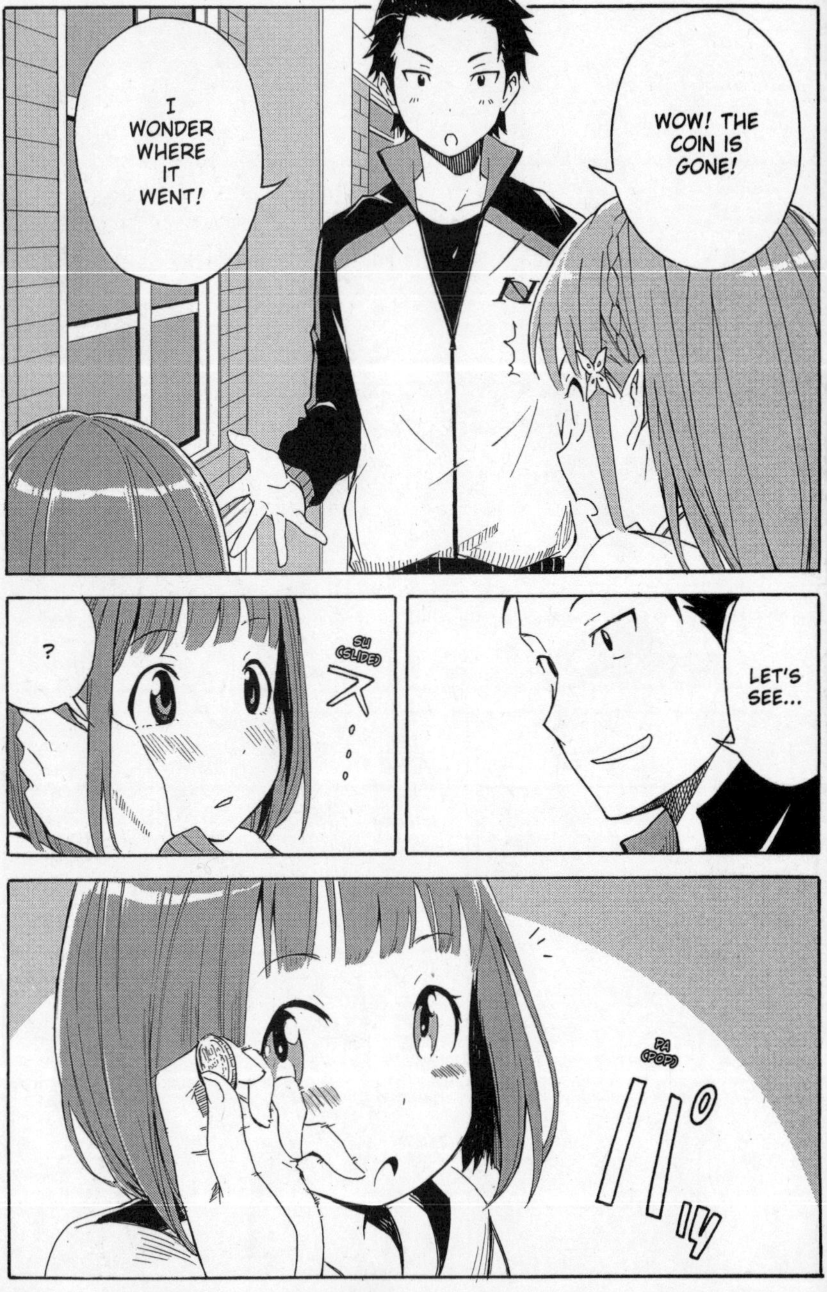
WOW! THE COIN IS GONE!
I WONDER WHERE IT WENT!
LET'S SEE...
SU (SLIDE)
ス
?
PA (POP)
パッ

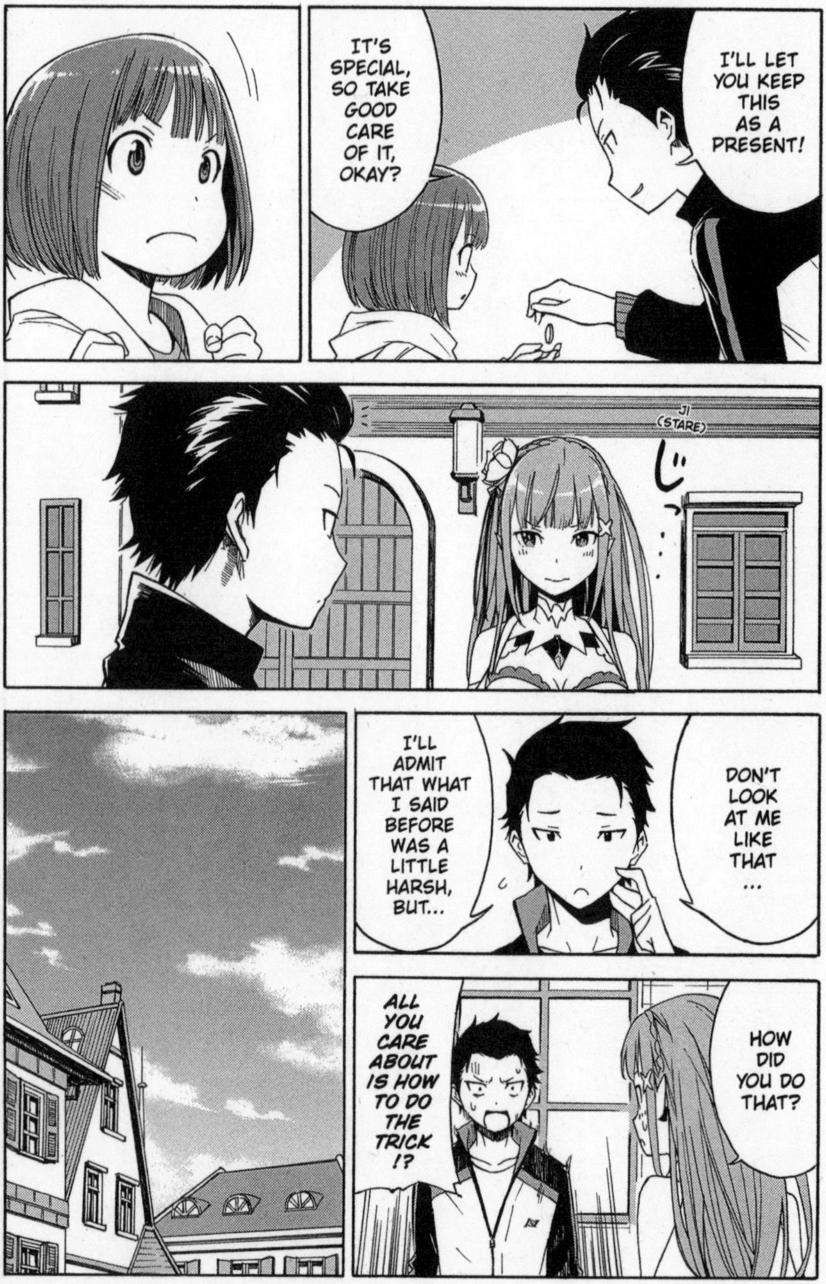
I'LL LET YOU KEEP THIS AS A PRESENT!
IT'S SPECIAL, SO TAKE GOOD CARE OF IT, OKAY?
JI (STARE)
じ
DON'T LOOK AT ME LIKE THAT...
I'LL ADMIT THAT WHAT I SAID BEFORE WAS A LITTLE HARSH, BUT...
HOW DID YOU DO THAT?
ALL YOU CARE ABOUT IS HOW TO DO THE TRICK!?

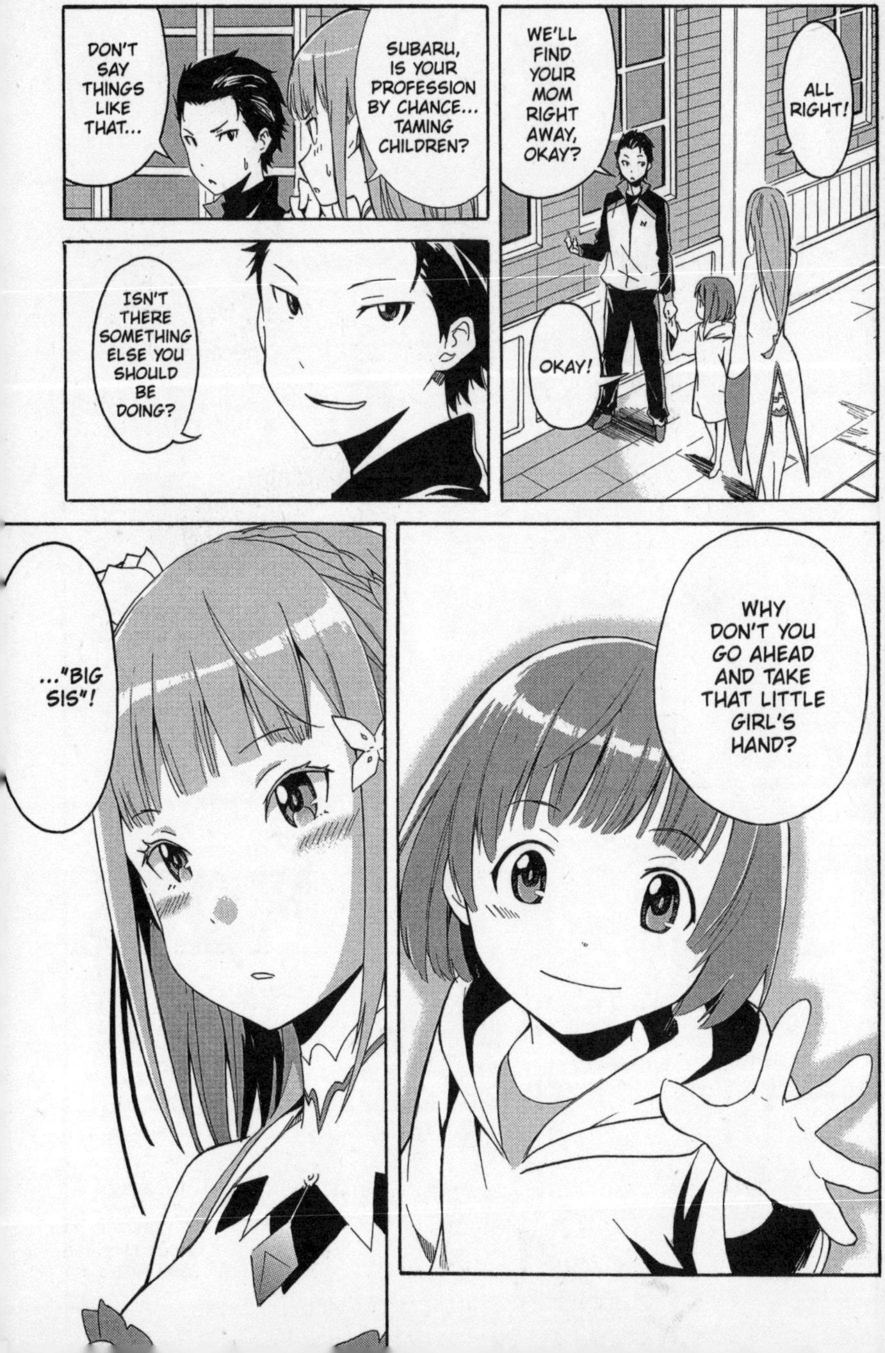
ALL RIGHT!
WE'LL FIND YOUR MOM RIGHT AWAY, OKAY?
OKAY!
SUBARU, IS YOUR PROFESSION BY CHANCE... TAMING CHILDREN?
DON'T SAY THINGS LIKE THAT...
ISN'T THERE SOMETHING ELSE YOU SHOULD BE DOING?
WHY DON'T YOU GO AHEAD AND TAKE THAT LITTLE GIRL'S HAND?
..."BIG SIS"!

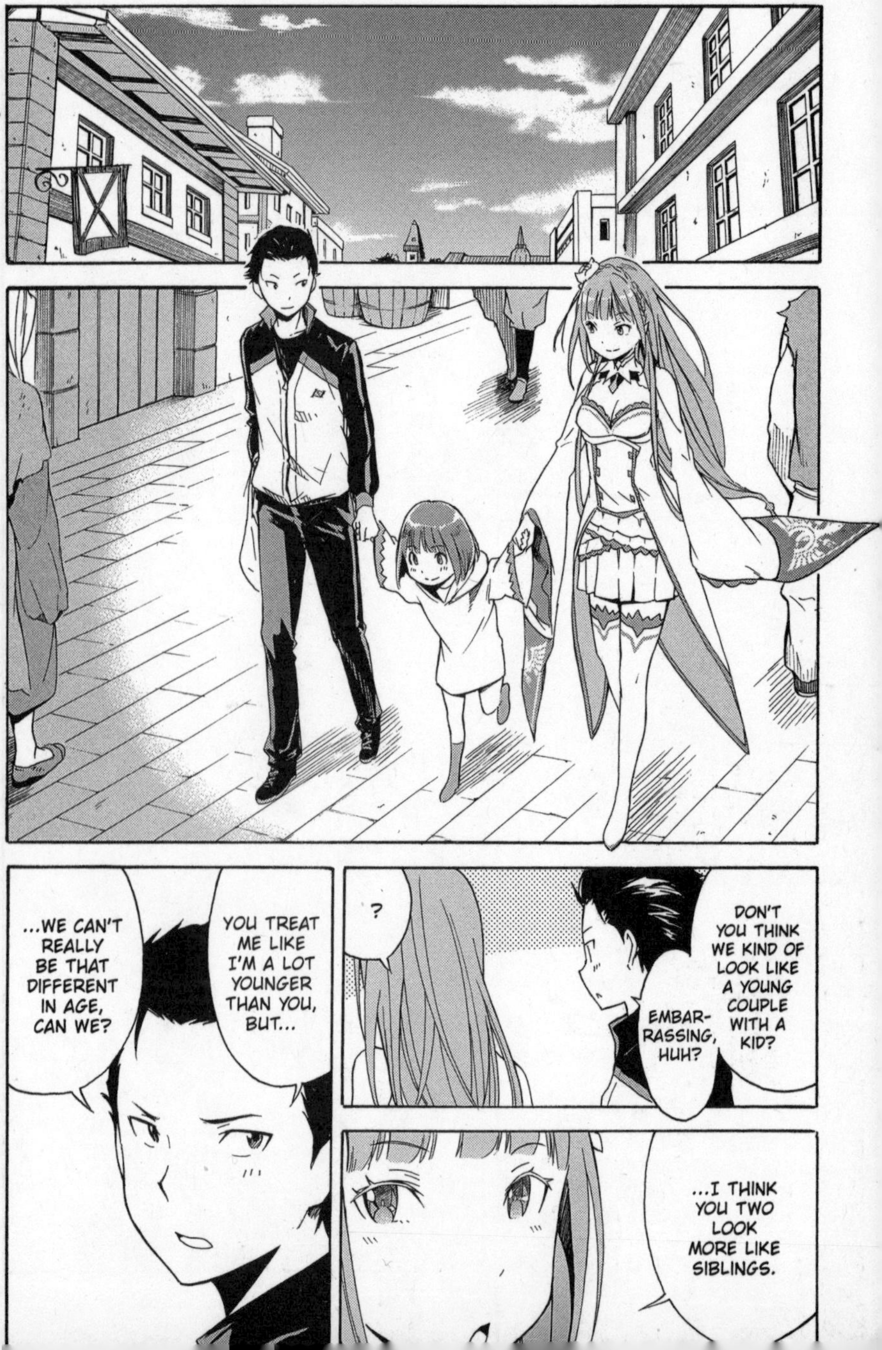
DON'T YOU THINK WE KIND OF LOOK LIKE A YOUNG COUPLE WITH A KID?
?
EMBAR-RASSING, HUH?
...I THINK YOU TWO LOOK MORE LIKE SIBLINGS.
YOU TREAT ME LIKE I'M A LOT YOUNGER THAN YOU, BUT...
...WE CAN'T REALLY BE THAT DIFFERENT IN AGE, CAN WE?

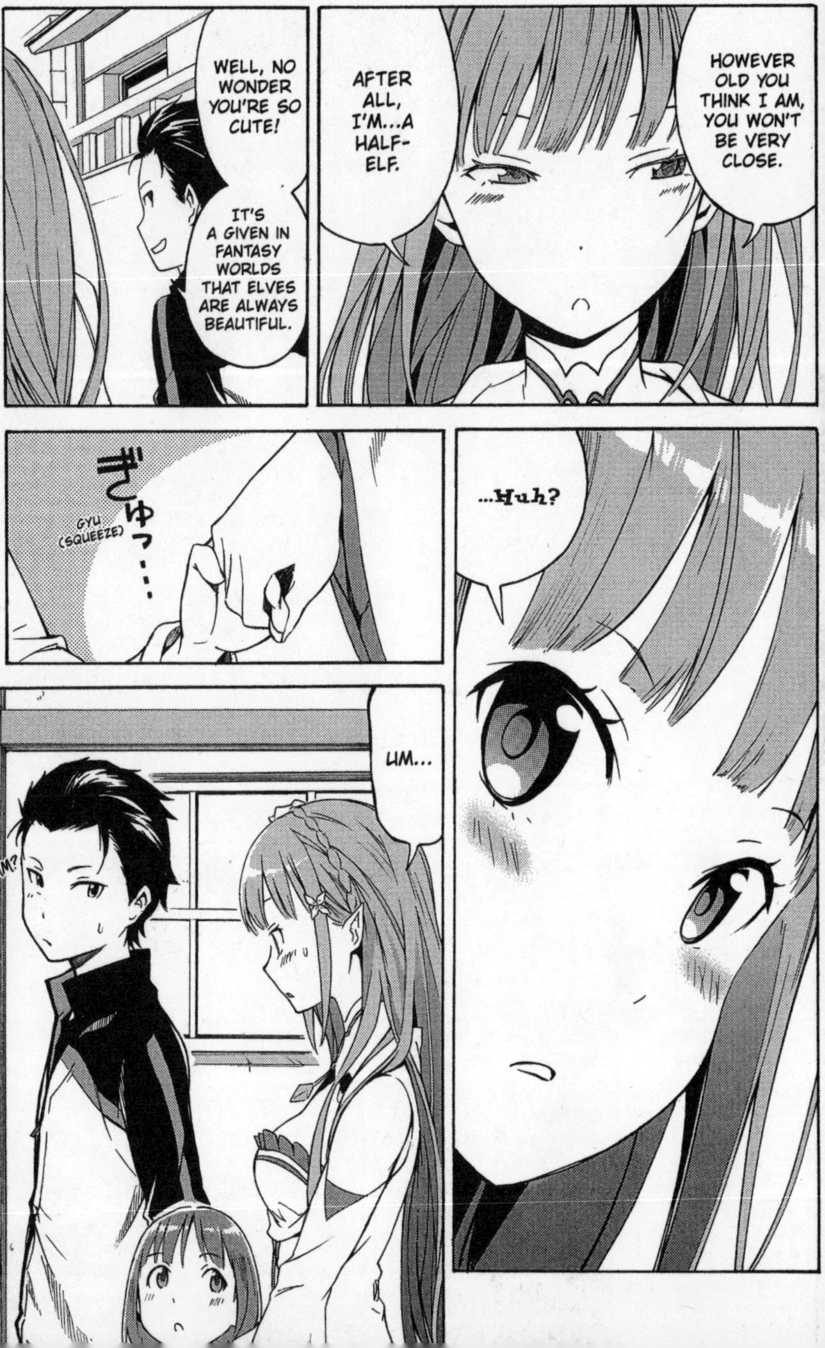
HOWEVER OLD YOU THINK I AM, YOU WON'T BE VERY CLOSE.
AFTER ALL, I'M...A HALF-ELF.
WELL, NO WONDER YOU'RE SO CUTE!
IT'S A GIVEN IN FANTASY WORLDS THAT ELVES ARE ALWAYS BEAUTIFUL.
...Huh?
ぎゅっ...
GYU (SQUEEZE)
UM...
HMM?

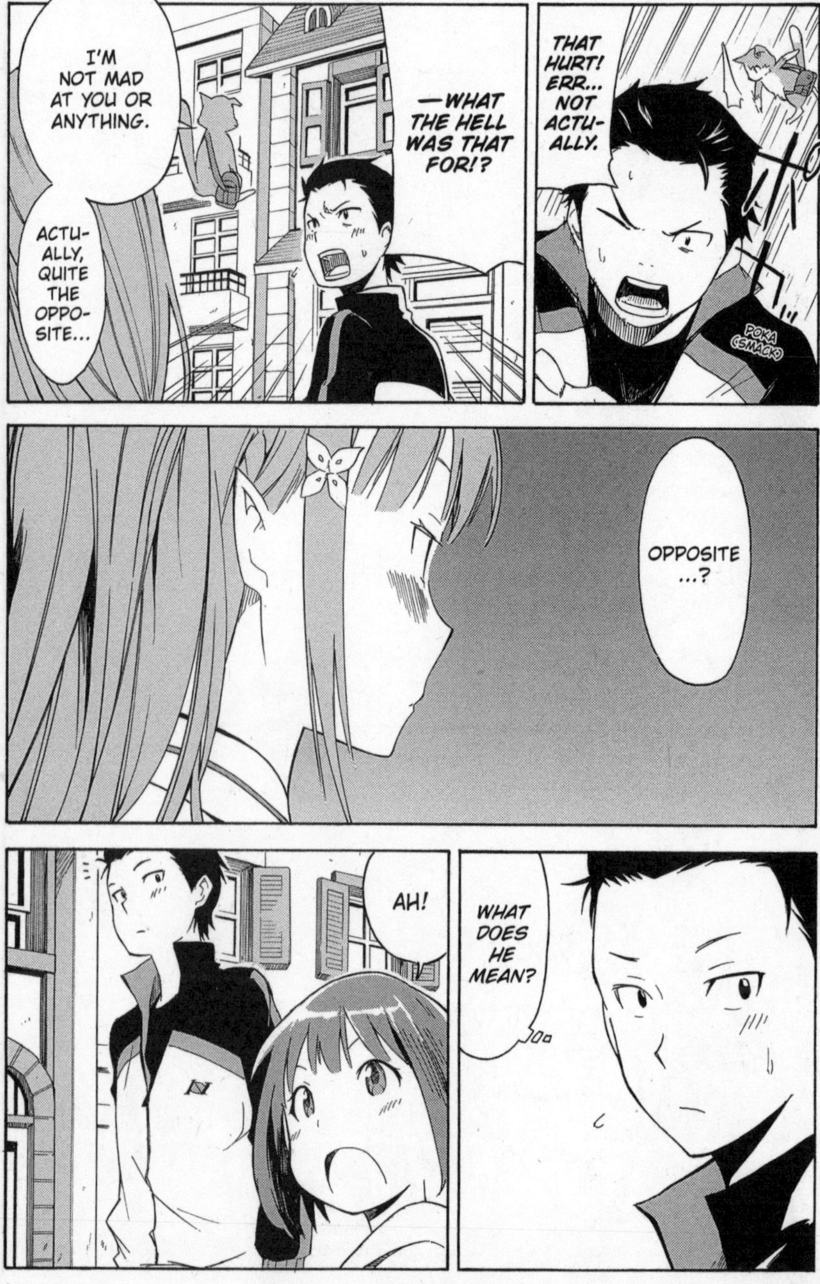
THAT HURT! ERR... NOT ACTU-ALLY.
POKA (SMACK)
—WHAT THE HELL WAS THAT FOR!?
I'M NOT MAD AT YOU OR ANYTHING.
ACTU-ALLY, QUITE THE OPPO-SITE...
OPPOSITE ...?
WHAT DOES HE MEAN?
AH!

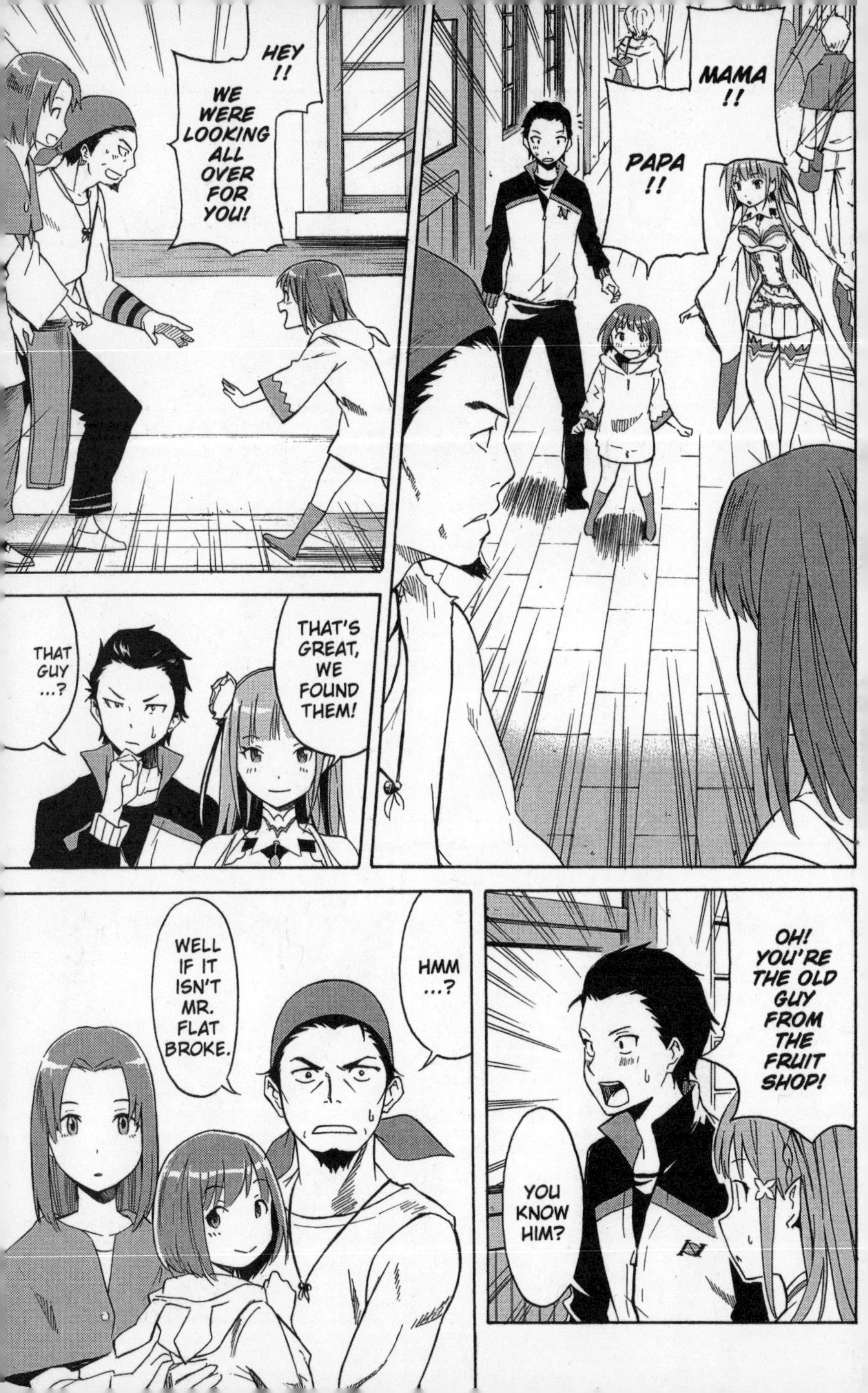
MAMA!!
PAPA!!
HEY!!
WE WERE LOOKING ALL OVER FOR YOU!
THAT'S GREAT, WE FOUND THEM!
THAT GUY...?
OH! YOU'RE THE OLD GUY FROM THE FRUIT SHOP!
YOU KNOW HIM?
HMM...?
WELL IF IT ISN'T MR. FLAT BROKE.

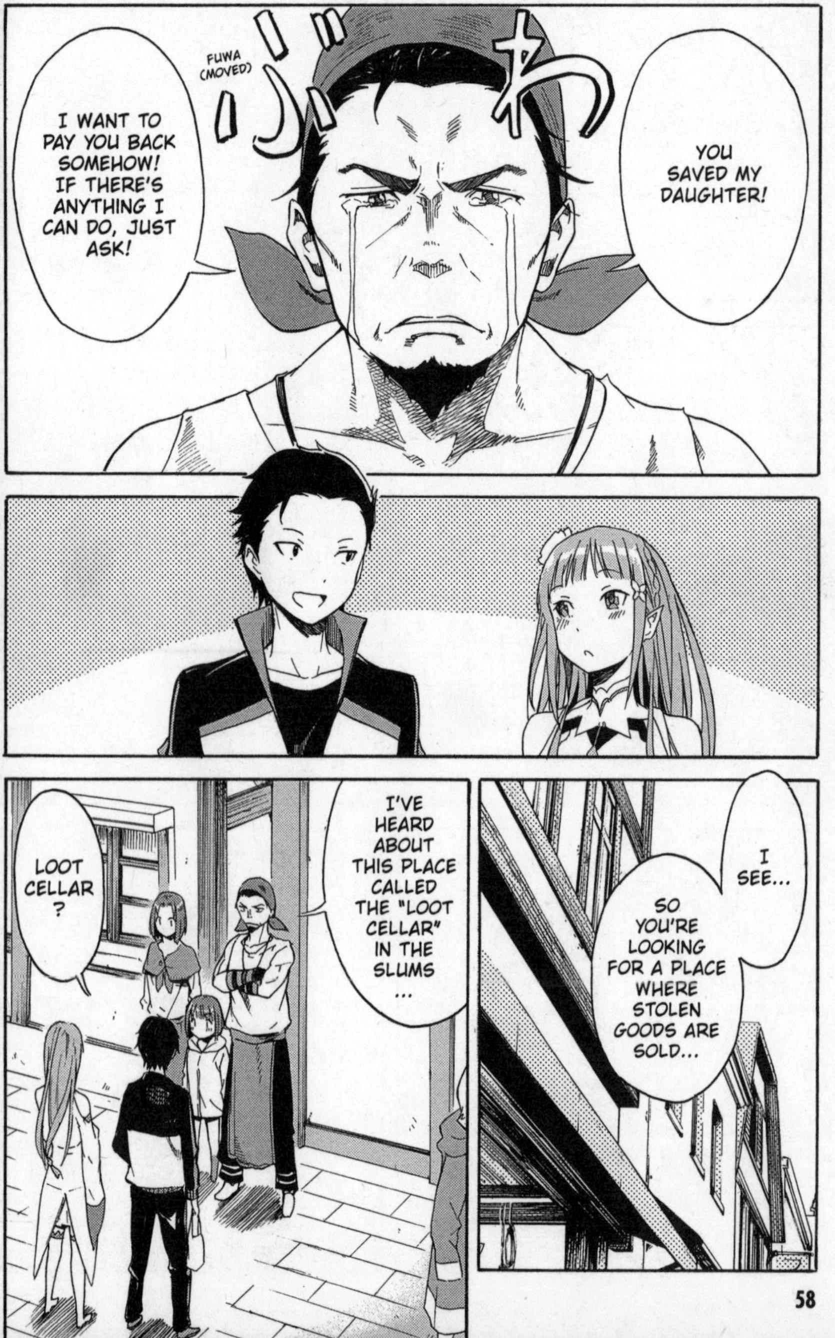
YOU SAVED MY DAUGHTER!
FUWA (MOVED)
I WANT TO PAY YOU BACK SOMEHOW! IF THERE'S ANYTHING I CAN DO, JUST ASK!
I SEE...
SO YOU'RE LOOKING FOR A PLACE WHERE STOLEN GOODS ARE SOLD...
I'VE HEARD ABOUT THIS PLACE CALLED THE "LOOT CELLAR" IN THE SLUMS...
LOOT CELLAR?

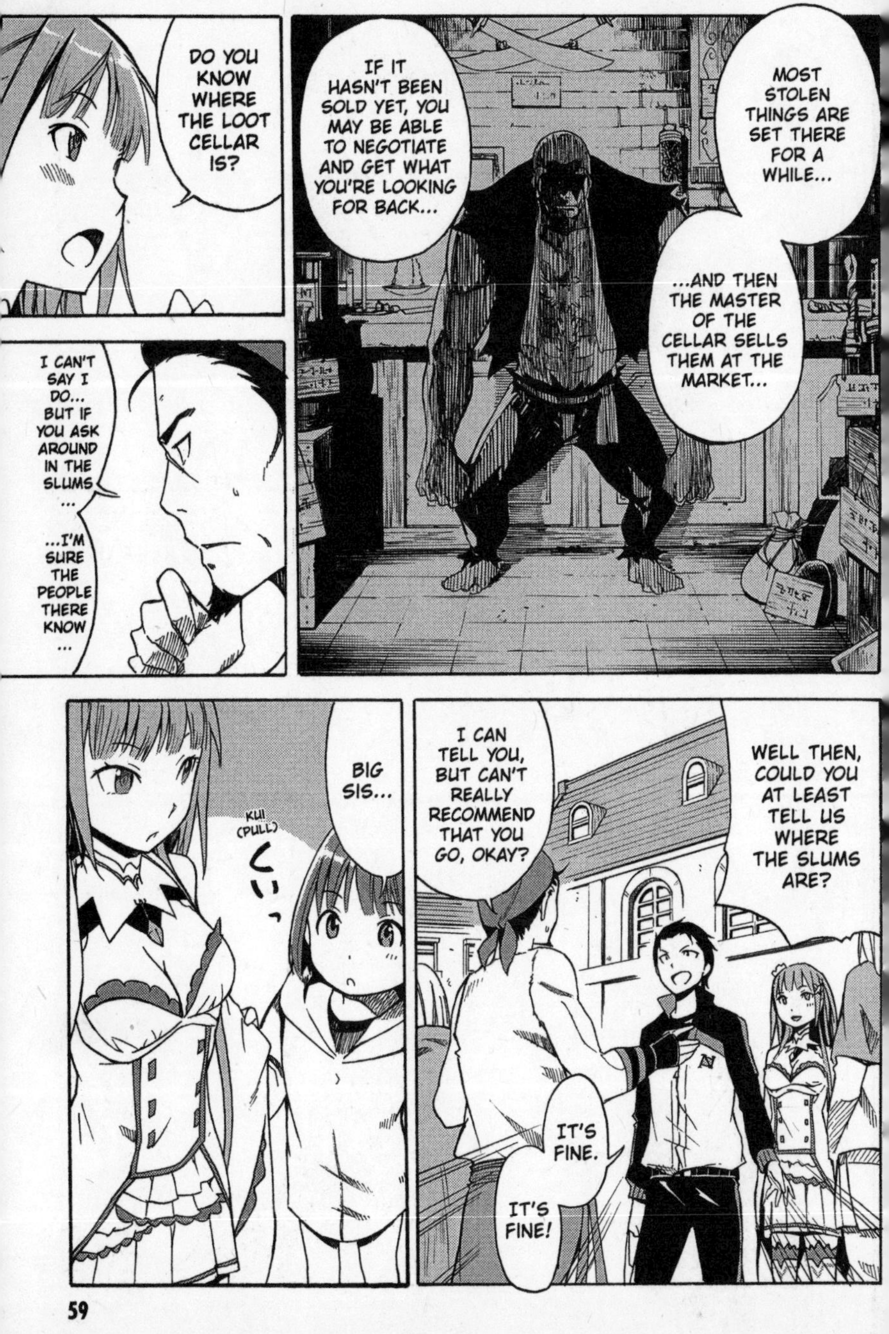
MOST STOLEN THINGS ARE SET THERE FOR A WHILE...
...AND THEN THE MASTER OF THE CELLAR SELLS THEM AT THE MARKET...
IF IT HASN'T BEEN SOLD YET, YOU MAY BE ABLE TO NEGOTIATE AND GET WHAT YOU'RE LOOKING FOR BACK...
DO YOU KNOW WHERE THE LOOT CELLAR IS?
I CAN'T SAY I DO... BUT IF YOU ASK AROUND IN THE SLUMS...
...I'M SURE THE PEOPLE THERE KNOW...
WELL THEN, COULD YOU AT LEAST TELL US WHERE THE SLUMS ARE?
I CAN TELL YOU, BUT CAN'T REALLY RECOMMEND THAT YOU GO, OKAY?
IT'S FINE.
IT'S FINE!
BIG SIS...
KUI (PULL)

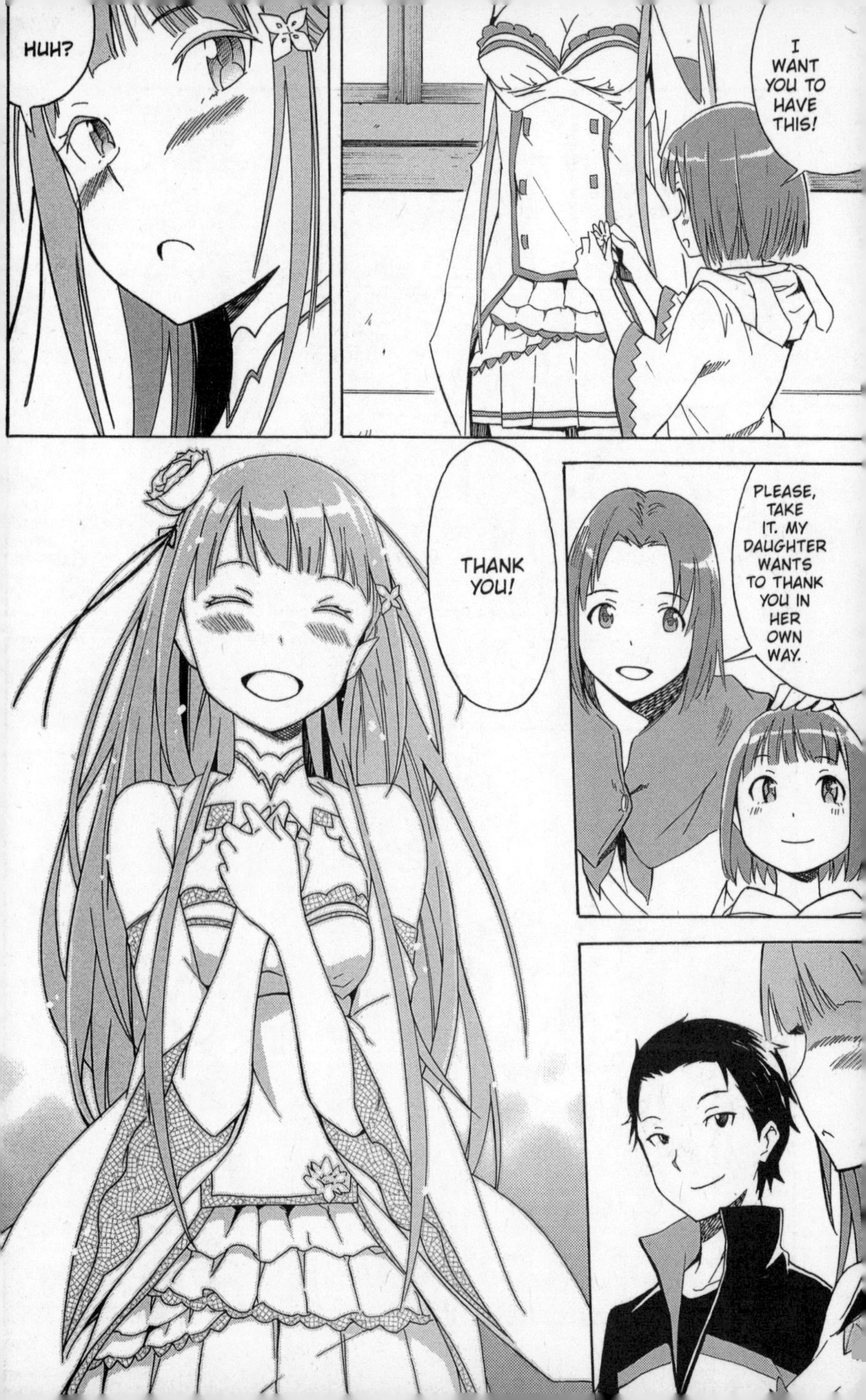
I WANT YOU TO HAVE THIS!
HUH?
PLEASE, TAKE IT. MY DAUGHTER WANTS TO THANK YOU IN HER OWN WAY.
THANK YOU!

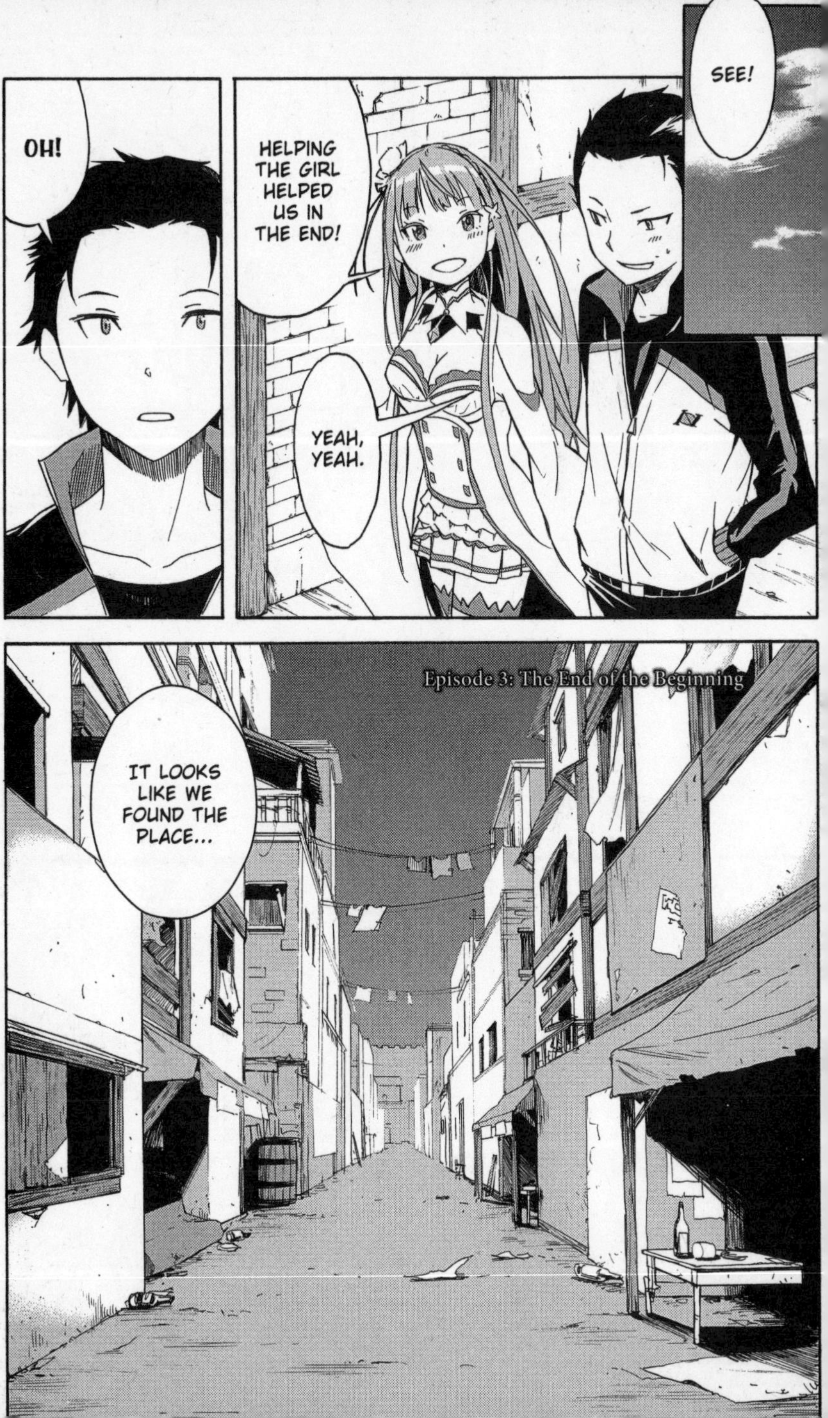
SEE!
HELPING THE GIRL HELPED US IN THE END!
YEAH, YEAH.
OH!
Episode 3: The End of the Beginning
IT LOOKS LIKE WE FOUND THE PLACE...

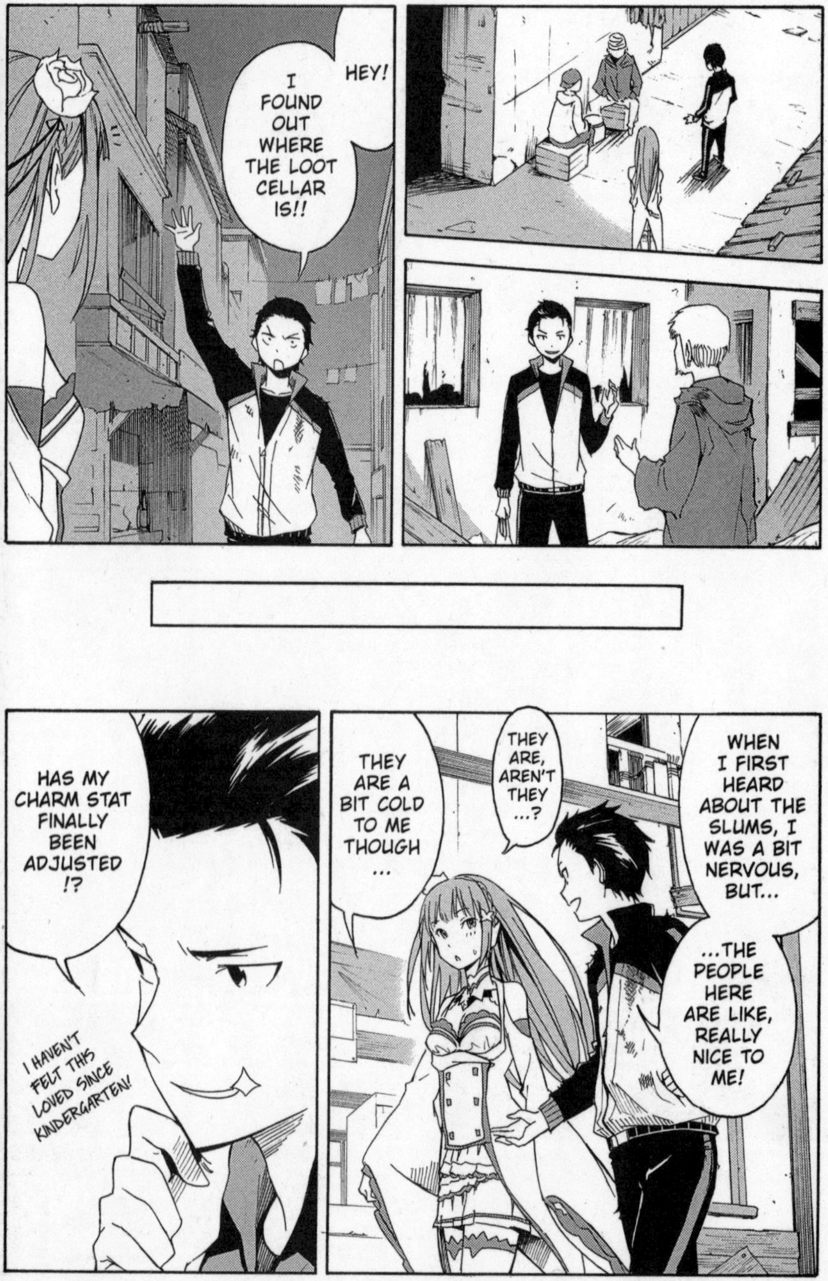
HEY!
I FOUND OUT WHERE THE LOOT CELLAR IS!!
WHEN I FIRST HEARD ABOUT THE SLUMS, I WAS A BIT NERVOUS, BUT...
...THE PEOPLE HERE ARE LIKE, REALLY NICE TO ME!
THEY ARE, AREN'T THEY ...?
THEY ARE A BIT COLD TO ME THOUGH ...
HAS MY CHARM STAT FINALLY BEEN ADJUSTED !?
I HAVEN'T FELT THIS LOVED SINCE KINDERGARTEN!

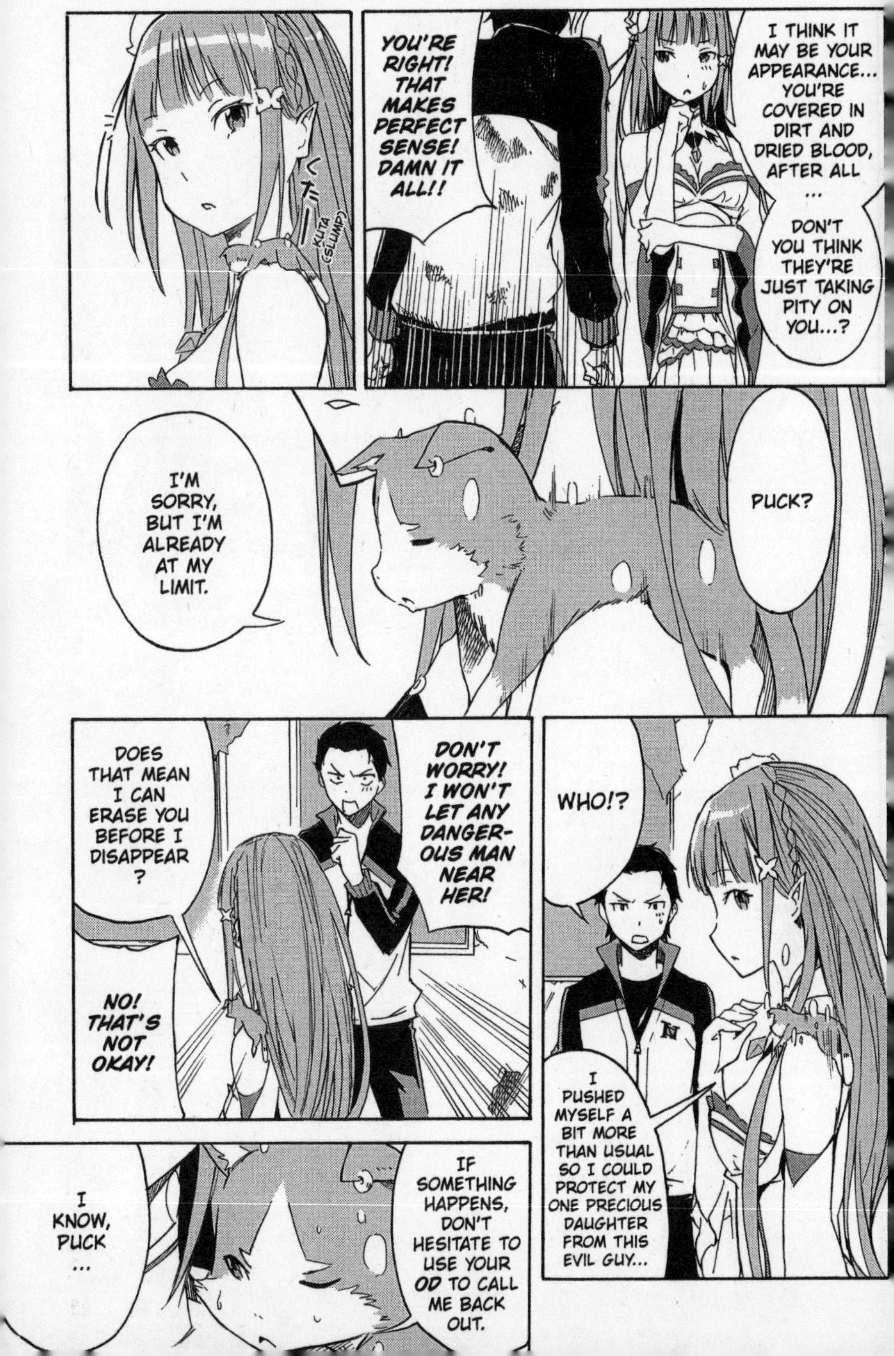
I THINK IT MAY BE YOUR APPEARANCE... YOU'RE COVERED IN DIRT AND DRIED BLOOD, AFTER ALL ...
DON'T YOU THINK THEY'RE JUST TAKING PITY ON YOU...?
YOU'RE RIGHT! THAT MAKES PERFECT SENSE! DAMN IT ALL!!
KUTA (SLUMP)
PUCK?
I'M SORRY, BUT I'M ALREADY AT MY LIMIT.
WHO!?
I PUSHED MYSELF A BIT MORE THAN USUAL SO I COULD PROTECT MY ONE PRECIOUS DAUGHTER FROM THIS EVIL GUY...
DON'T WORRY! I WON'T LET ANY DANGEROUS MAN NEAR HER!
DOES THAT MEAN I CAN ERASE YOU BEFORE I DISAPPEAR?
NO! THAT'S NOT OKAY!
IF SOMETHING HAPPENS, DON'T HESITATE TO USE YOUR OD TO CALL ME BACK OUT.
I KNOW, PUCK ...

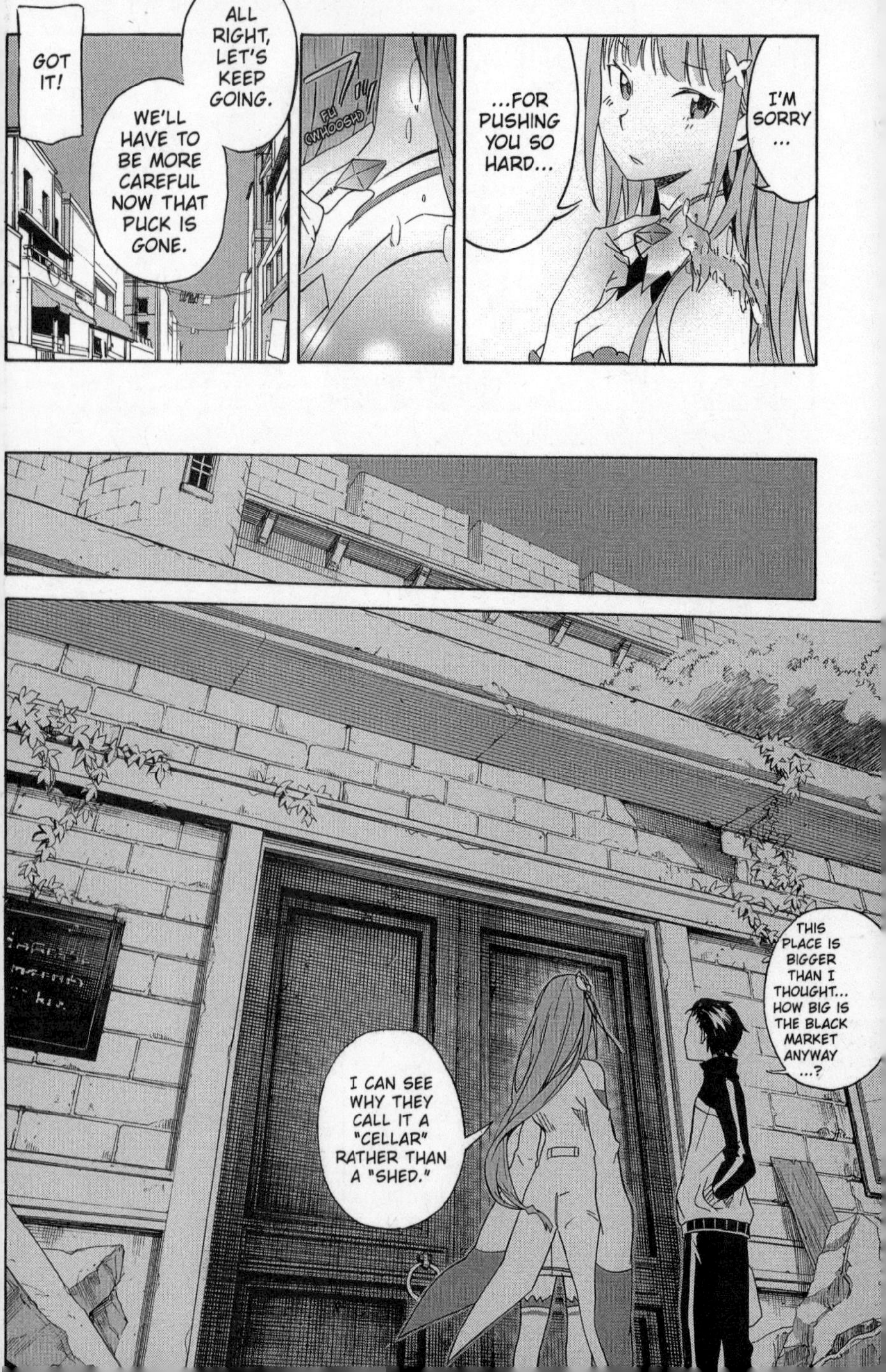
I'M SORRY...
...FOR PUSHING YOU SO HARD...
FU (WHOOSH)
ALL RIGHT, LET'S KEEP GOING.
WE'LL HAVE TO BE MORE CAREFUL NOW THAT PUCK IS GONE.
GOT IT!
THIS PLACE IS BIGGER THAN I THOUGHT... HOW BIG IS THE BLACK MARKET ANYWAY...?
I CAN SEE WHY THEY CALL IT A "CELLAR" RATHER THAN A "SHED."

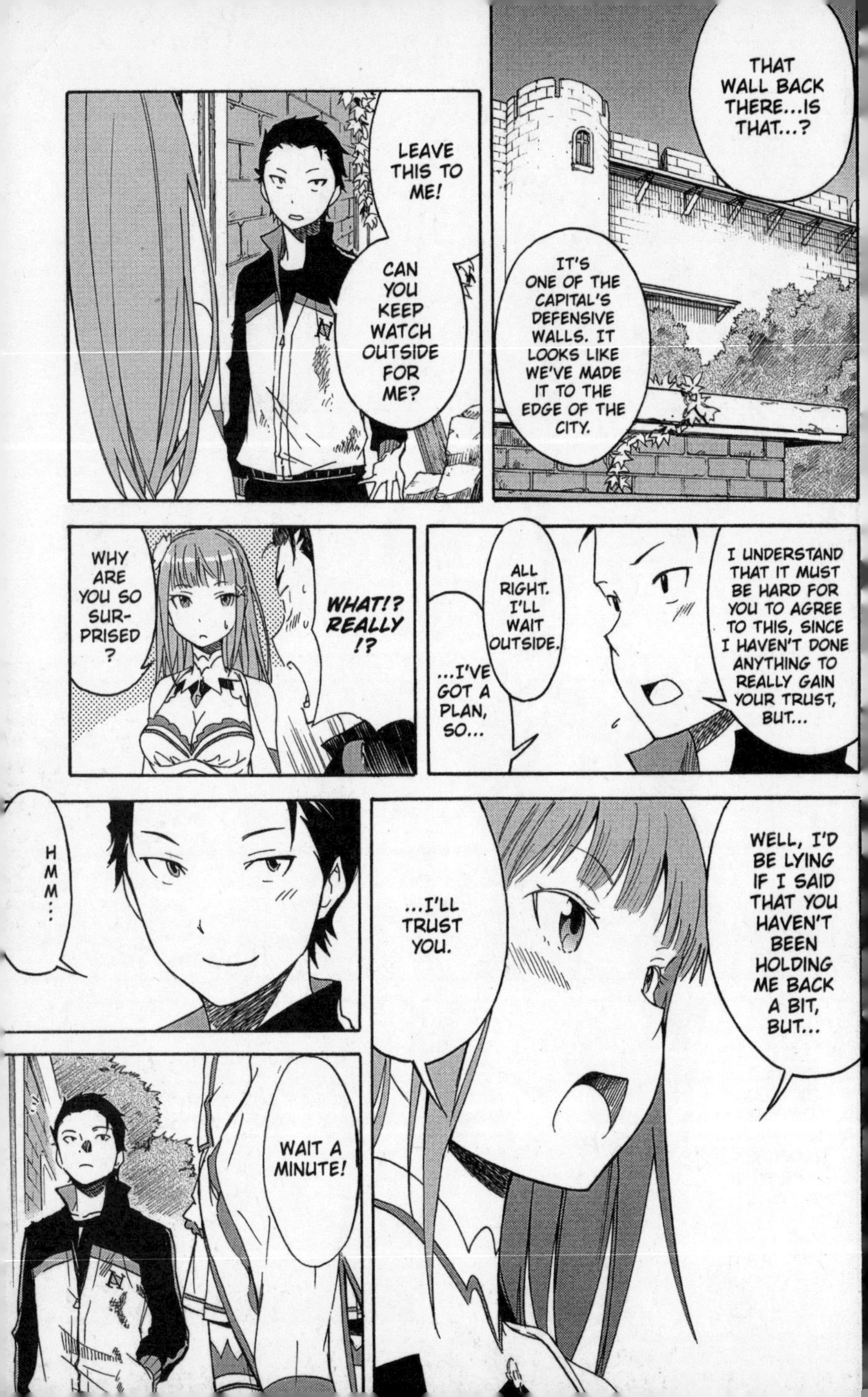
THAT WALL BACK THERE...IS THAT...?
IT'S ONE OF THE CAPITAL'S DEFENSIVE WALLS. IT LOOKS LIKE WE'VE MADE IT TO THE EDGE OF THE CITY.
LEAVE THIS TO ME!
CAN YOU KEEP WATCH OUTSIDE FOR ME?
I UNDERSTAND THAT IT MUST BE HARD FOR YOU TO AGREE TO THIS, SINCE I HAVEN'T DONE ANYTHING TO REALLY GAIN YOUR TRUST, BUT...
...I'VE GOT A PLAN, SO...
ALL RIGHT. I'LL WAIT OUTSIDE.
WHAT!? REALLY!?
WHY ARE YOU SO SUR-PRISED?
WELL, I'D BE LYING IF I SAID THAT YOU HAVEN'T BEEN HOLDING ME BACK A BIT, BUT...
...I'LL TRUST YOU.
HMM...
WAIT A MINUTE!

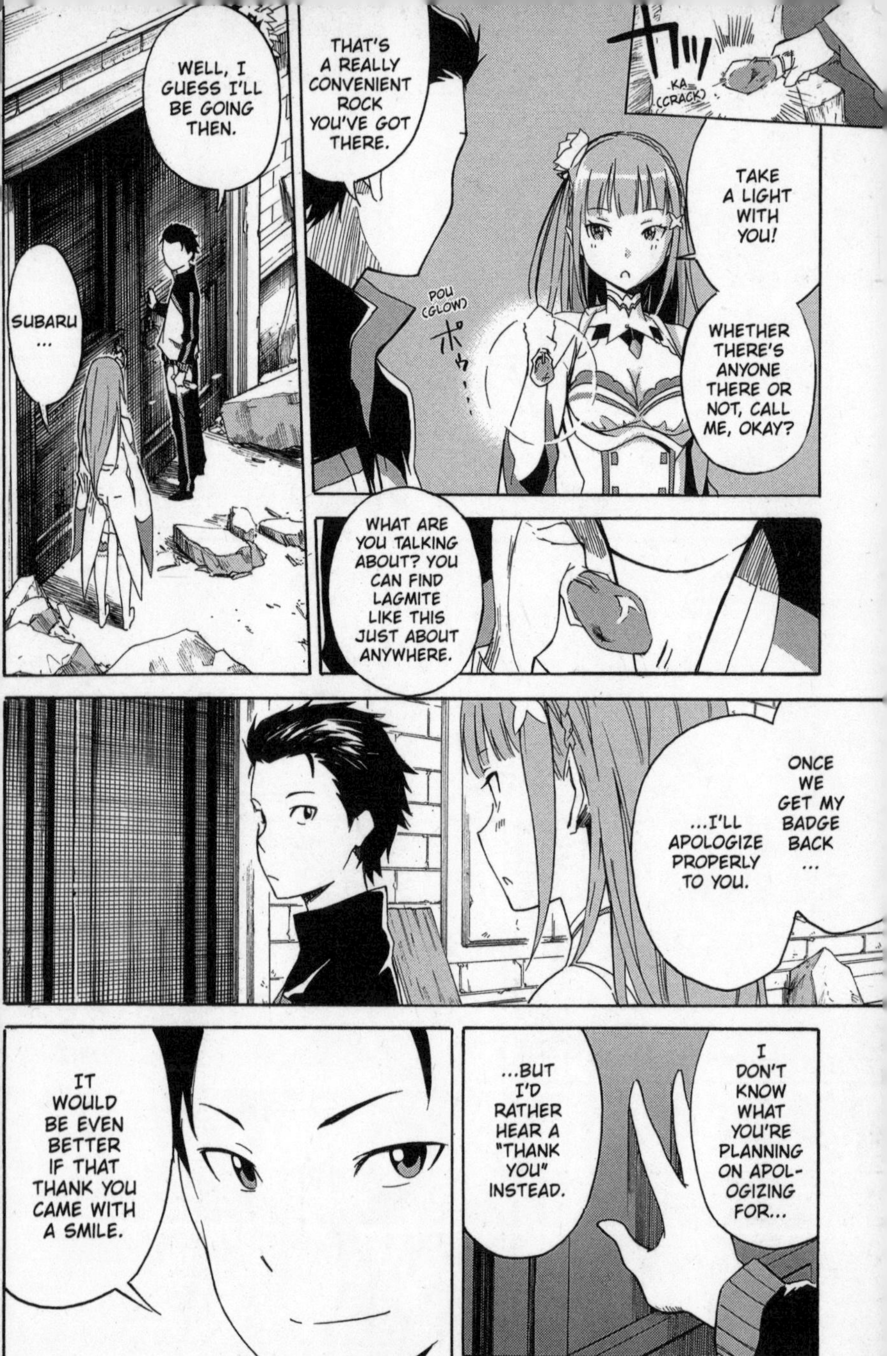
KA (CRACK)
TAKE A LIGHT WITH YOU!
WHETHER THERE'S ANYONE THERE OR NOT, CALL ME, OKAY?
POU (GLOW)
THAT'S A REALLY CONVENIENT ROCK YOU'VE GOT THERE.
WHAT ARE YOU TALKING ABOUT? YOU CAN FIND LAGMITE LIKE THIS JUST ABOUT ANYWHERE.
WELL, I GUESS I'LL BE GOING THEN.
SUBARU...
ONCE WE GET MY BADGE BACK...
...I'LL APOLOGIZE PROPERLY TO YOU.
I DON'T KNOW WHAT YOU'RE PLANNING ON APOLOGIZING FOR...
...BUT I'D RATHER HEAR A "THANK YOU" INSTEAD.
IT WOULD BE EVEN BETTER IF THAT THANK YOU CAME WITH A SMILE.

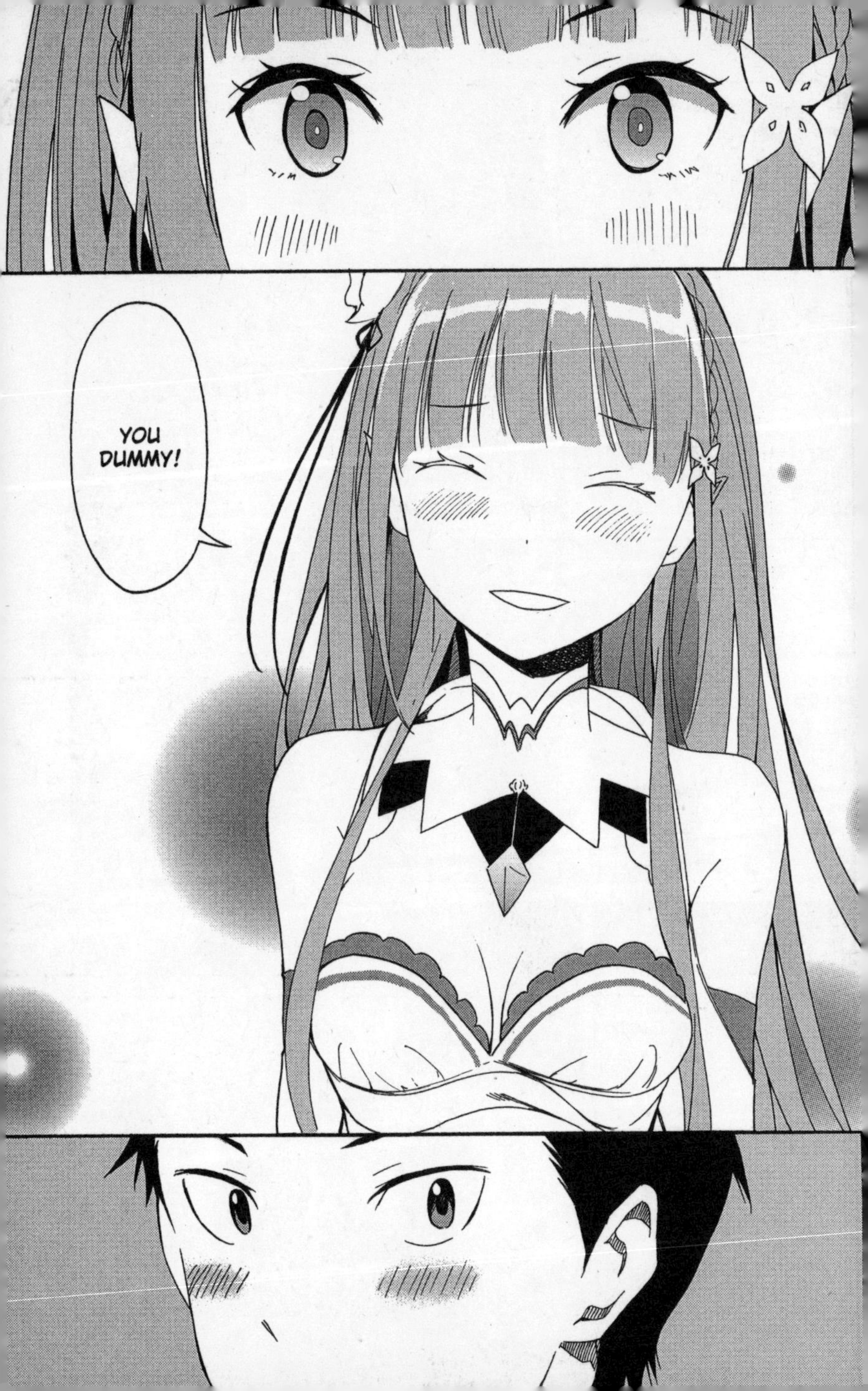
YOU DUMMY!

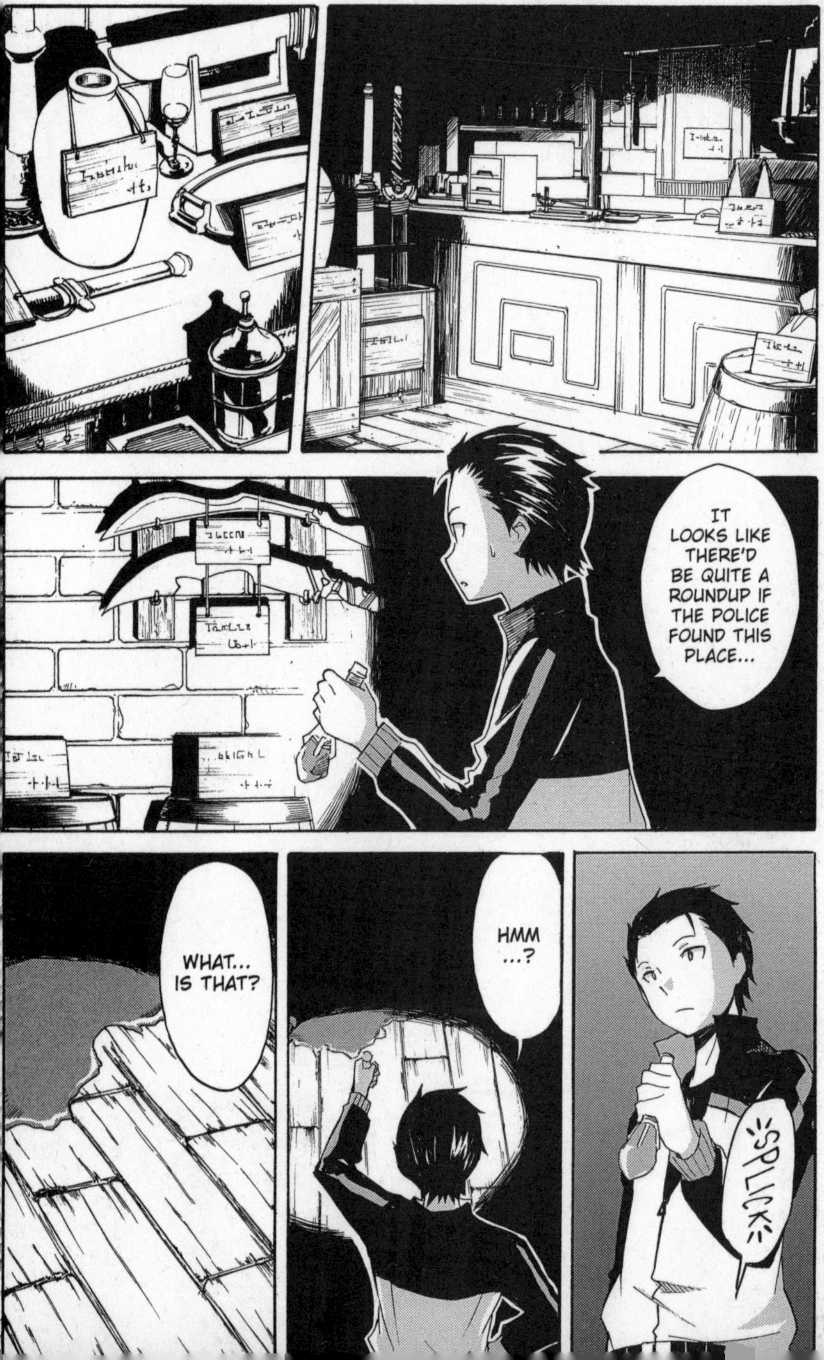
IT LOOKS LIKE THERE'D BE QUITE A ROUNDUP IF THE POLICE FOUND THIS PLACE...
SPLICK
HMM ...?
WHAT... IS THAT?

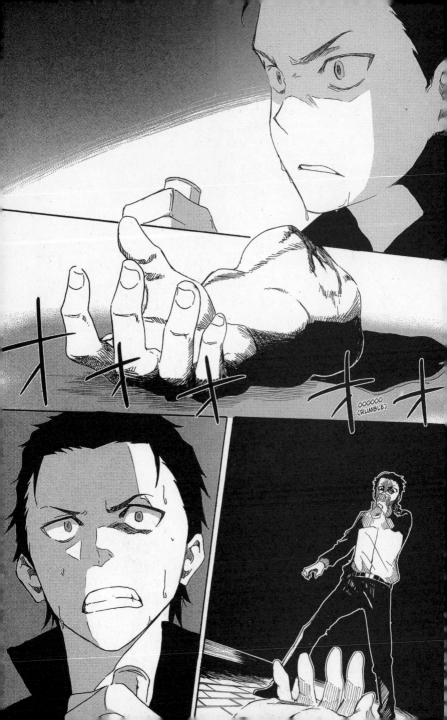

OOOOOO
(RUMBLE)

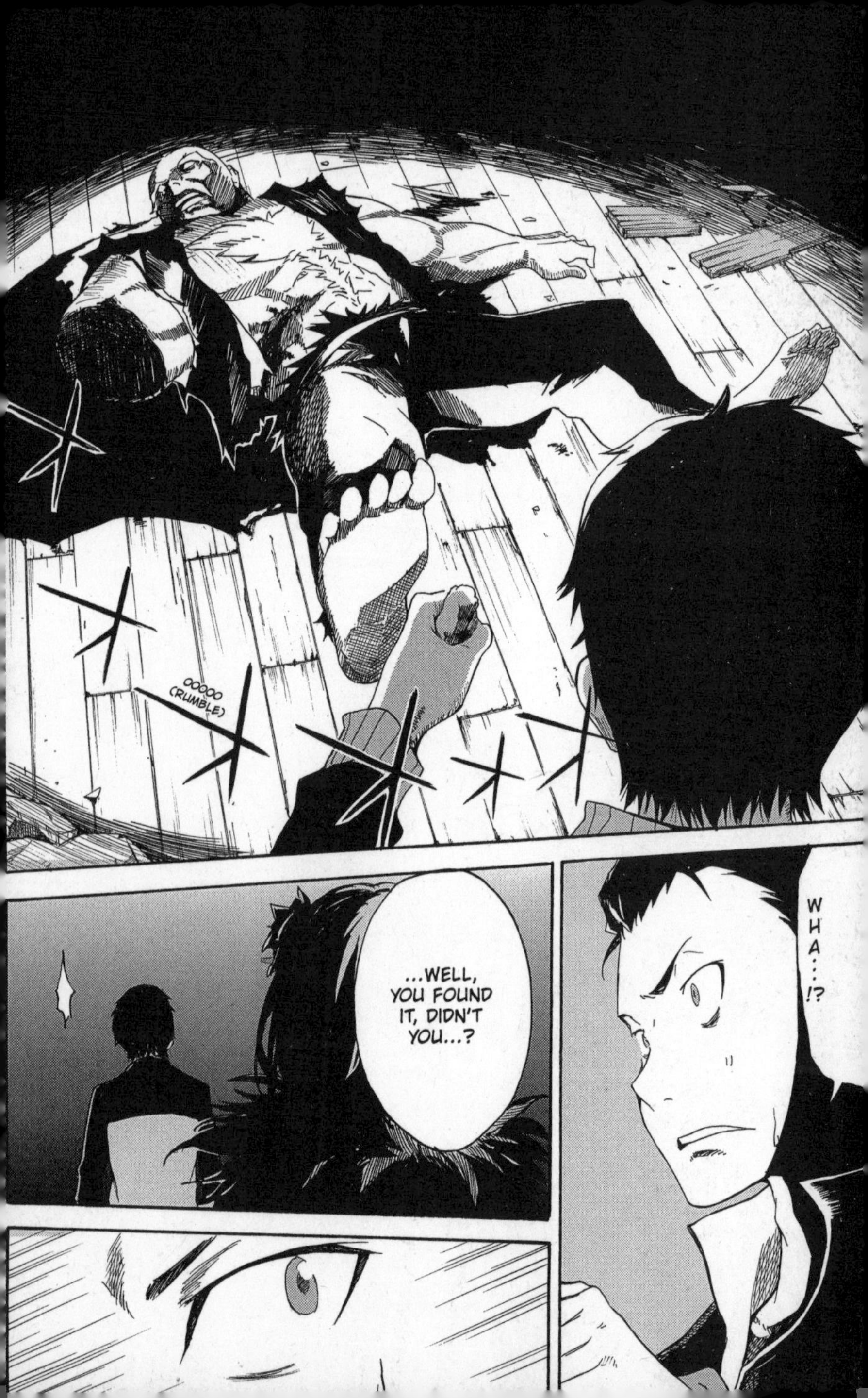
OOOOO (RUMBLE)
WHA...!?
...WELL, YOU FOUND IT, DIDN'T YOU...?

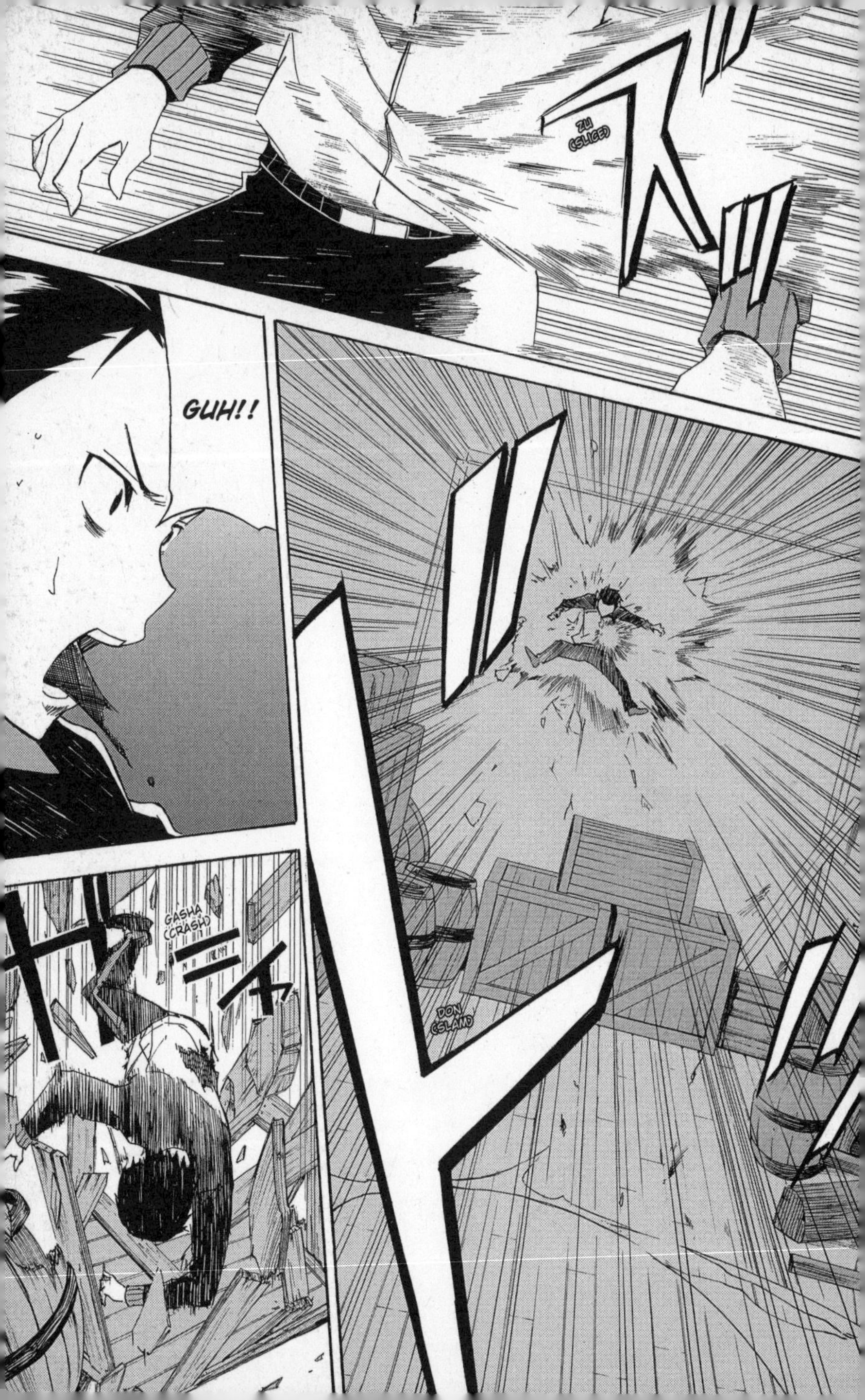
ZU (SLICE)
DON (SLAM)
GUH!!
GASHA (CRASH)

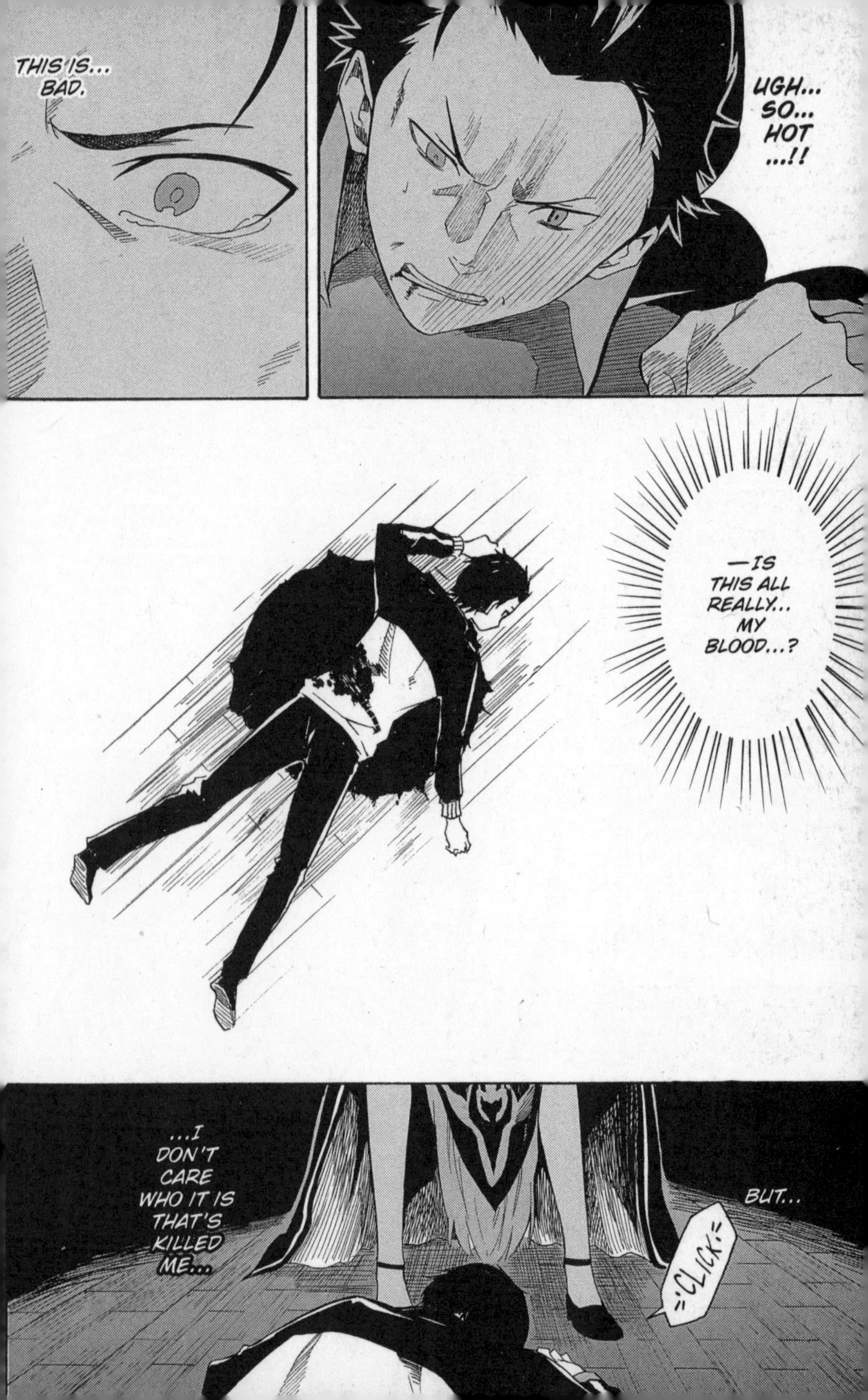
UGH... SO... HOT ...!!
THIS IS... BAD.
—IS THIS ALL REALLY... MY BLOOD...?
BUT...
CLICK
...I DON'T CARE WHO IT IS THAT'S KILLED ME...

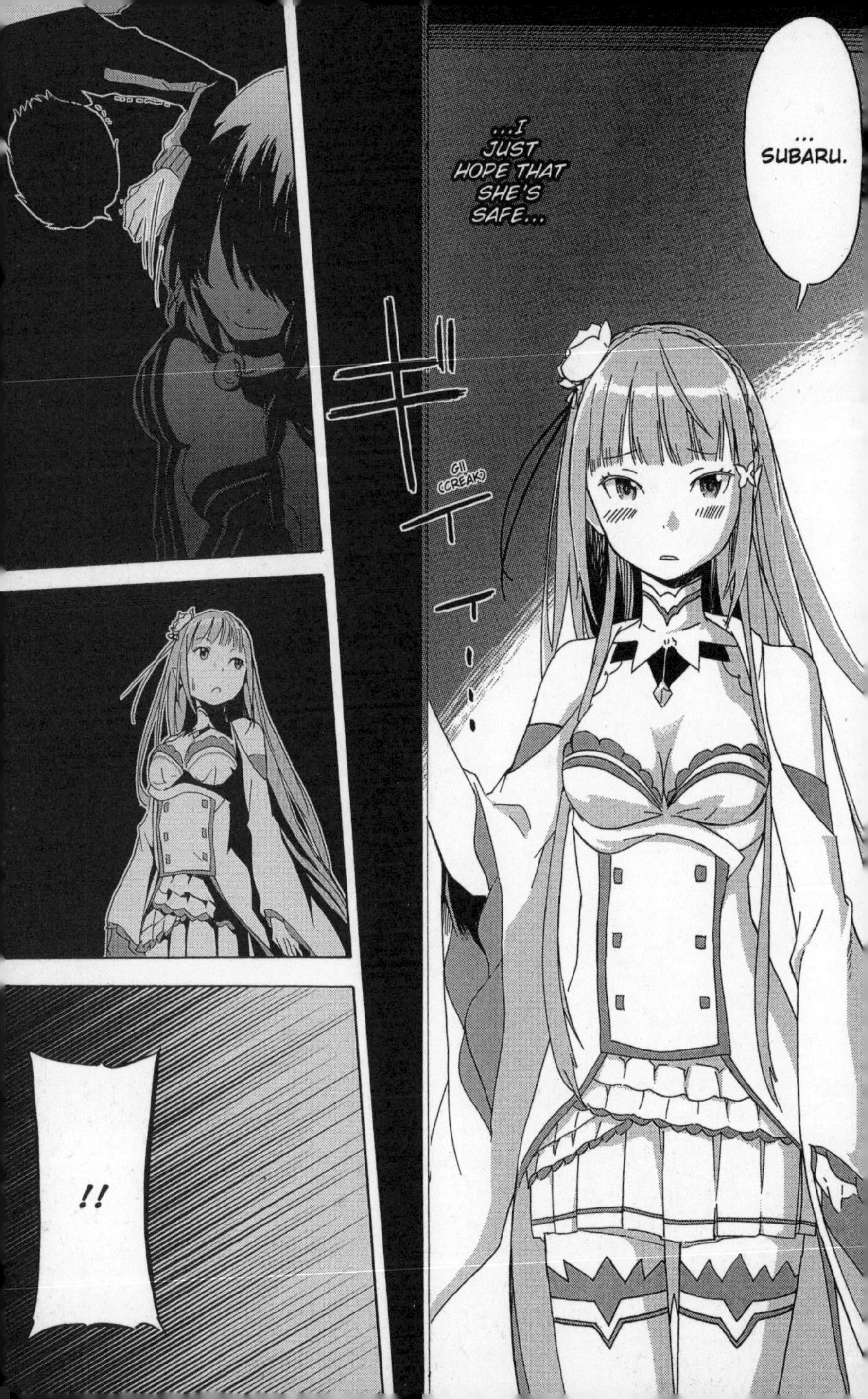
...SUBARU.
...I JUST HOPE THAT SHE'S SAFE...
GII (CREAK)
!!

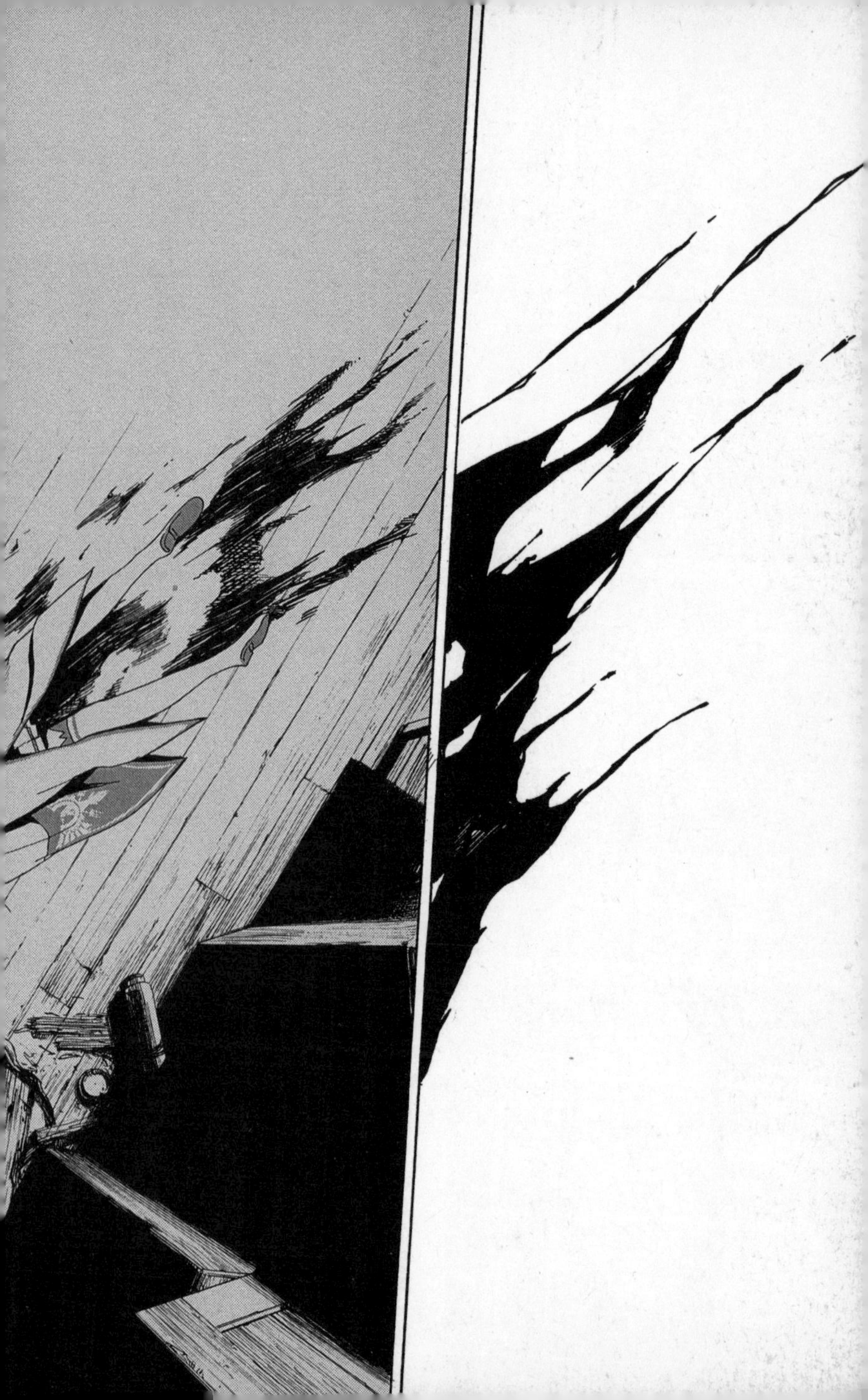

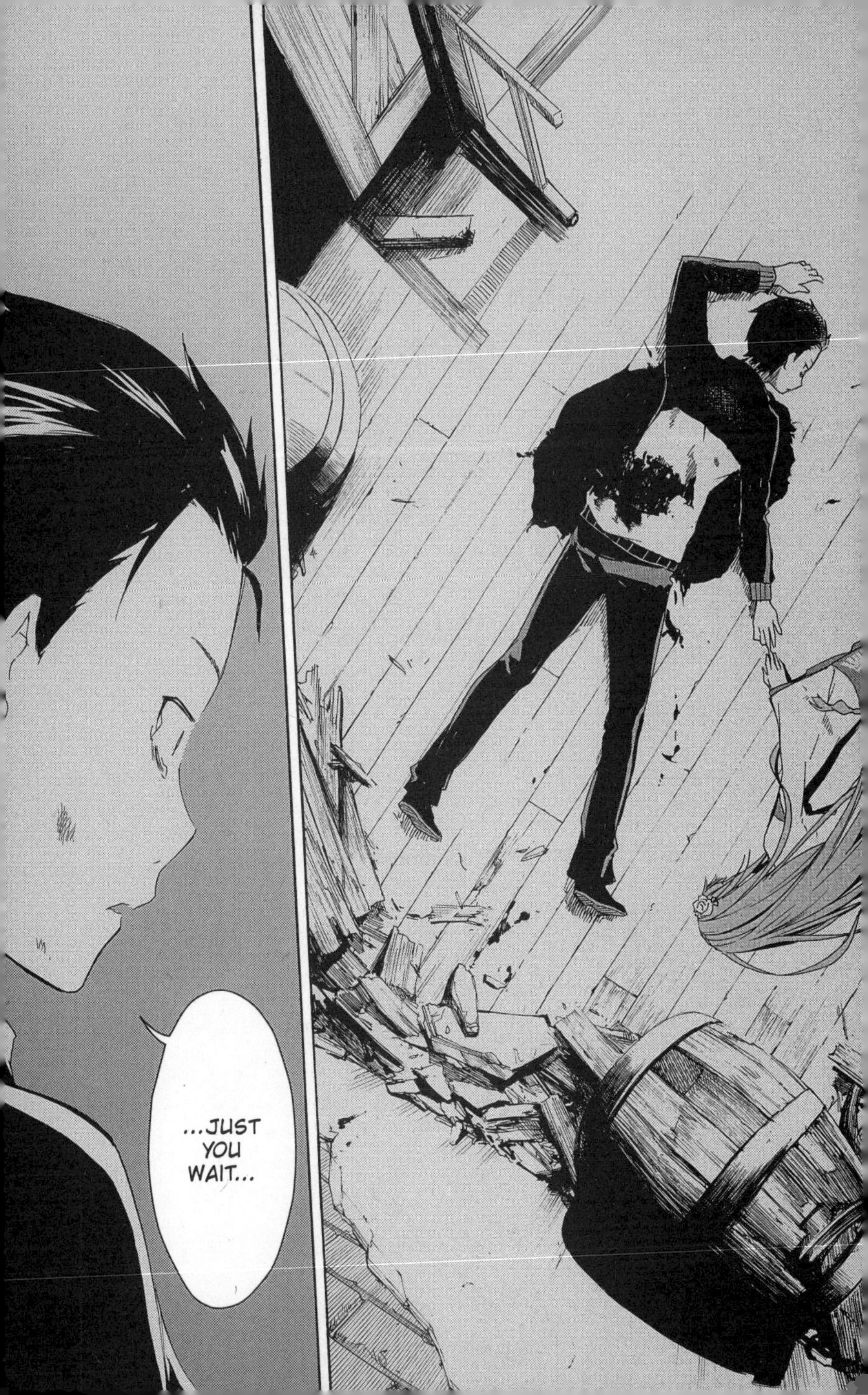
...JUST YOU WAIT...

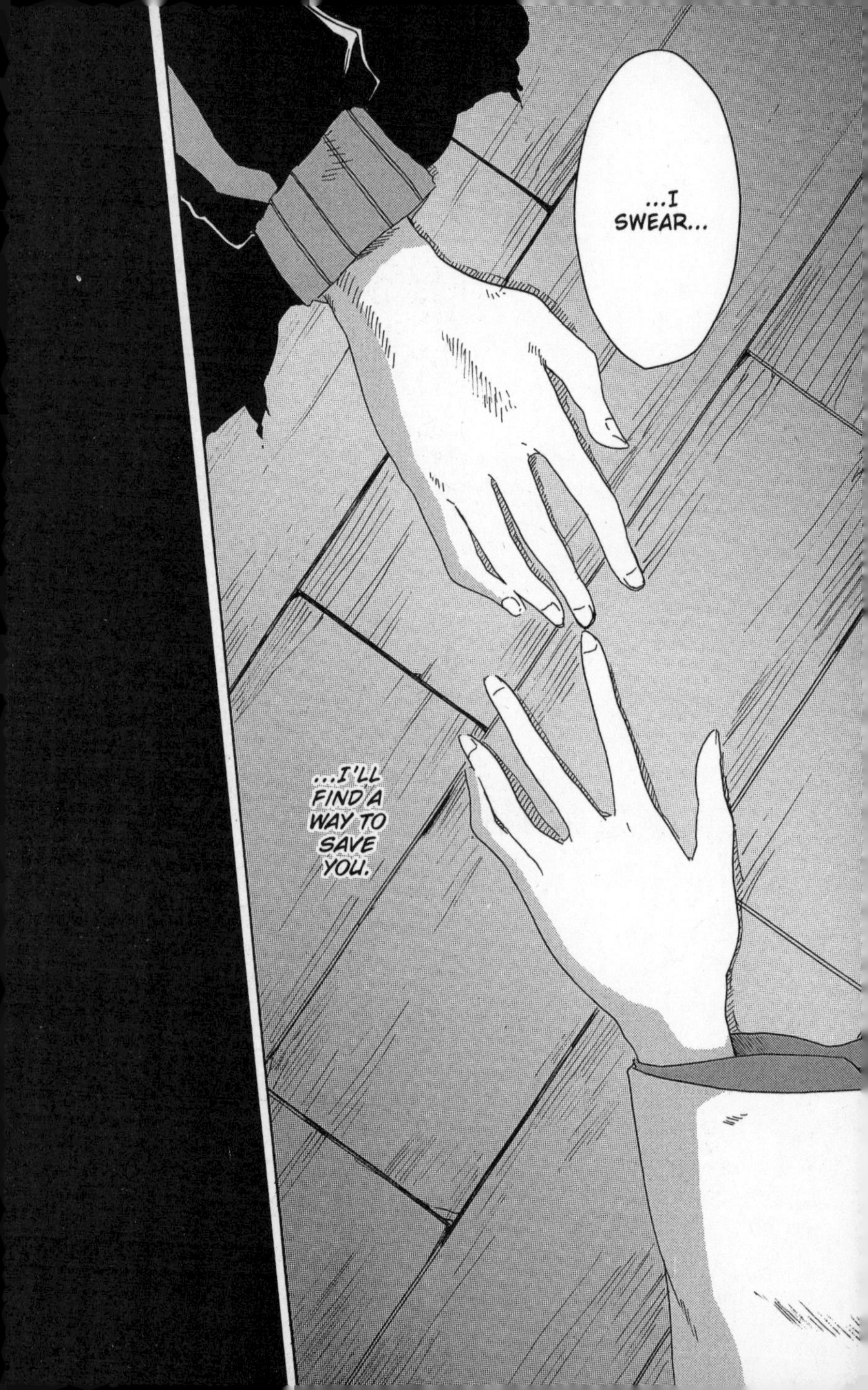
...I SWEAR...
...I'LL FIND A WAY TO SAVE YOU.

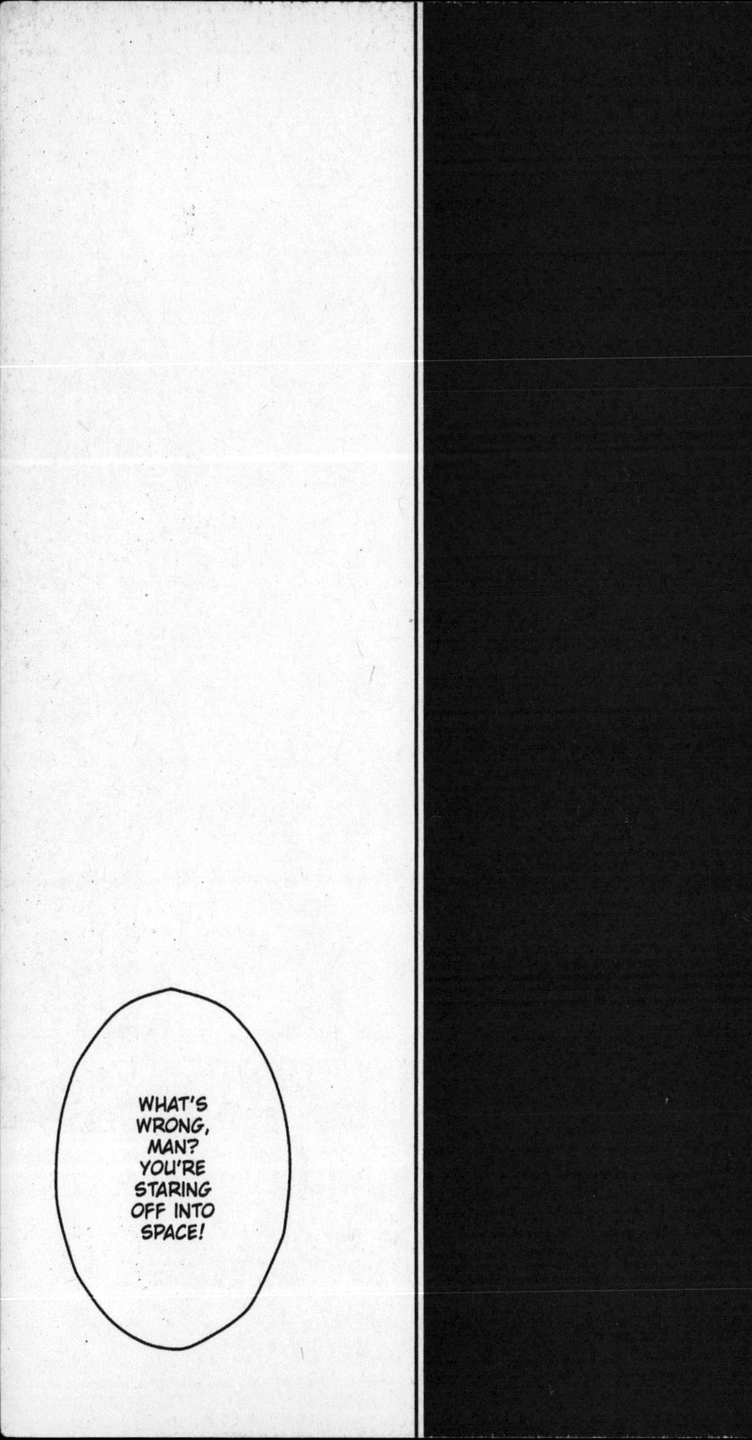
WHAT'S WRONG, MAN? YOU'RE STARING OFF INTO SPACE!

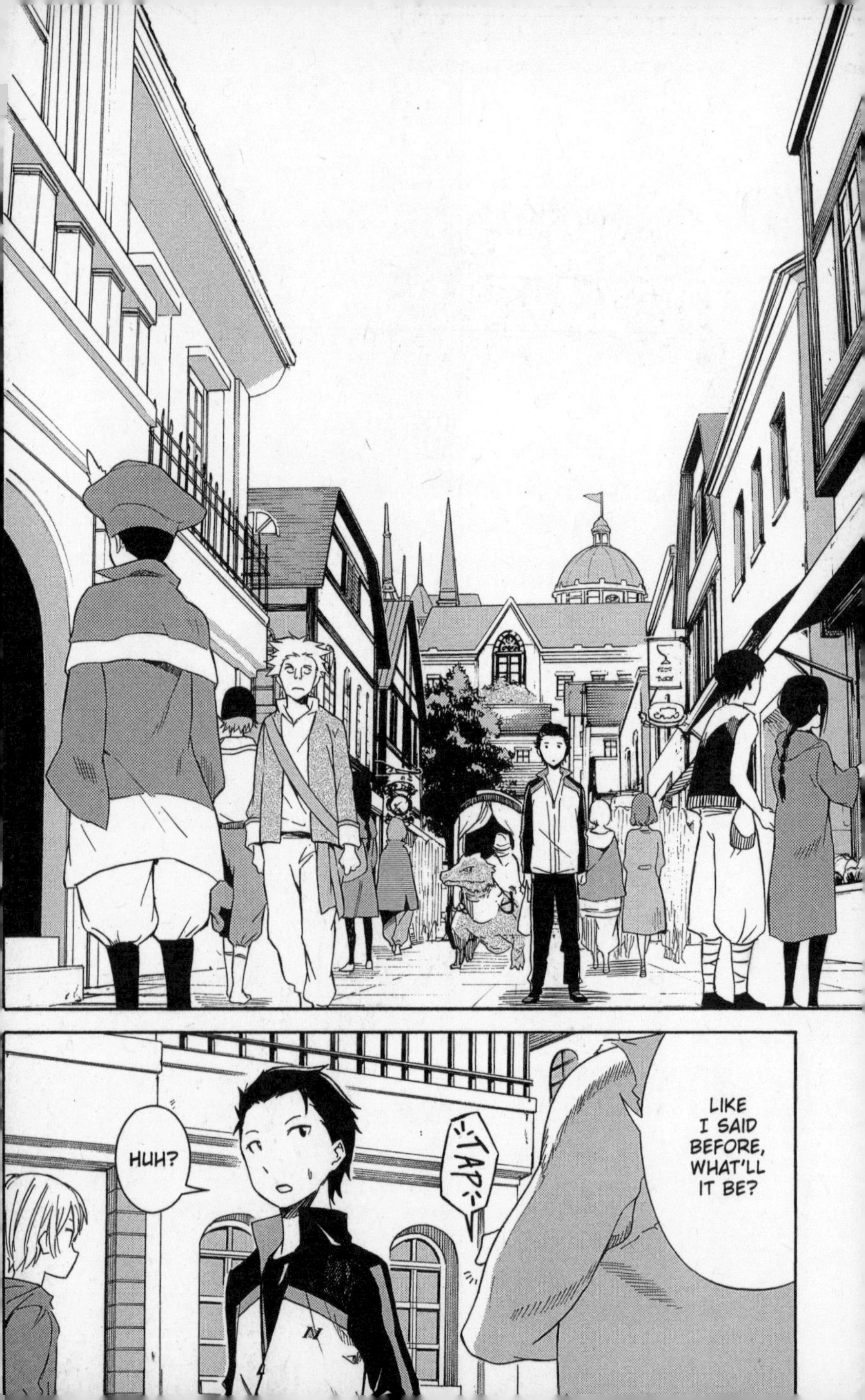
LIKE I SAID BEFORE, WHAT'LL IT BE?
TAP
HUH?

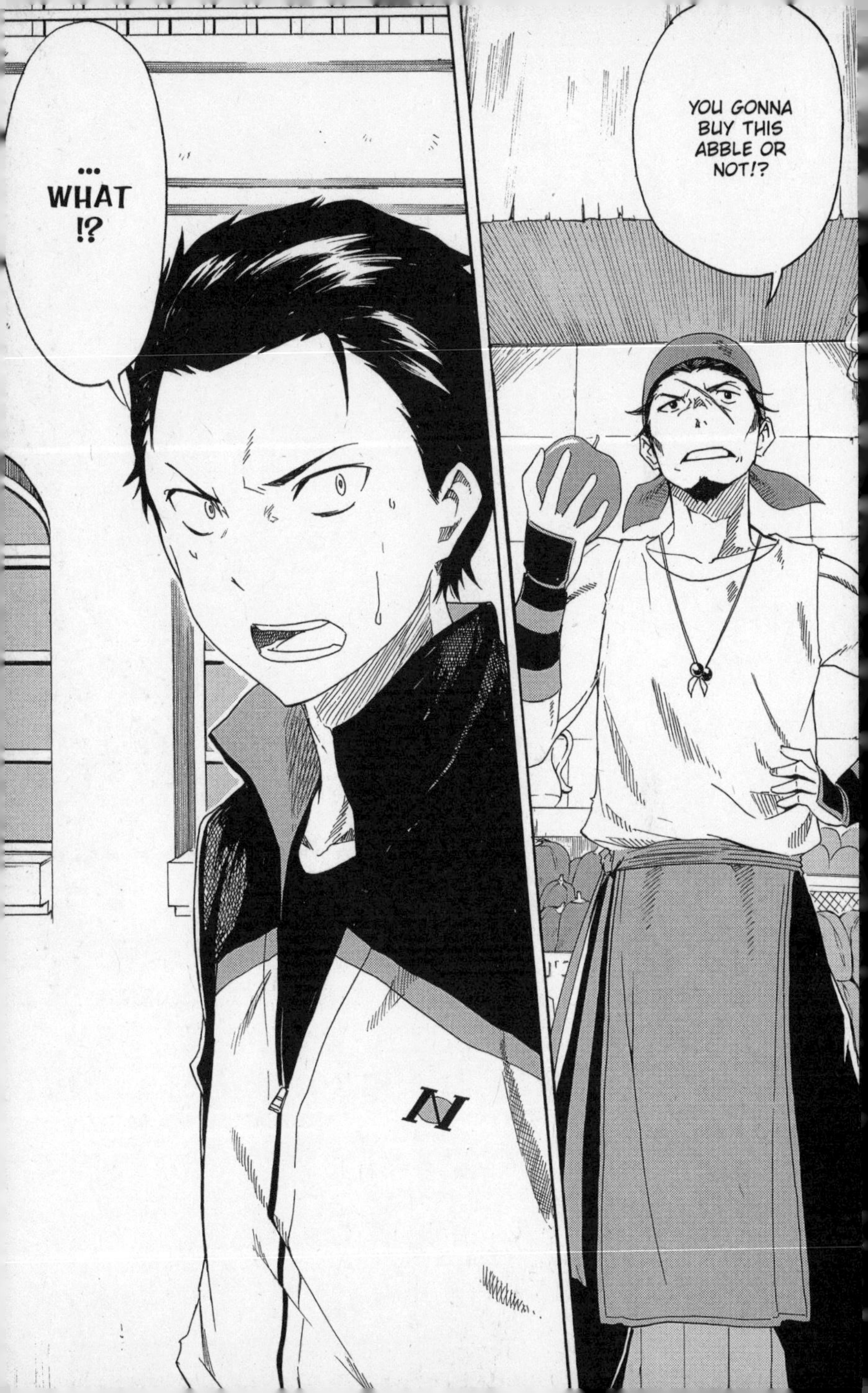
YOU GONNA BUY THIS ABBLE OR NOT!?
... WHAT !?

The only ability Subaru Natsuki gets when he's summoned to another world is time travel via his own death. But to save her, he'll die as many times as it takes.

Re:ZERO -Starting Life in Another World-

Chapter 1: A Day in the Capital

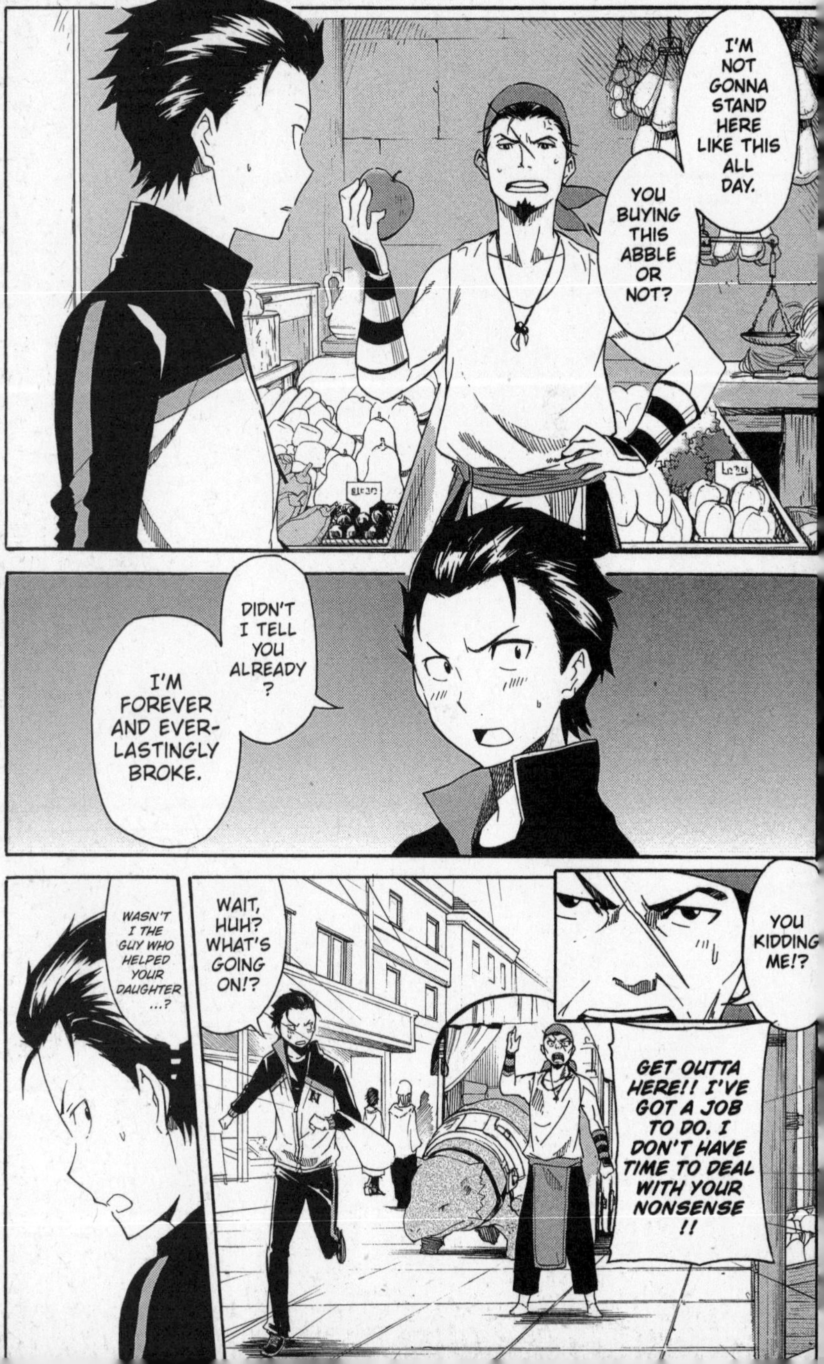
I'M NOT GONNA STAND HERE LIKE THIS ALL DAY.
YOU BUYING THIS ABBLE OR NOT?
DIDN'T I TELL YOU ALREADY?
I'M FOREVER AND EVER-LASTINGLY BROKE.
YOU KIDDING ME!?
GET OUTTA HERE!! I'VE GOT A JOB TO DO. I DON'T HAVE TIME TO DEAL WITH YOUR NONSENSE!!
WAIT, HUH? WHAT'S GOING ON!?
WASN'T I THE GUY WHO HELPED YOUR DAUGHTER...?

Episode 4: The Bitter Taste of Alcohol

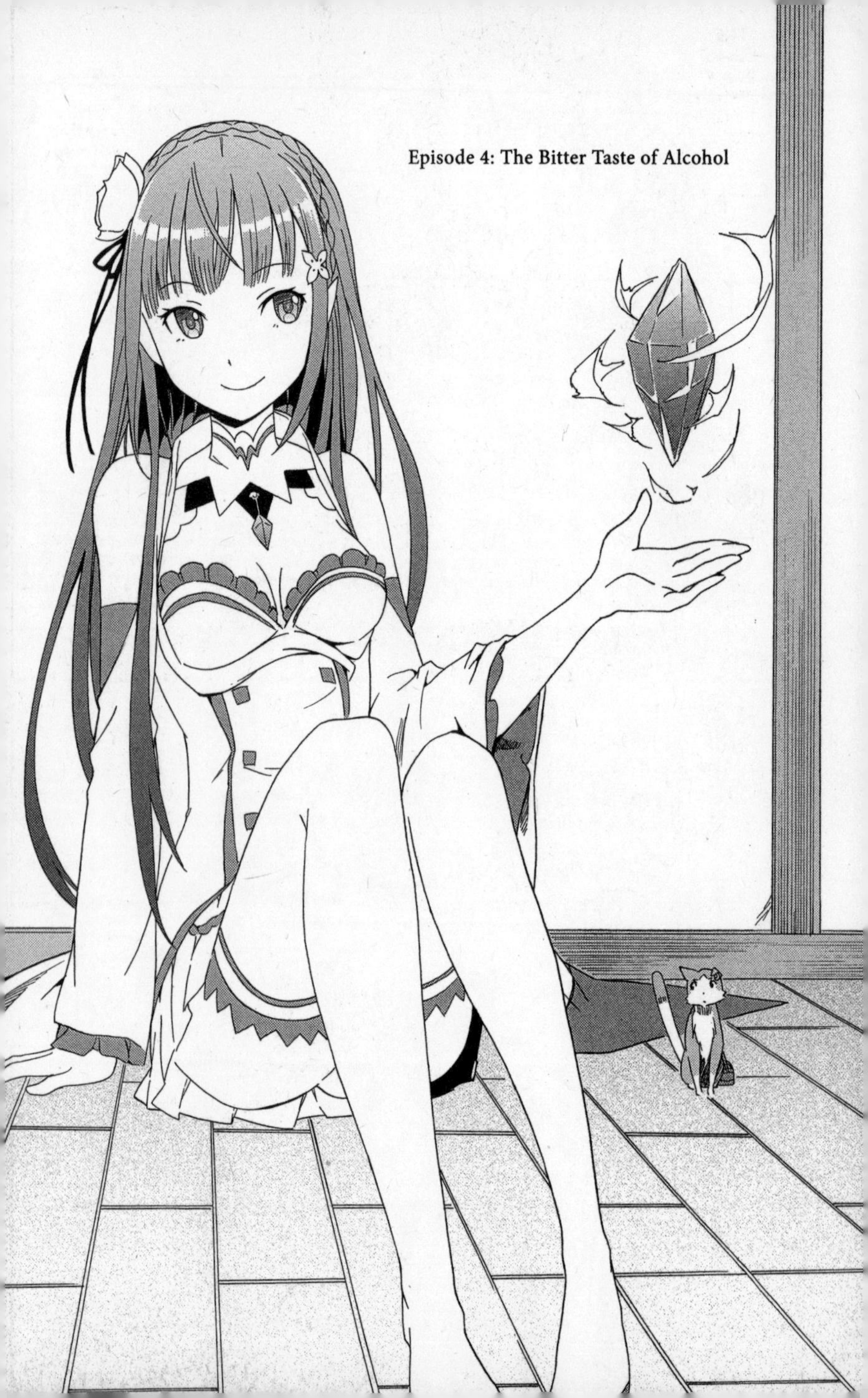

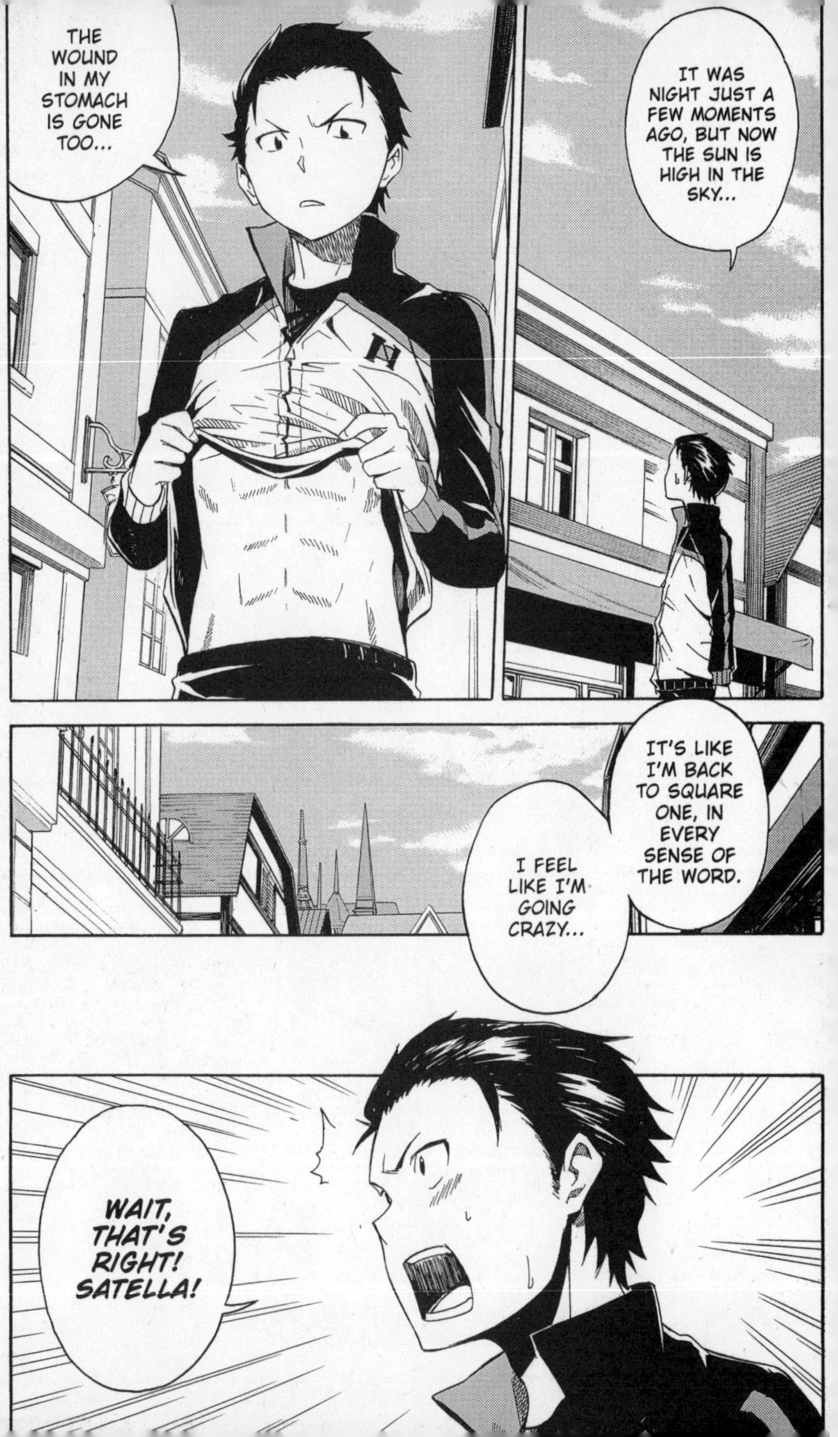
IT WAS NIGHT JUST A FEW MOMENTS AGO, BUT NOW THE SUN IS HIGH IN THE SKY...
THE WOUND IN MY STOMACH IS GONE TOO...
IT'S LIKE I'M BACK TO SQUARE ONE, IN EVERY SENSE OF THE WORD.
I FEEL LIKE I'M GOING CRAZY...
WAIT, THAT'S RIGHT! SATELLA!

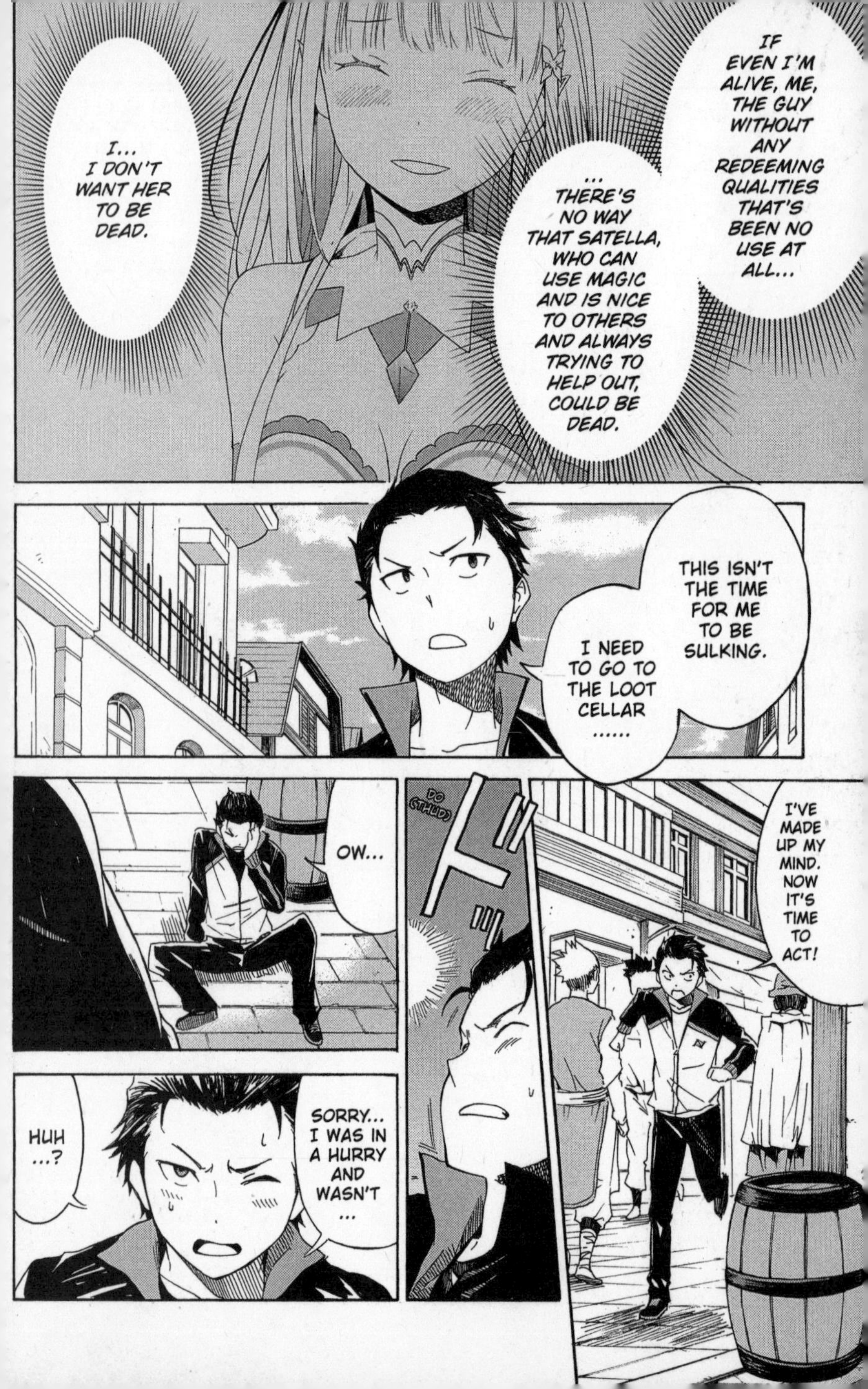
IF EVEN I'M ALIVE, ME, THE GUY WITHOUT ANY REDEEMING QUALITIES THAT'S BEEN NO USE AT ALL...
...THERE'S NO WAY THAT SATELLA, WHO CAN USE MAGIC AND IS NICE TO OTHERS AND ALWAYS TRYING TO HELP OUT, COULD BE DEAD.
I... I DON'T WANT HER TO BE DEAD.
THIS ISN'T THE TIME FOR ME TO BE SULKING.
I NEED TO GO TO THE LOOT CELLAR ......
I'VE MADE UP MY MIND. NOW IT'S TIME TO ACT!
DO (THUD)
OW...
SORRY... I WAS IN A HURRY AND WASN'T ...
HUH ...?

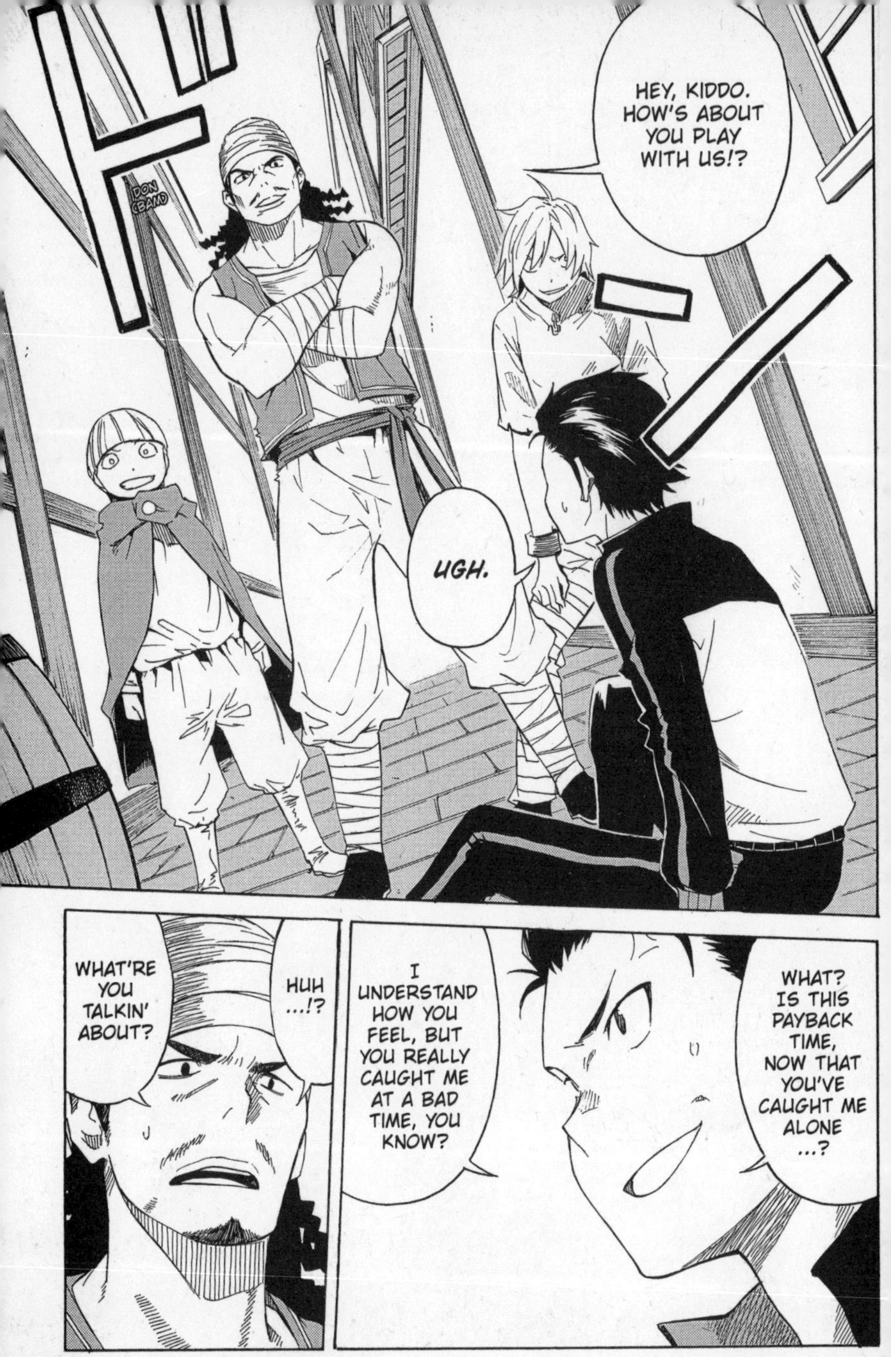
HEY, KIDDO. HOW'S ABOUT YOU PLAY WITH US!?
DON (BAM)
UGH.
WHAT? IS THIS PAYBACK TIME, NOW THAT YOU'VE CAUGHT ME ALONE ...?
I UNDERSTAND HOW YOU FEEL, BUT YOU REALLY CAUGHT ME AT A BAD TIME, YOU KNOW?
HUH ...!?
WHAT'RE YOU TALKIN' ABOUT?

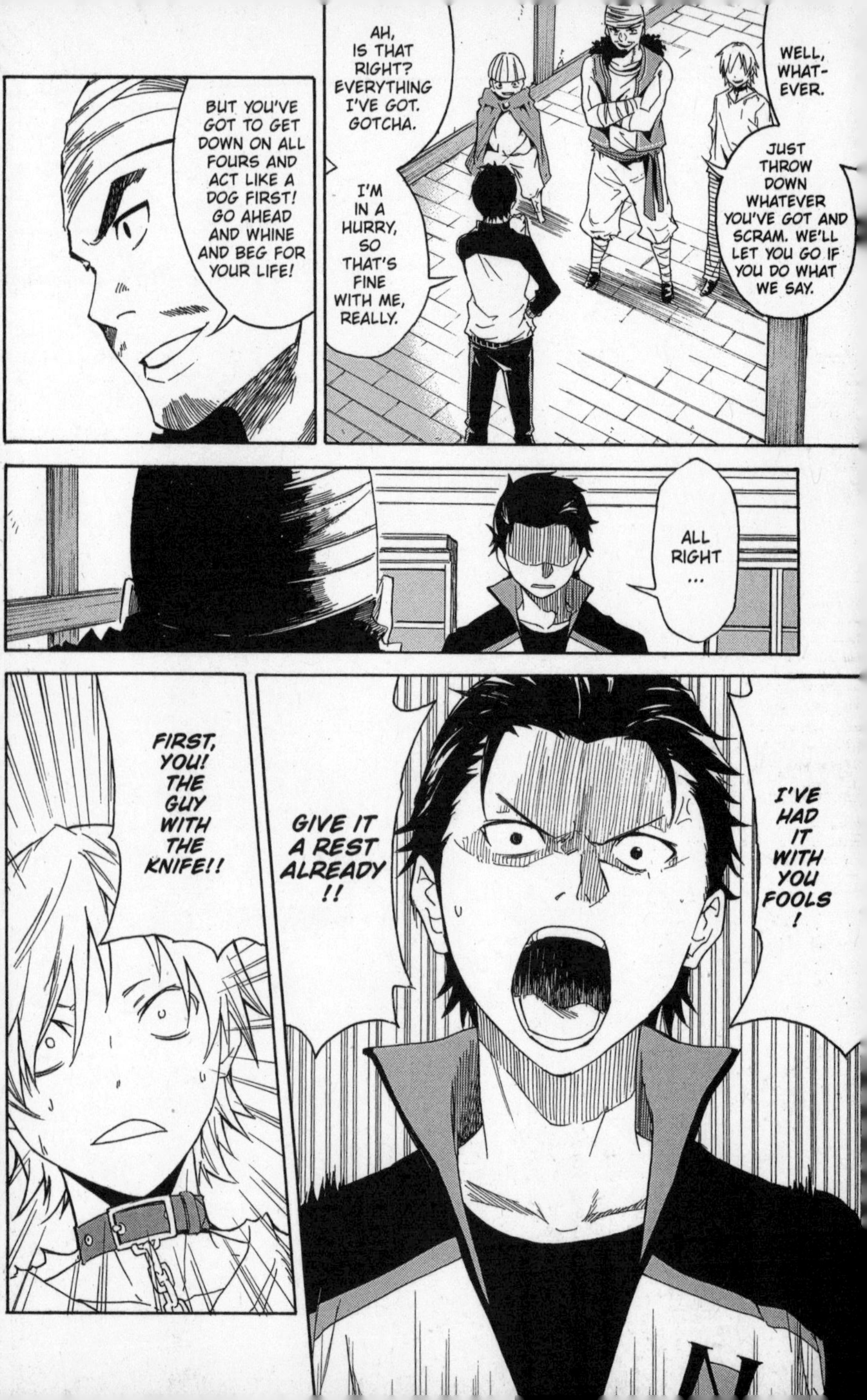
WELL, WHATEVER.
JUST THROW DOWN WHATEVER YOU'VE GOT AND SCRAM. WE'LL LET YOU GO IF YOU DO WHAT WE SAY.
AH, IS THAT RIGHT? EVERYTHING I'VE GOT. GOTCHA.
I'M IN A HURRY, SO THAT'S FINE WITH ME, REALLY.
BUT YOU'VE GOT TO GET DOWN ON ALL FOURS AND ACT LIKE A DOG FIRST! GO AHEAD AND WHINE AND BEG FOR YOUR LIFE!
ALL RIGHT ...
I'VE HAD IT WITH YOU FOOLS!
GIVE IT A REST ALREADY!!
FIRST, YOU! THE GUY WITH THE KNIFE!!

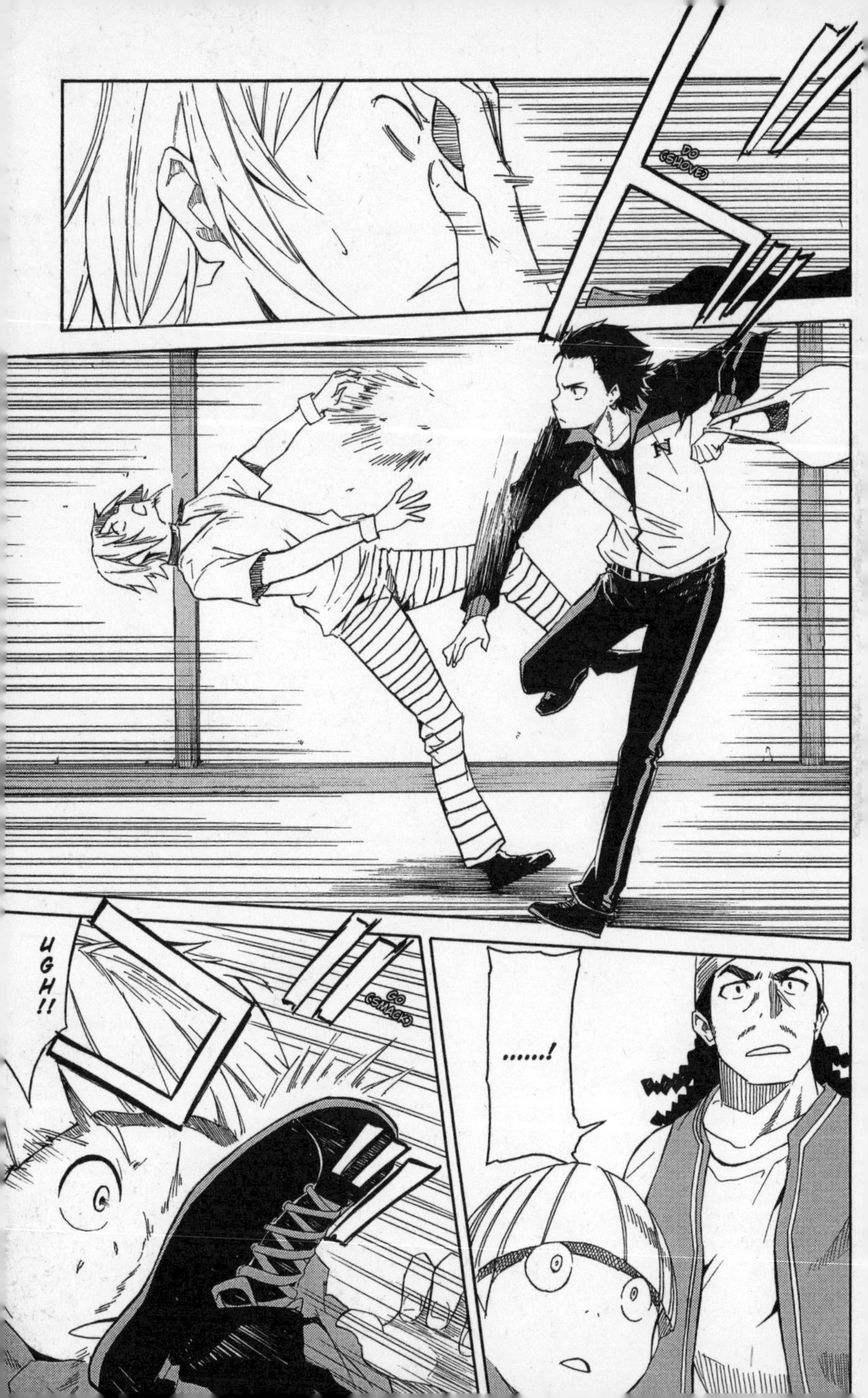
DO (SHOVE)
......!
GO (SMACK)
UGH!!

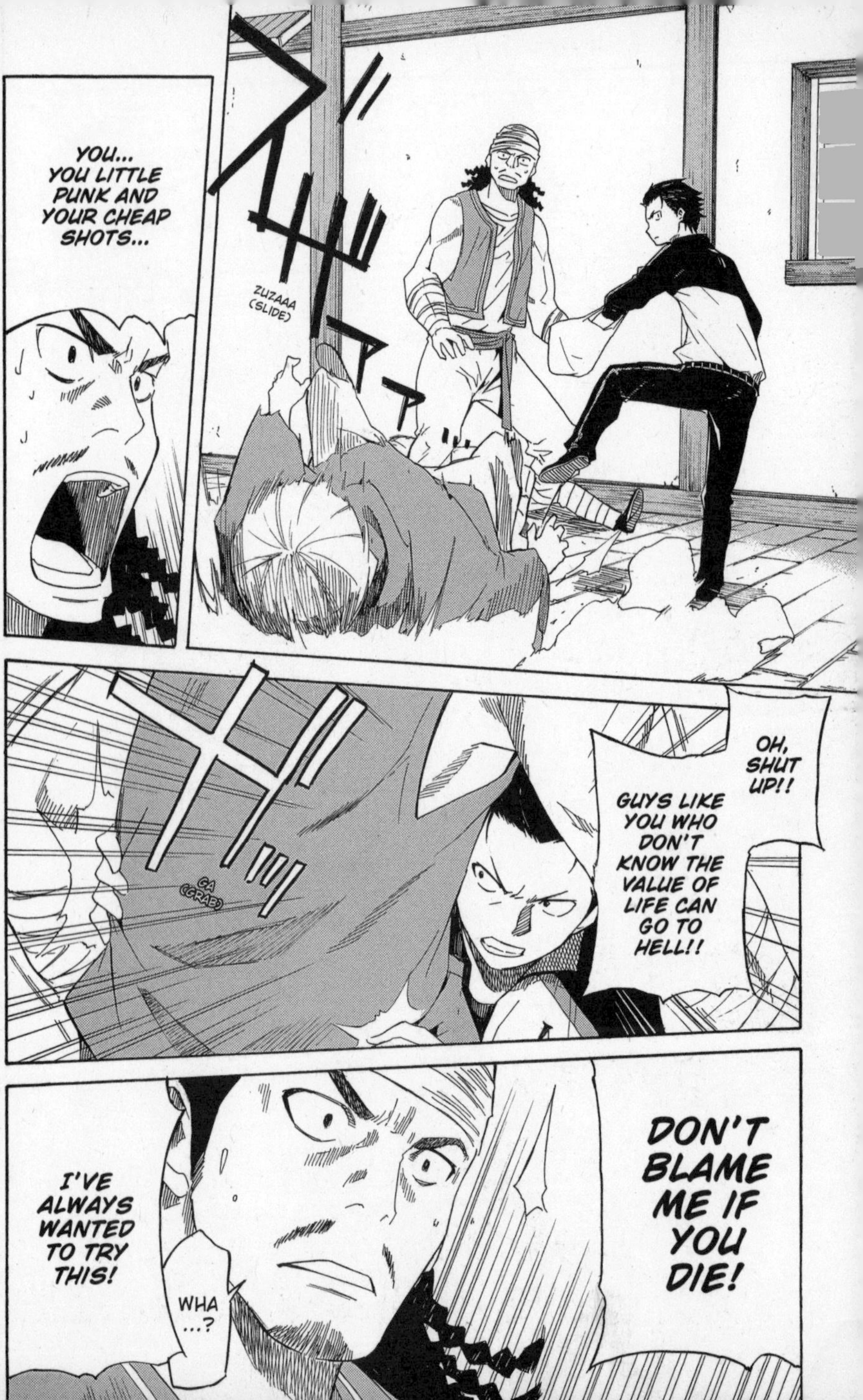
ZUZAAA (SLIDE)
YOU... YOU LITTLE PUNK AND YOUR CHEAP SHOTS...
OH, SHUT UP!!
GUYS LIKE YOU WHO DON'T KNOW THE VALUE OF LIFE CAN GO TO HELL!!
GA (GRAB)
DON'T BLAME ME IF YOU DIE!
I'VE ALWAYS WANTED TO TRY THIS!
WHA ...?

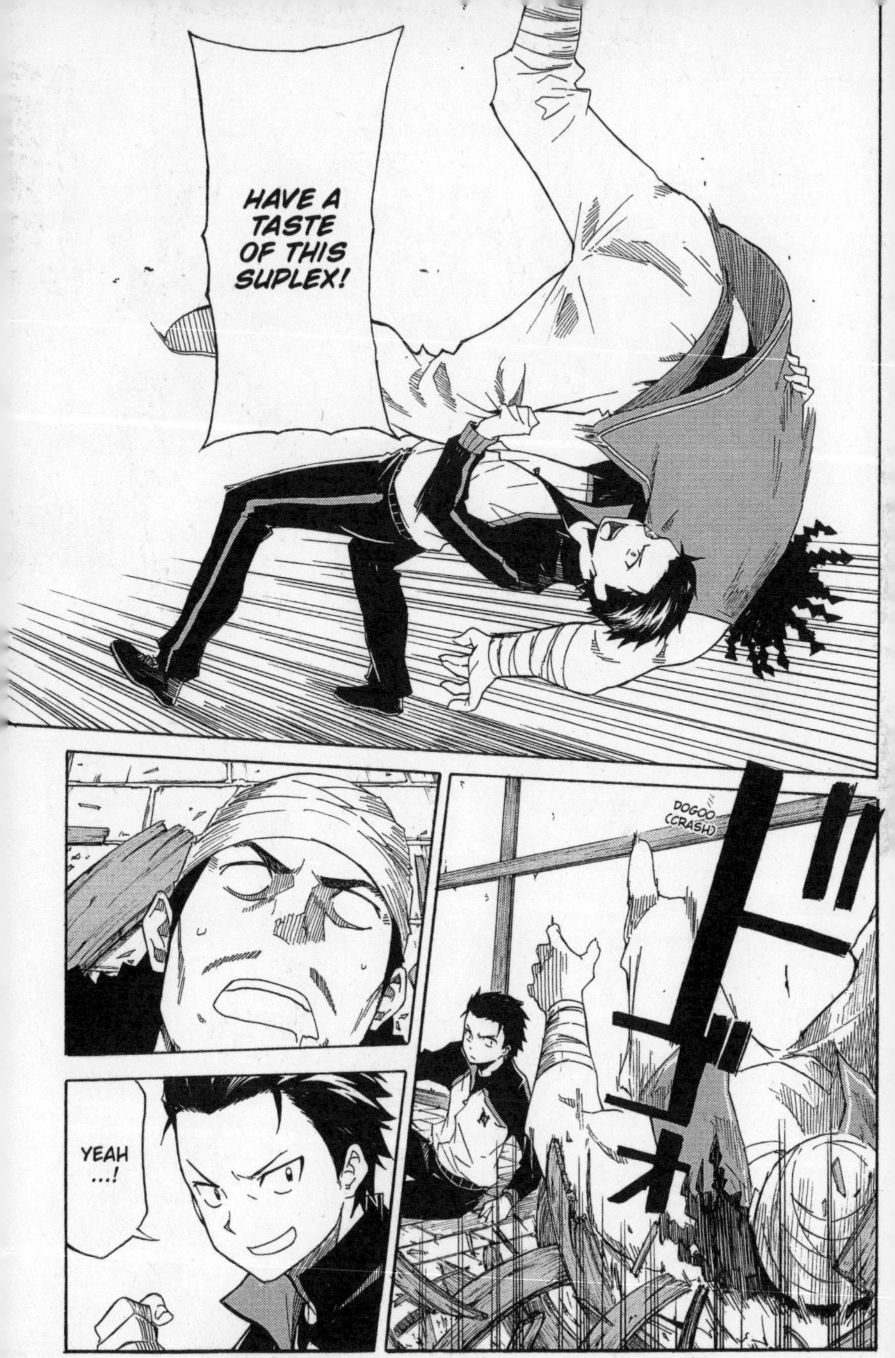
HAVE A TASTE OF THIS SUPLEX!
DOGOO (CRASH)
YEAH ...!

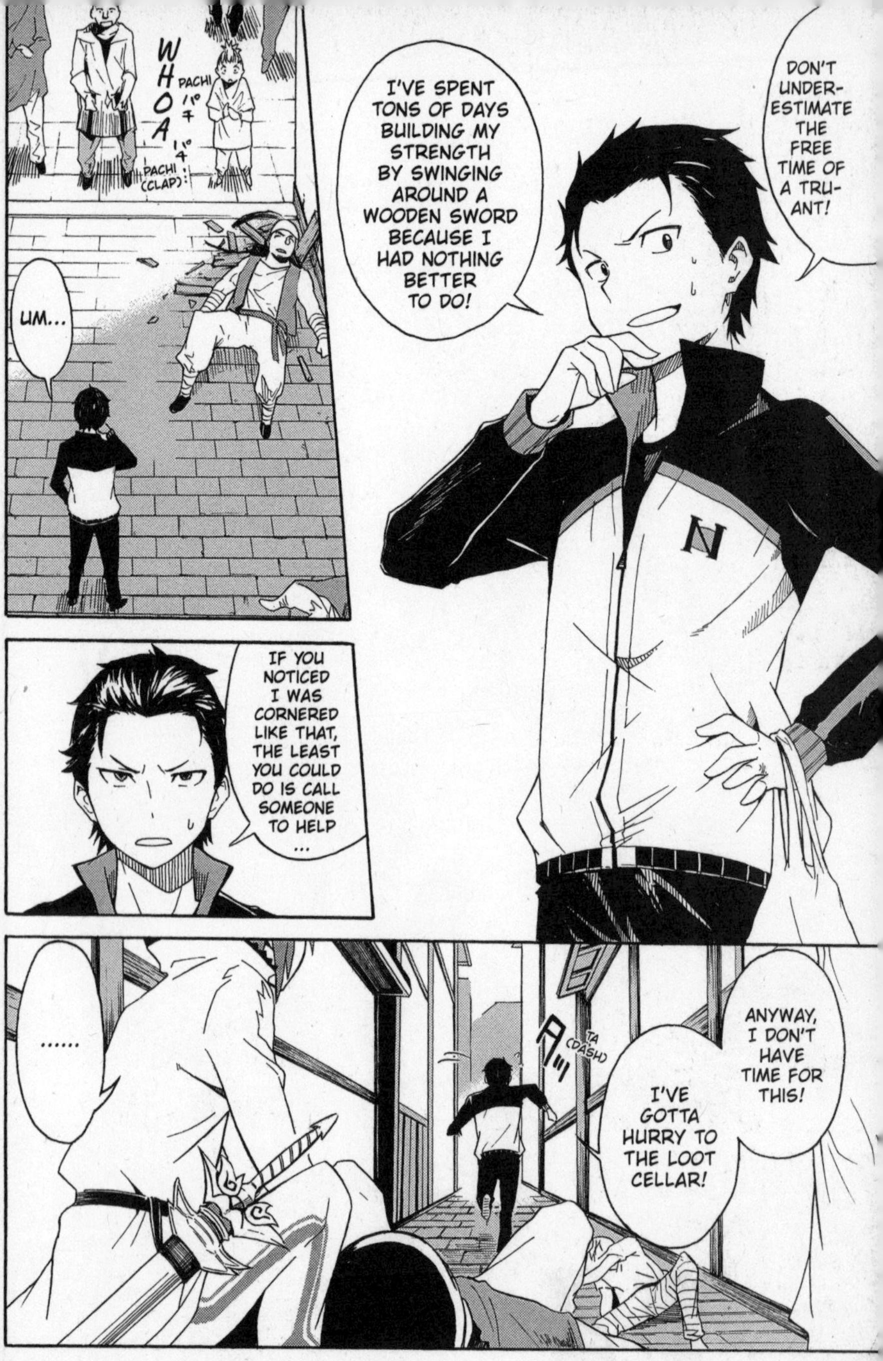
DON'T UNDER-ESTIMATE THE FREE TIME OF A TRU-ANT!
I'VE SPENT TONS OF DAYS BUILDING MY STRENGTH BY SWINGING AROUND A WOODEN SWORD BECAUSE I HAD NOTHING BETTER TO DO!
WHOA
PACHI
PACHI (CLAP)
UM...
IF YOU NOTICED I WAS CORNERED LIKE THAT, THE LEAST YOU COULD DO IS CALL SOMEONE TO HELP ...
ANYWAY, I DON'T HAVE TIME FOR THIS!
I'VE GOTTA HURRY TO THE LOOT CELLAR!
TA (DASH)
......

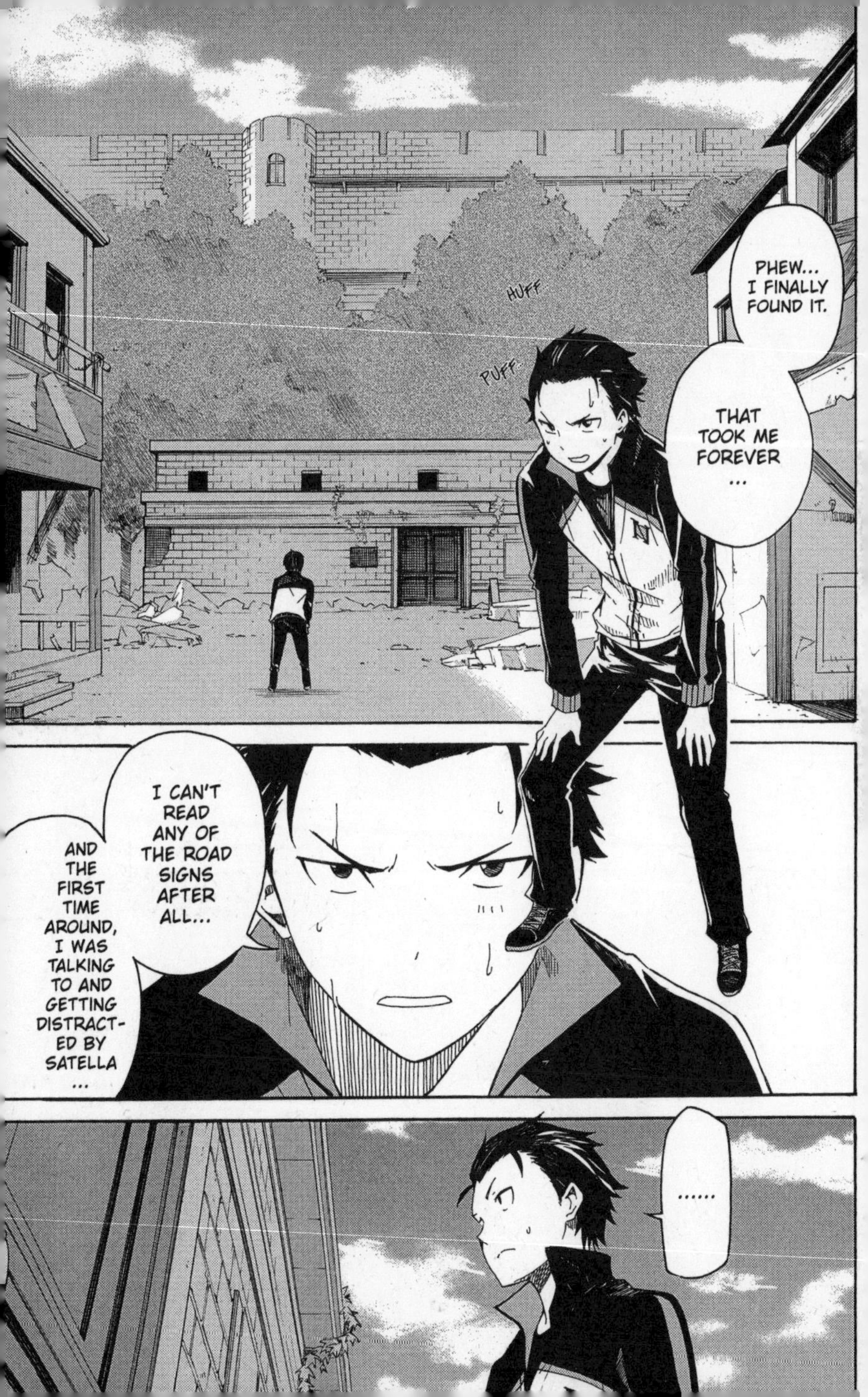
PHEW... I FINALLY FOUND IT.
THAT TOOK ME FOREVER ...
HUFF
PUFF
I CAN'T READ ANY OF THE ROAD SIGNS AFTER ALL...
AND THE FIRST TIME AROUND, I WAS TALKING TO AND GETTING DISTRACT-ED BY SATELLA ...
......

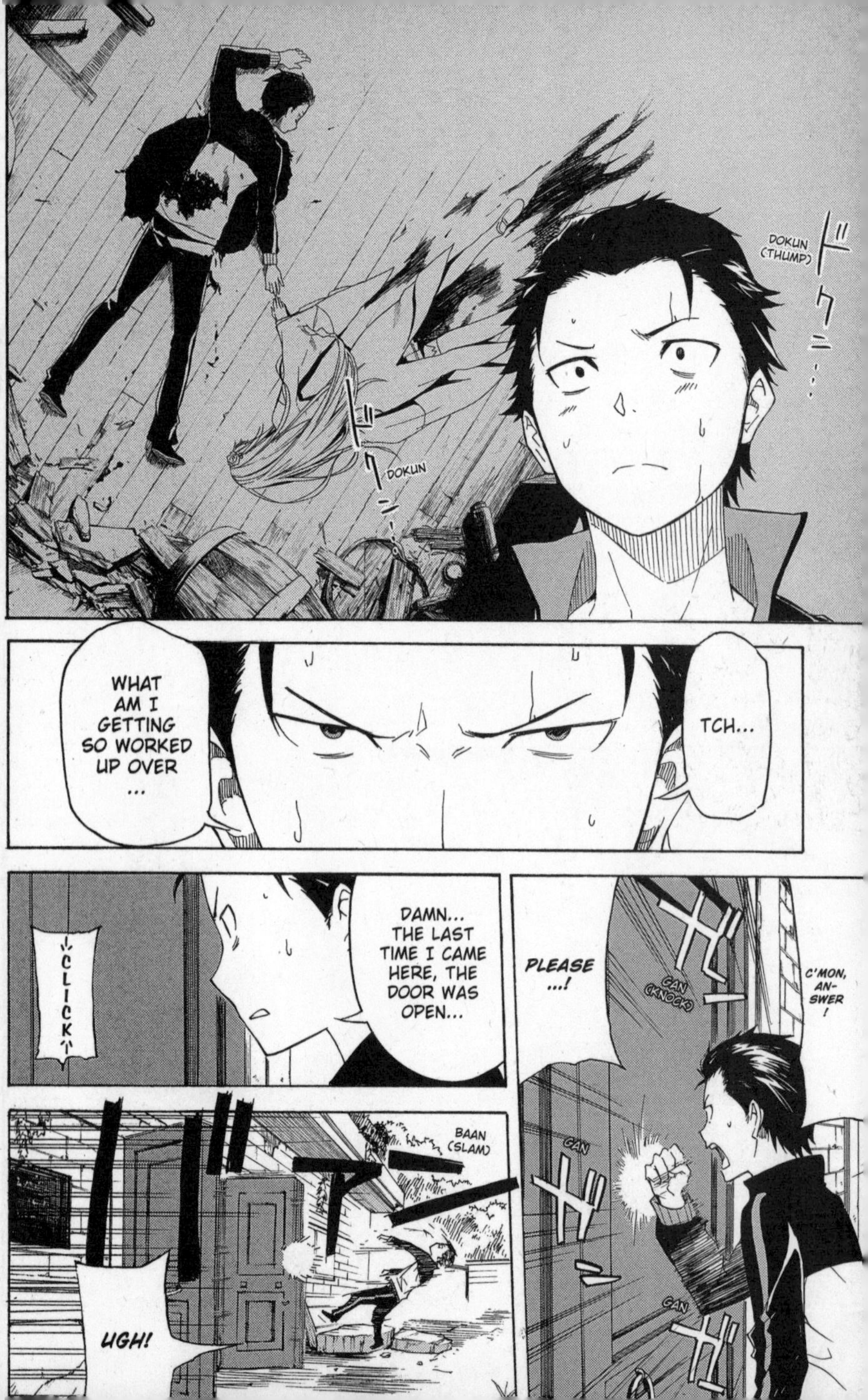
DOKUN (THUMP)
DOKUN
TCH...
WHAT AM I GETTING SO WORKED UP OVER ...
C'MON, ANSWER!
GAN (KNOCK)
PLEASE ...!
GAN
GAN
DAMN... THE LAST TIME I CAME HERE, THE DOOR WAS OPEN...
CLICK
BAAN (SLAM)
UGH!

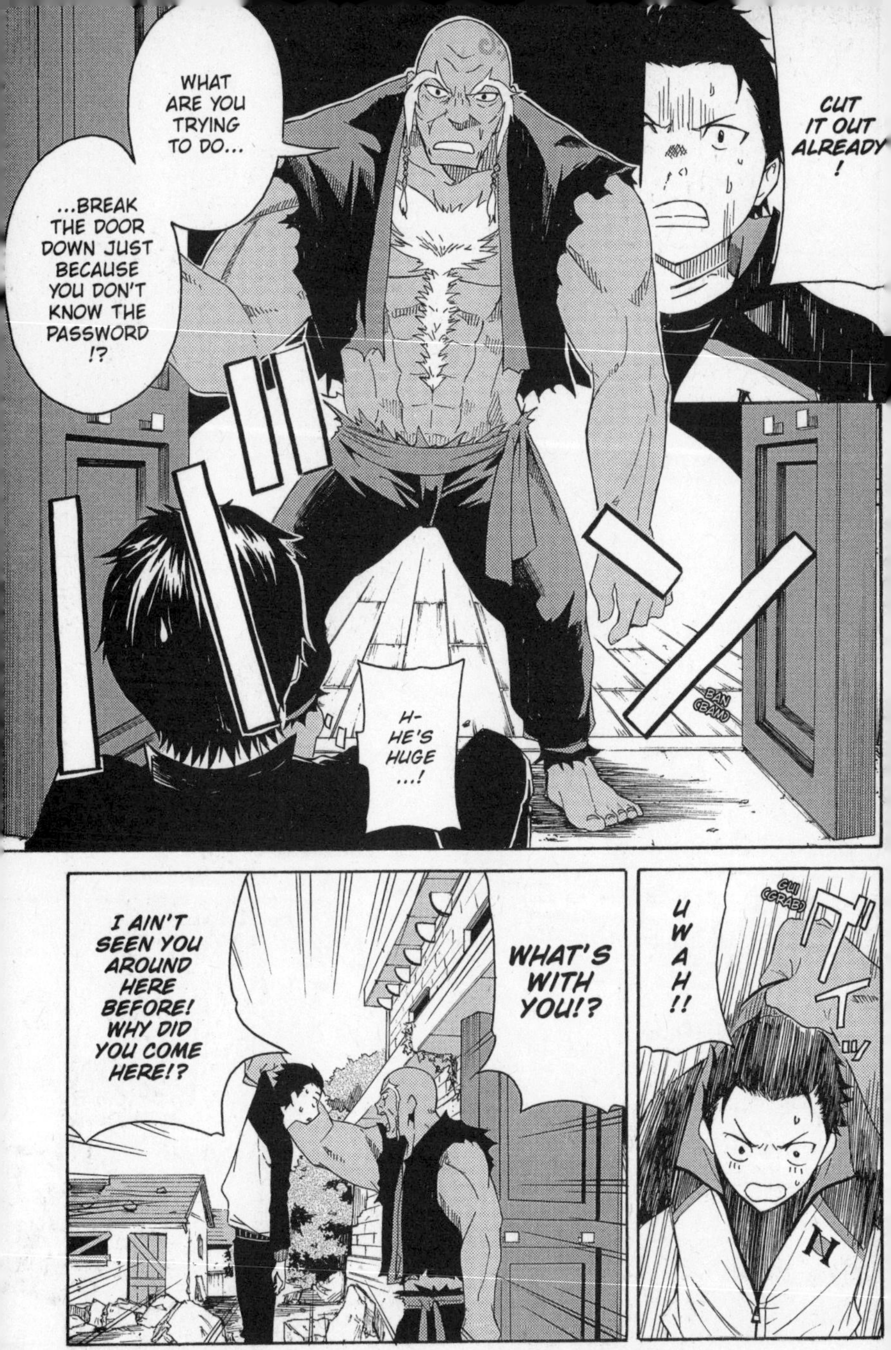
CUT IT OUT ALREADY!
WHAT ARE YOU TRYING TO DO...
...BREAK THE DOOR DOWN JUST BECAUSE YOU DON'T KNOW THE PASSWORD!?
BAN (BAM)
H- HE'S HUGE...!
GUI (GRAB)
UWAH!!
WHAT'S WITH YOU!?
I AIN'T SEEN YOU AROUND HERE BEFORE! WHY DID YOU COME HERE!?

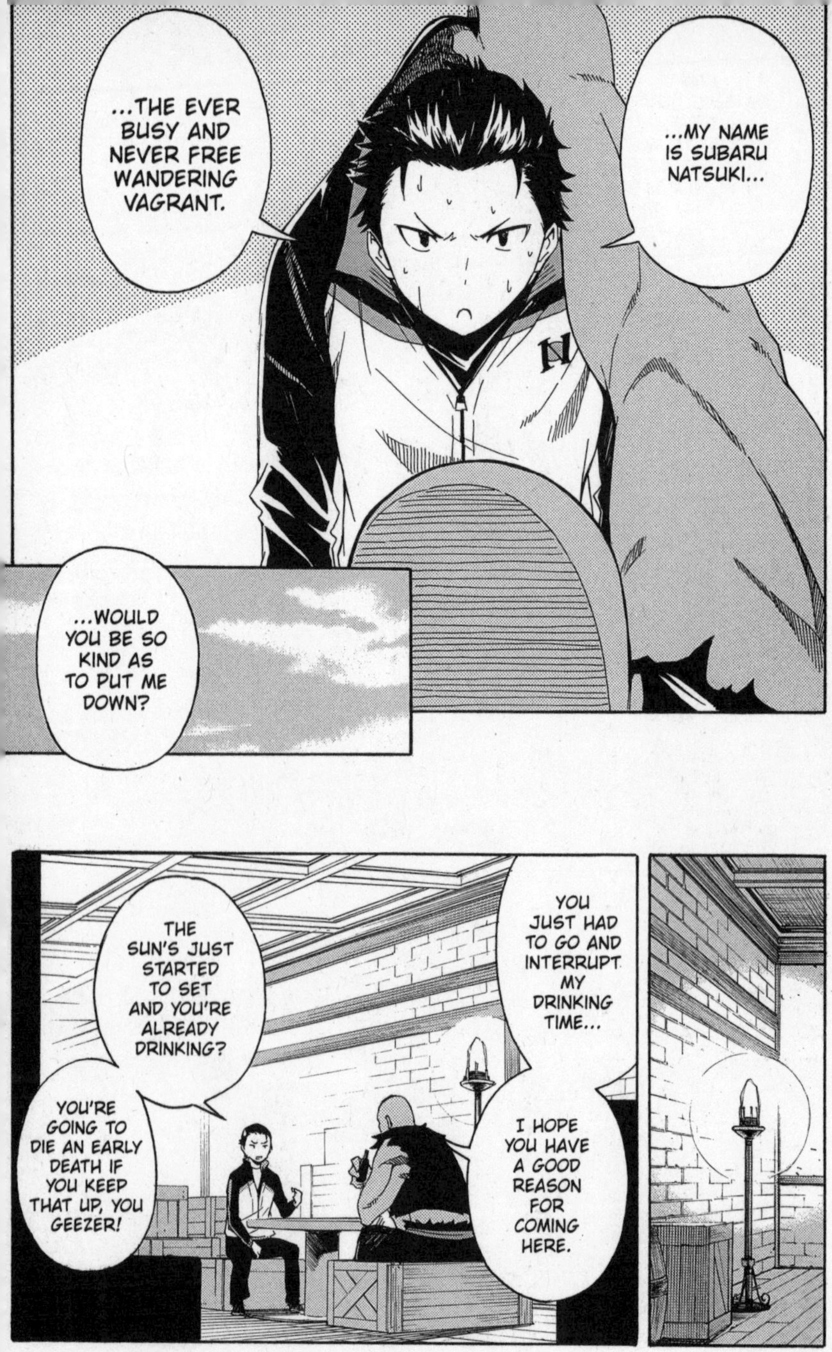

...MY NAME IS SUBARU NATSUKI...
...THE EVER BUSY AND NEVER FREE WANDERING VAGRANT.
...WOULD YOU BE SO KIND AS TO PUT ME DOWN?
YOU JUST HAD TO GO AND INTERRUPT MY DRINKING TIME...
THE SUN'S JUST STARTED TO SET AND YOU'RE ALREADY DRINKING?
I HOPE YOU HAVE A GOOD REASON FOR COMING HERE.
YOU'RE GOING TO DIE AN EARLY DEATH IF YOU KEEP THAT UP, YOU GEEZER!

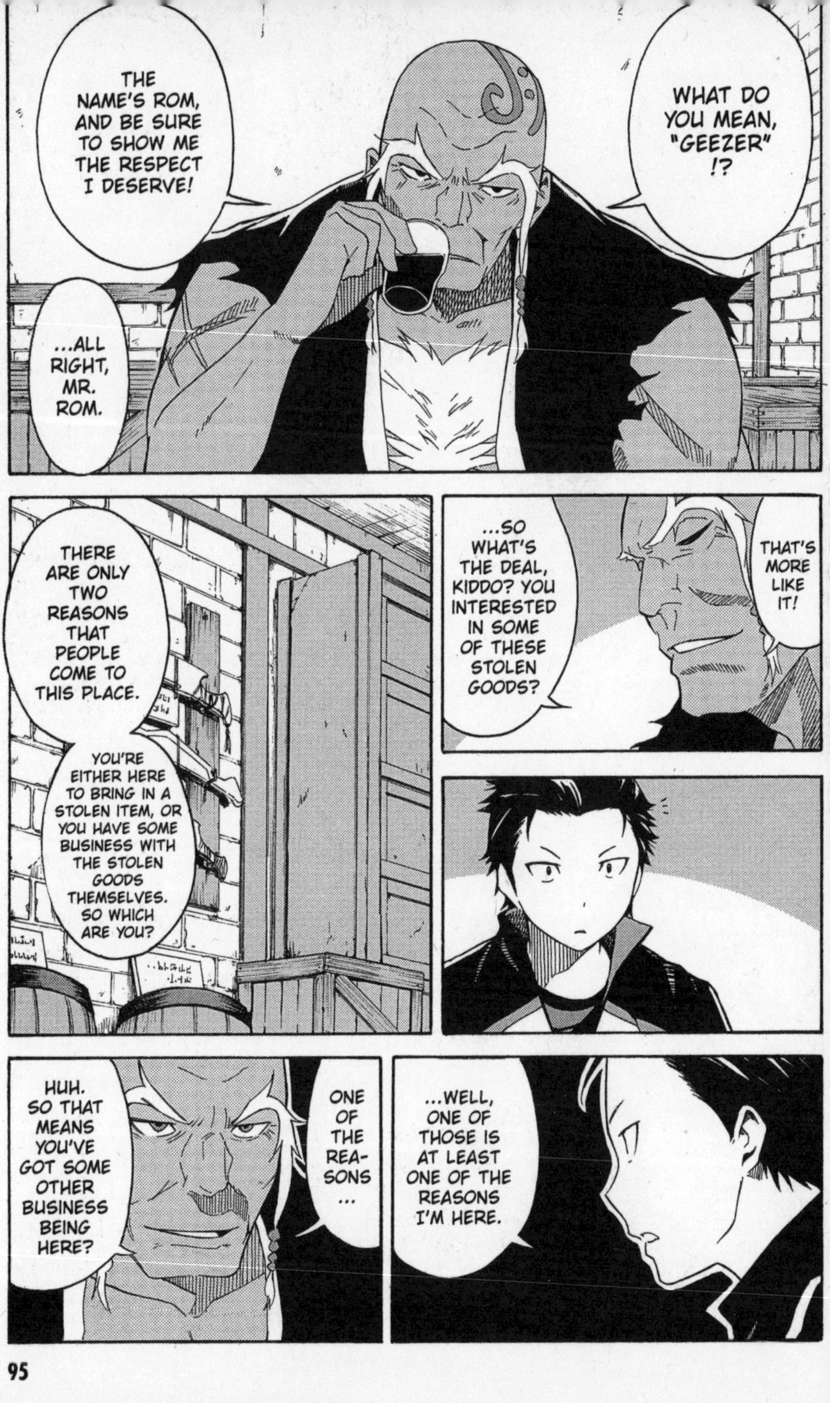
WHAT DO YOU MEAN, "GEEZER" !?
THE NAME'S ROM, AND BE SURE TO SHOW ME THE RESPECT I DESERVE!
...ALL RIGHT, MR. ROM.
THAT'S MORE LIKE IT!
...SO WHAT'S THE DEAL, KIDDO? YOU INTERESTED IN SOME OF THESE STOLEN GOODS?
THERE ARE ONLY TWO REASONS THAT PEOPLE COME TO THIS PLACE.
YOU'RE EITHER HERE TO BRING IN A STOLEN ITEM, OR YOU HAVE SOME BUSINESS WITH THE STOLEN GOODS THEMSELVES. SO WHICH ARE YOU?
...WELL, ONE OF THOSE IS AT LEAST ONE OF THE REASONS I'M HERE.
ONE OF THE REA-SONS ...
HUH. SO THAT MEANS YOU'VE GOT SOME OTHER BUSINESS BEING HERE?

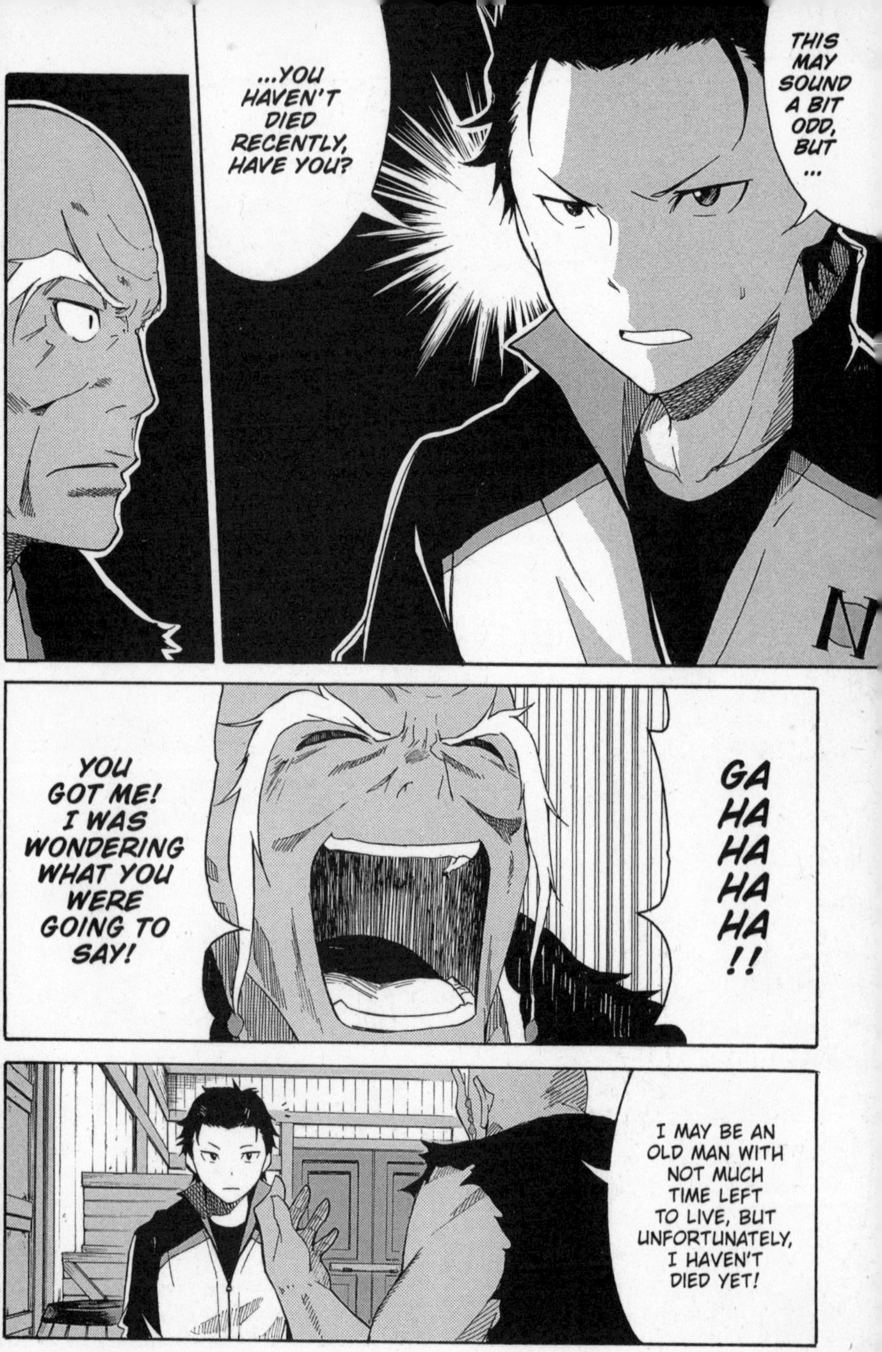
THIS MAY SOUND A BIT ODD, BUT...
...YOU HAVEN'T DIED RECENTLY, HAVE YOU?
GA HA HA HA HA!!
YOU GOT ME! I WAS WONDERING WHAT YOU WERE GOING TO SAY!
I MAY BE AN OLD MAN WITH NOT MUCH TIME LEFT TO LIVE, BUT UNFORTUNATELY, I HAVEN'T DIED YET!

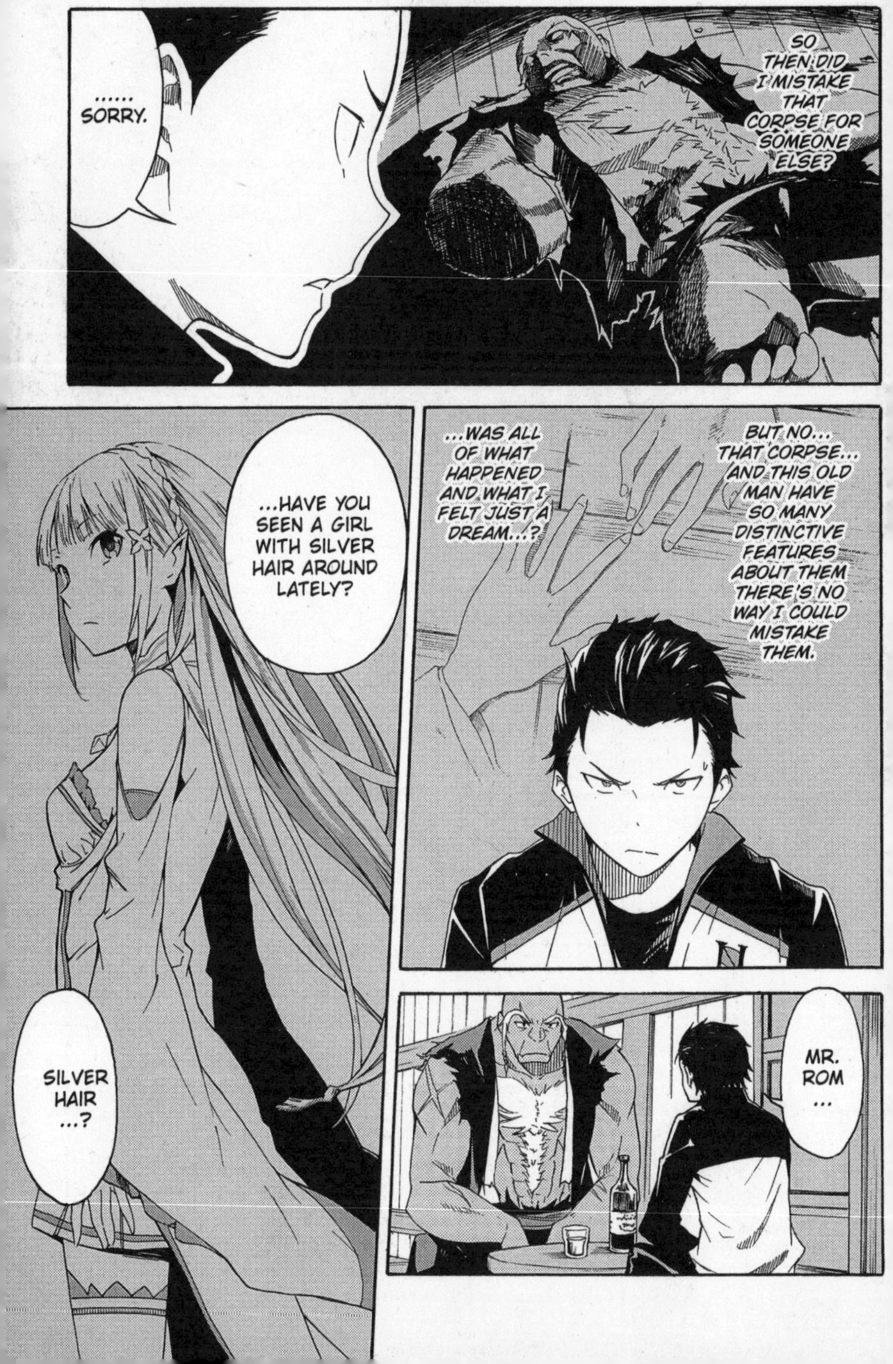
SO THEN DID I MISTAKE THAT CORPSE FOR SOMEONE ELSE?
......SORRY.
BUT NO... THAT CORPSE... AND THIS OLD MAN HAVE SO MANY DISTINCTIVE FEATURES ABOUT THEM THERE'S NO WAY I COULD MISTAKE THEM.
...WAS ALL OF WHAT HAPPENED AND WHAT I FELT JUST A DREAM...?
MR. ROM ...
...HAVE YOU SEEN A GIRL WITH SILVER HAIR AROUND LATELY?
SILVER HAIR ...?

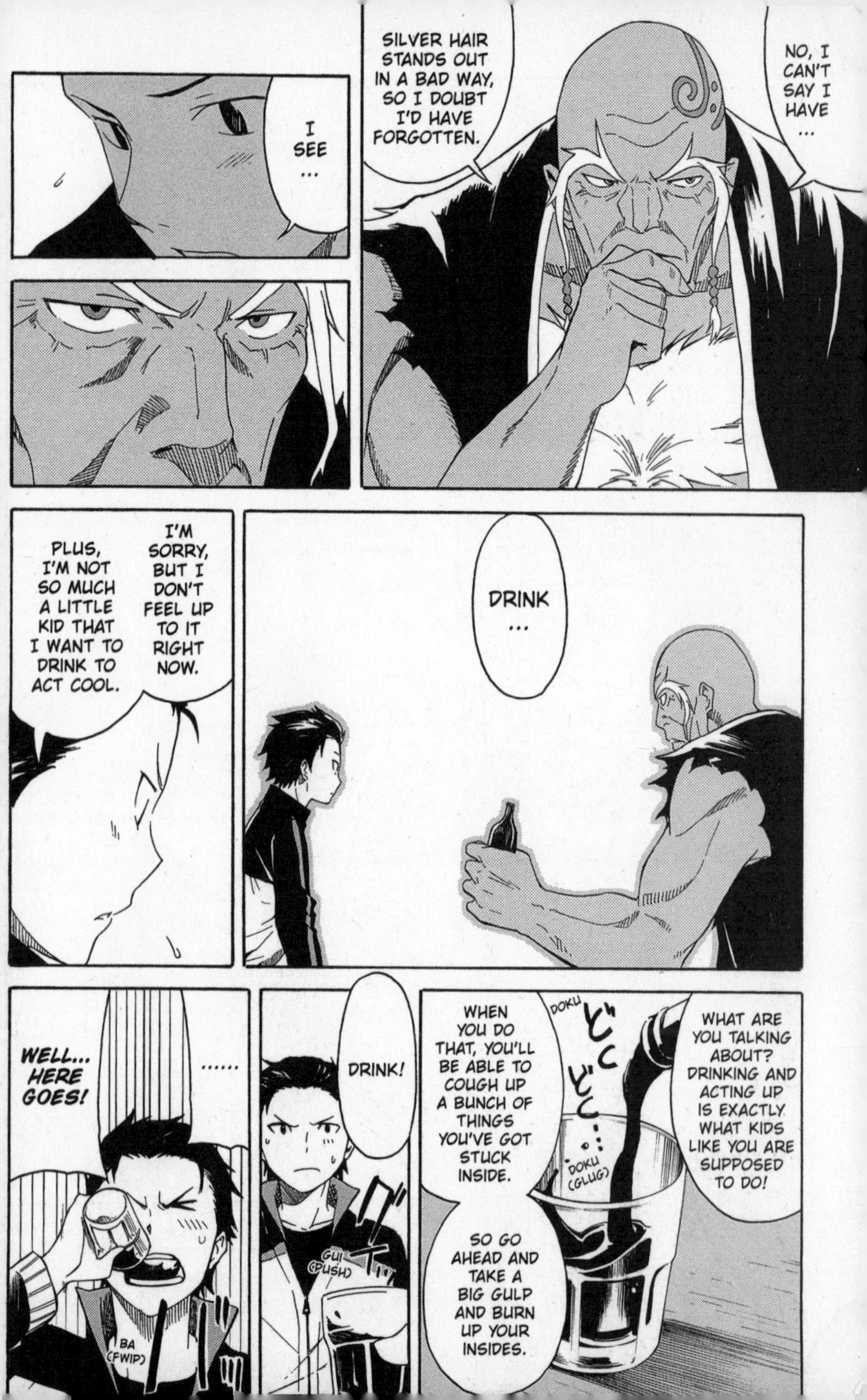

NO, I CAN'T SAY I HAVE ...
SILVER HAIR STANDS OUT IN A BAD WAY, SO I DOUBT I'D HAVE FORGOTTEN.
I SEE ...
DRINK ...
I'M SORRY, BUT I DON'T FEEL UP TO IT RIGHT NOW.
PLUS, I'M NOT SO MUCH A LITTLE KID THAT I WANT TO DRINK TO ACT COOL.
WHAT ARE YOU TALKING ABOUT? DRINKING AND ACTING UP IS EXACTLY WHAT KIDS LIKE YOU ARE SUPPOSED TO DO!
DOKU
どくどく
DOKU (GLUG)
WHEN YOU DO THAT, YOU'LL BE ABLE TO COUGH UP A BUNCH OF THINGS YOU'VE GOT STUCK INSIDE.
SO GO AHEAD AND TAKE A BIG GULP AND BURN UP YOUR INSIDES.
DRINK!
GUI (PUSH)
......
WELL... HERE GOES!
BA (FWIP)

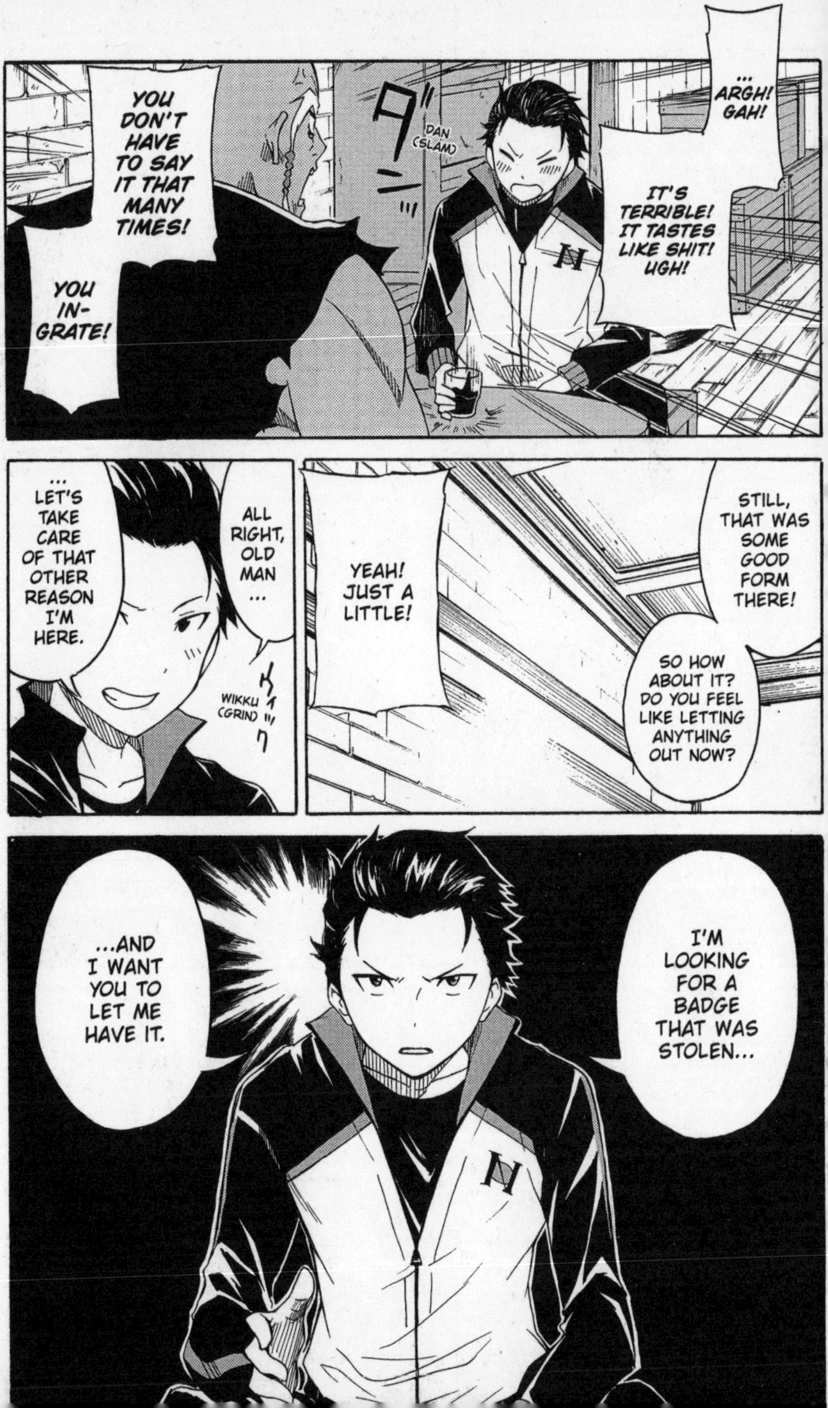
... ARGH! GAH!
IT'S TERRIBLE! IT TASTES LIKE SHIT! UGH!
DAN (SLAM)
YOU DON'T HAVE TO SAY IT THAT MANY TIMES!
YOU IN-GRATE!
STILL, THAT WAS SOME GOOD FORM THERE!
SO HOW ABOUT IT? DO YOU FEEL LIKE LETTING ANYTHING OUT NOW?
YEAH! JUST A LITTLE!
ALL RIGHT, OLD MAN ...
WIKKU (GRIN)
... LET'S TAKE CARE OF THAT OTHER REASON I'M HERE.
I'M LOOKING FOR A BADGE THAT WAS STOLEN...
...AND I WANT YOU TO LET ME HAVE IT.

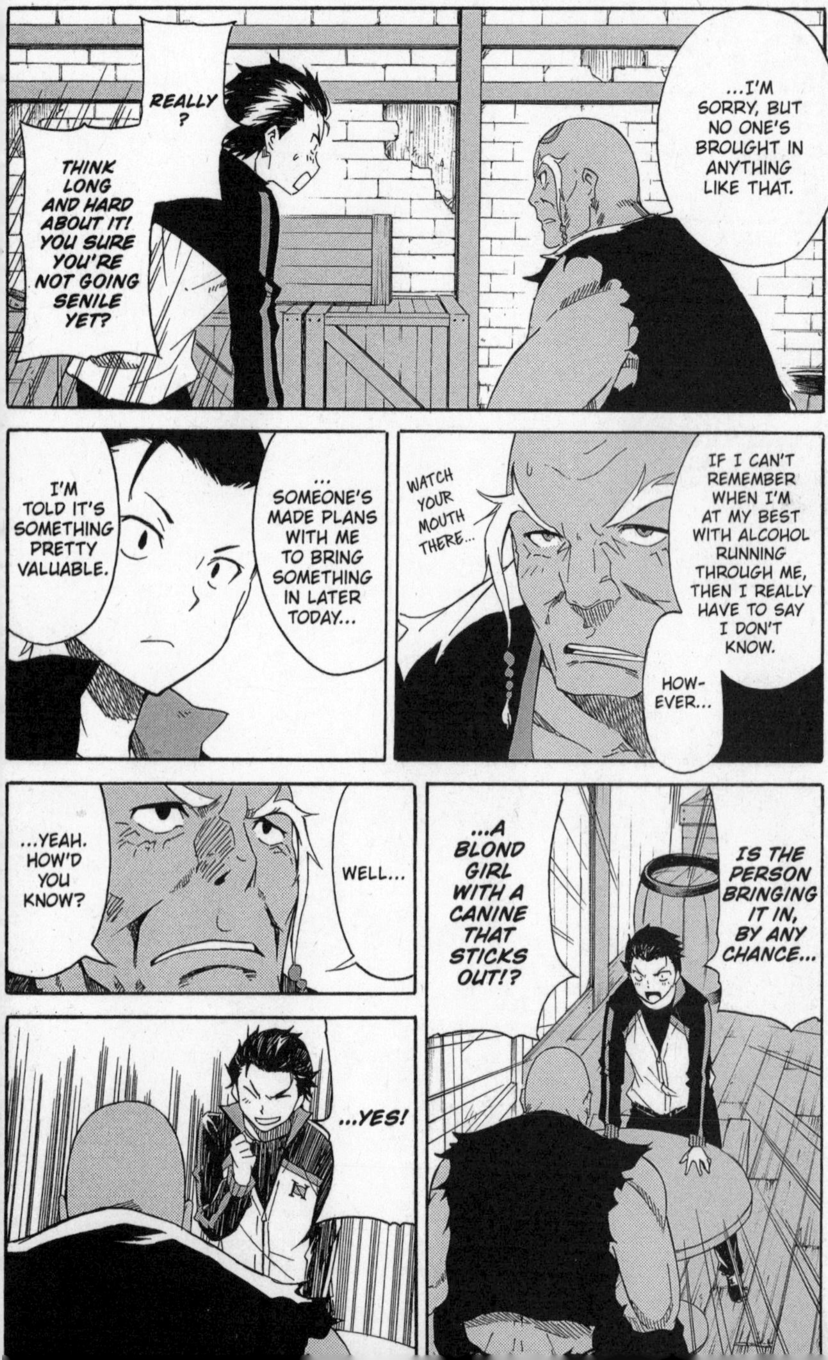
...I'M SORRY, BUT NO ONE'S BROUGHT IN ANYTHING LIKE THAT.
REALLY?
THINK LONG AND HARD ABOUT IT! YOU SURE YOU'RE NOT GOING SENILE YET?
WATCH YOUR MOUTH THERE...
IF I CAN'T REMEMBER WHEN I'M AT MY BEST WITH ALCOHOL RUNNING THROUGH ME, THEN I REALLY HAVE TO SAY I DON'T KNOW.
HOW-EVER...
... SOMEONE'S MADE PLANS WITH ME TO BRING SOMETHING IN LATER TODAY...
I'M TOLD IT'S SOMETHING PRETTY VALUABLE.
IS THE PERSON BRINGING IT IN, BY ANY CHANCE...
...A BLOND GIRL WITH A CANINE THAT STICKS OUT!?
WELL...
...YEAH. HOW'D YOU KNOW?
...YES!

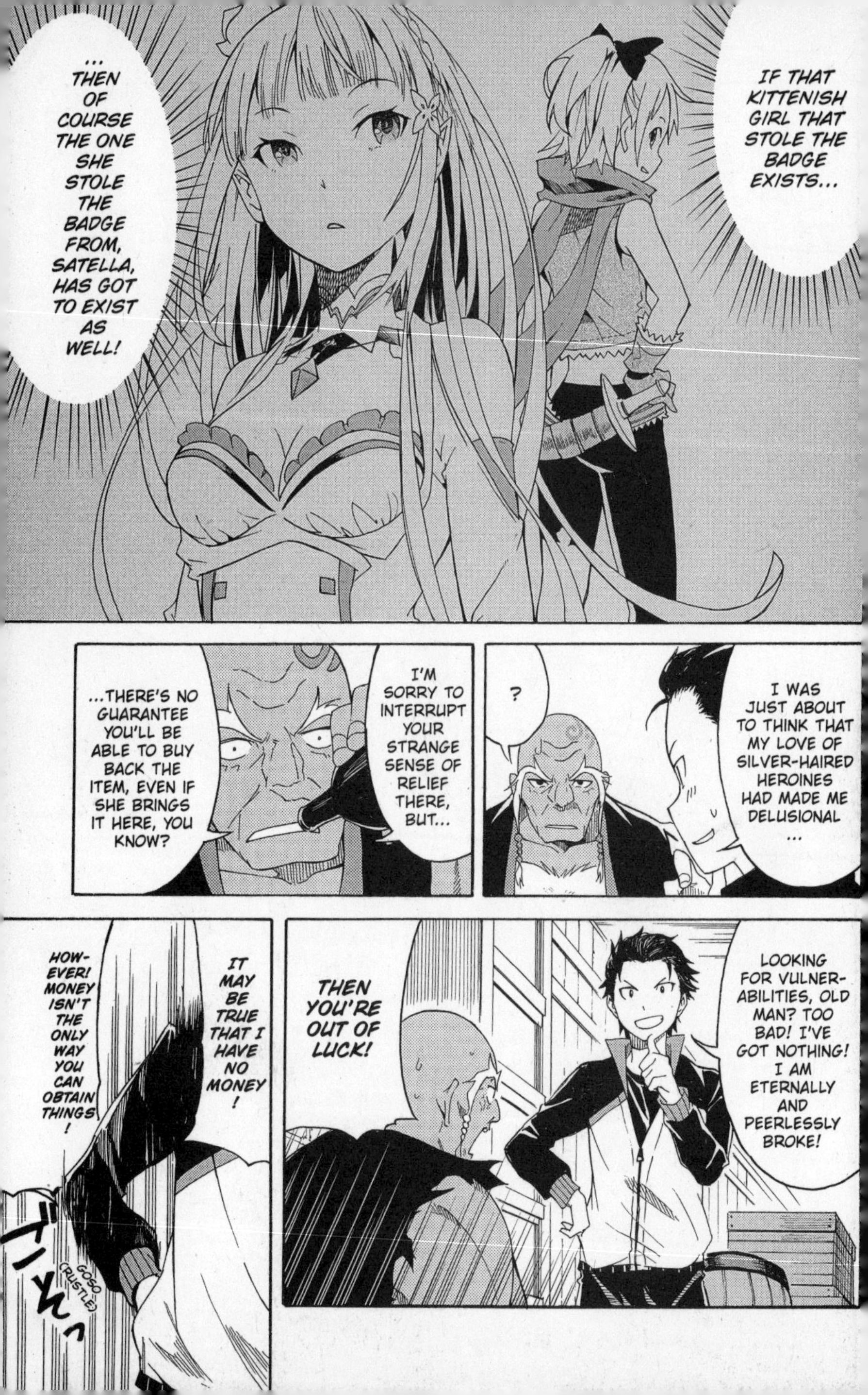
IF THAT KITTENISH GIRL THAT STOLE THE BADGE EXISTS...
...THEN OF COURSE THE ONE SHE STOLE THE BADGE FROM, SATELLA, HAS GOT TO EXIST AS WELL!
I WAS JUST ABOUT TO THINK THAT MY LOVE OF SILVER-HAIRED HEROINES HAD MADE ME DELUSIONAL...
?
I'M SORRY TO INTERRUPT YOUR STRANGE SENSE OF RELIEF THERE, BUT...
...THERE'S NO GUARANTEE YOU'LL BE ABLE TO BUY BACK THE ITEM, EVEN IF SHE BRINGS IT HERE, YOU KNOW?
LOOKING FOR VULNER-ABILITIES, OLD MAN? TOO BAD! I'VE GOT NOTHING! I AM ETERNALLY AND PEERLESSLY BROKE!
THEN YOU'RE OUT OF LUCK!
IT MAY BE TRUE THAT I HAVE NO MONEY!
HOW-EVER! MONEY ISN'T THE ONLY WAY YOU CAN OBTAIN THINGS!
GOSO (RUSTLE)

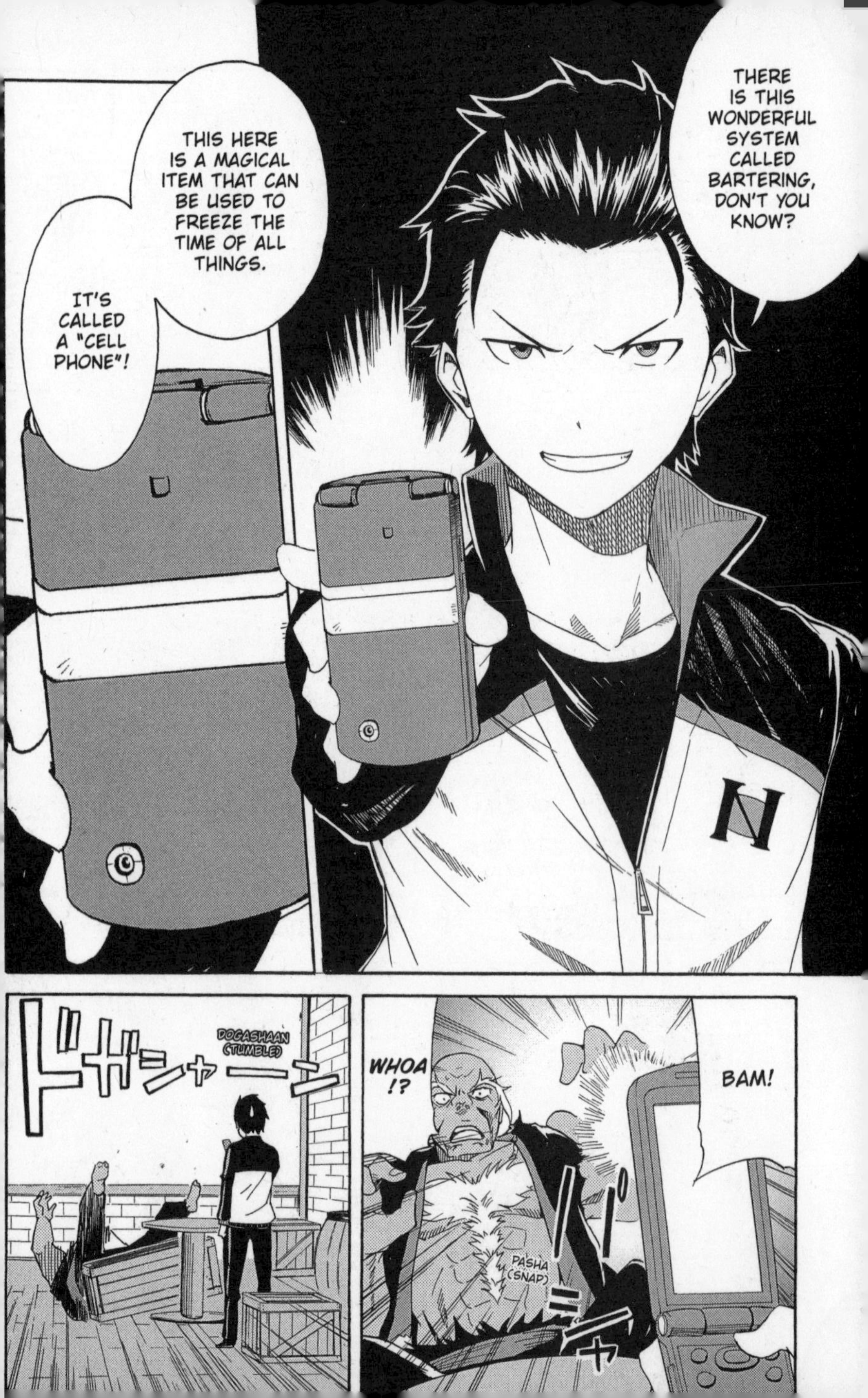
THERE IS THIS WONDERFUL SYSTEM CALLED BARTERING, DON'T YOU KNOW?
THIS HERE IS A MAGICAL ITEM THAT CAN BE USED TO FREEZE THE TIME OF ALL THINGS.
IT'S CALLED A "CELL PHONE"!
BAM!
WHOA !?
PASHA (SNAP)
ドガシャーン
DOGASHAAN (TUMBLED)

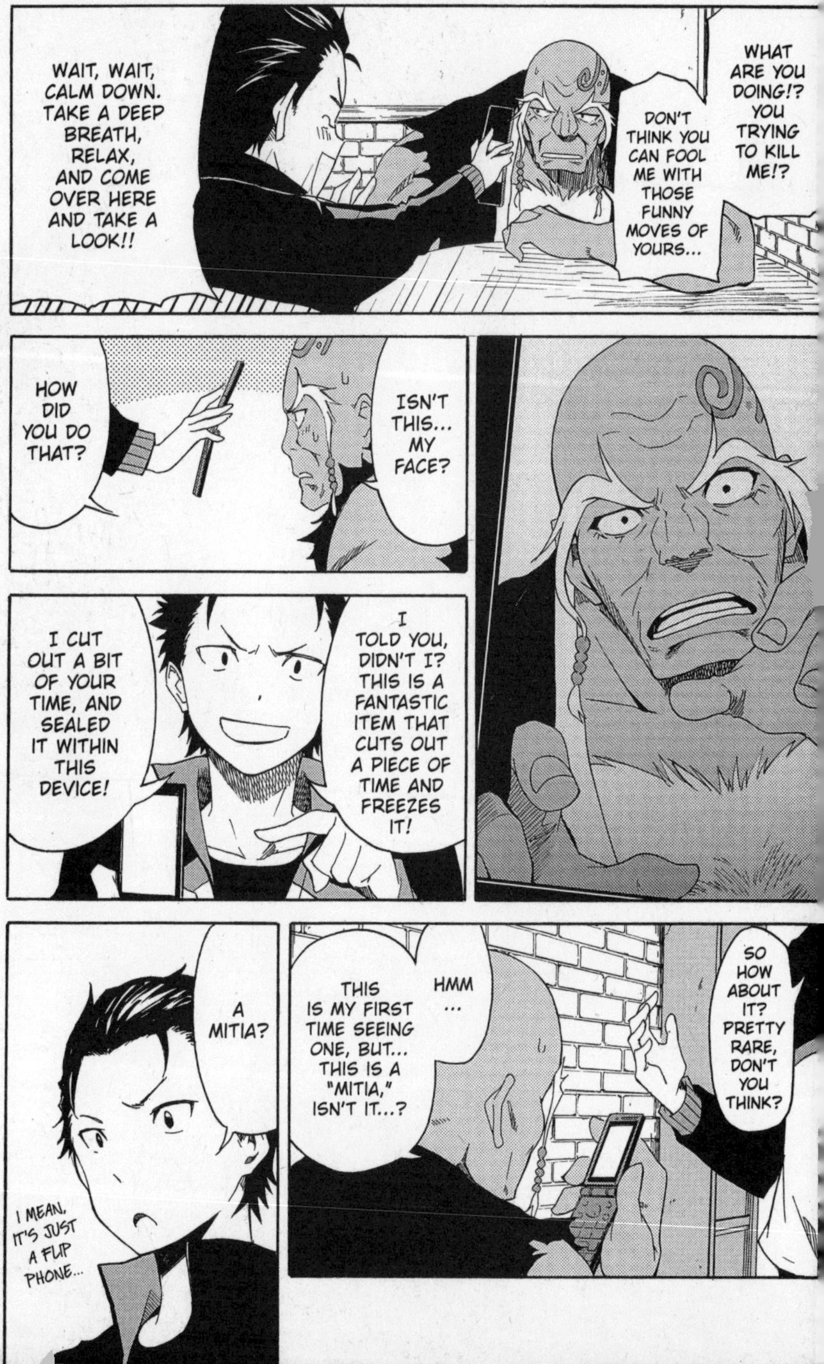
WHAT ARE YOU DOING!? YOU TRYING TO KILL ME!?
DON'T THINK YOU CAN FOOL ME WITH THOSE FUNNY MOVES OF YOURS...
WAIT, WAIT, CALM DOWN. TAKE A DEEP BREATH, RELAX, AND COME OVER HERE AND TAKE A LOOK!!
ISN'T THIS... MY FACE?
HOW DID YOU DO THAT?
I TOLD YOU, DIDN'T I? THIS IS A FANTASTIC ITEM THAT CUTS OUT A PIECE OF TIME AND FREEZES IT!
I CUT OUT A BIT OF YOUR TIME, AND SEALED IT WITHIN THIS DEVICE!
SO HOW ABOUT IT? PRETTY RARE, DON'T YOU THINK?
HMM ...
THIS IS MY FIRST TIME SEEING ONE, BUT... THIS IS A "MITIA," ISN'T IT...?
A MITIA?
I MEAN, IT'S JUST A FLIP PHONE...

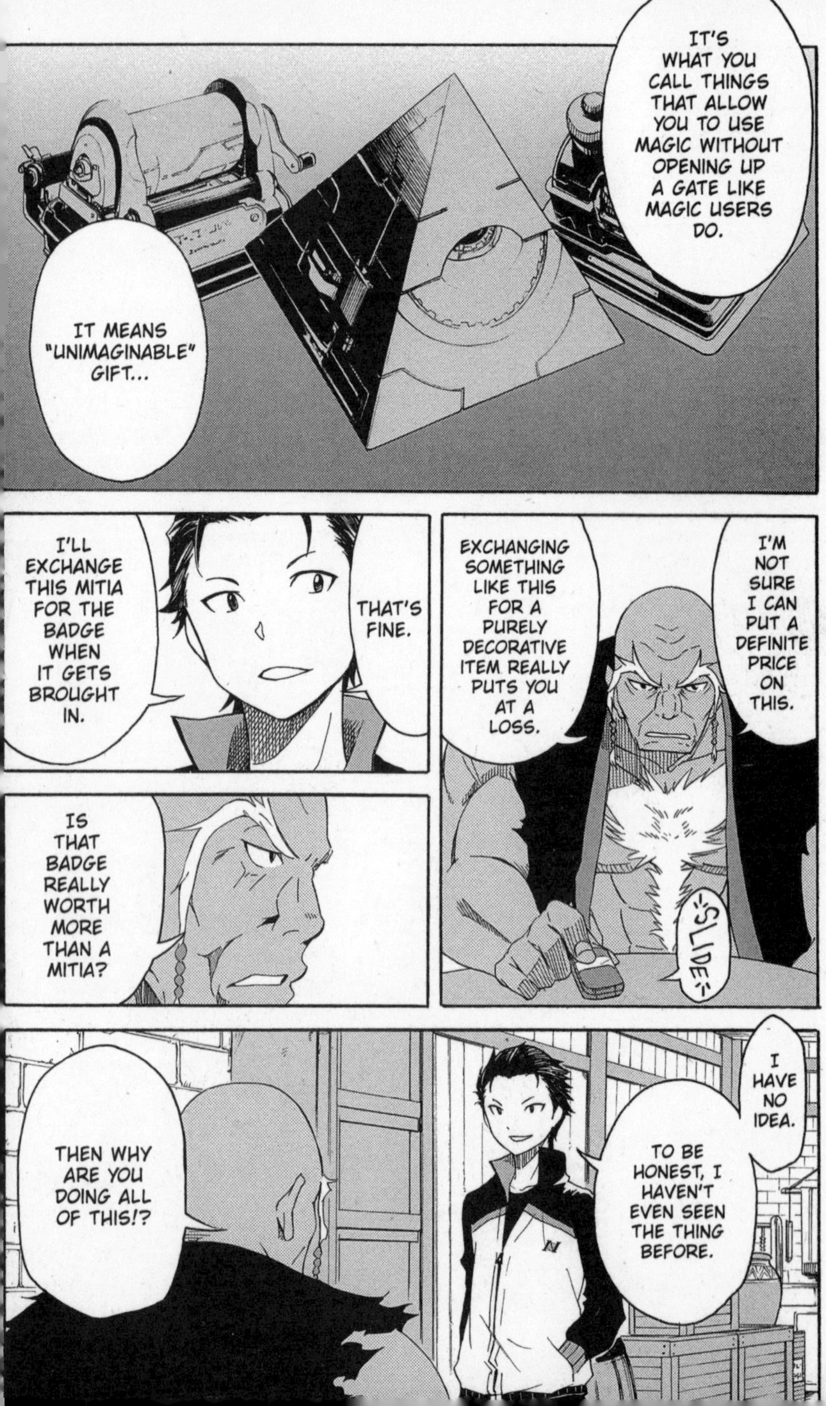
IT'S WHAT YOU CALL THINGS THAT ALLOW YOU TO USE MAGIC WITHOUT OPENING UP A GATE LIKE MAGIC USERS DO.
IT MEANS "UNIMAGINABLE" GIFT...
I'M NOT SURE I CAN PUT A DEFINITE PRICE ON THIS.
EXCHANGING SOMETHING LIKE THIS FOR A PURELY DECORATIVE ITEM REALLY PUTS YOU AT A LOSS.
SLIDE
THAT'S FINE.
I'LL EXCHANGE THIS MITIA FOR THE BADGE WHEN IT GETS BROUGHT IN.
IS THAT BADGE REALLY WORTH MORE THAN A MITIA?
I HAVE NO IDEA.
TO BE HONEST, I HAVEN'T EVEN SEEN THE THING BEFORE.
THEN WHY ARE YOU DOING ALL OF THIS!?

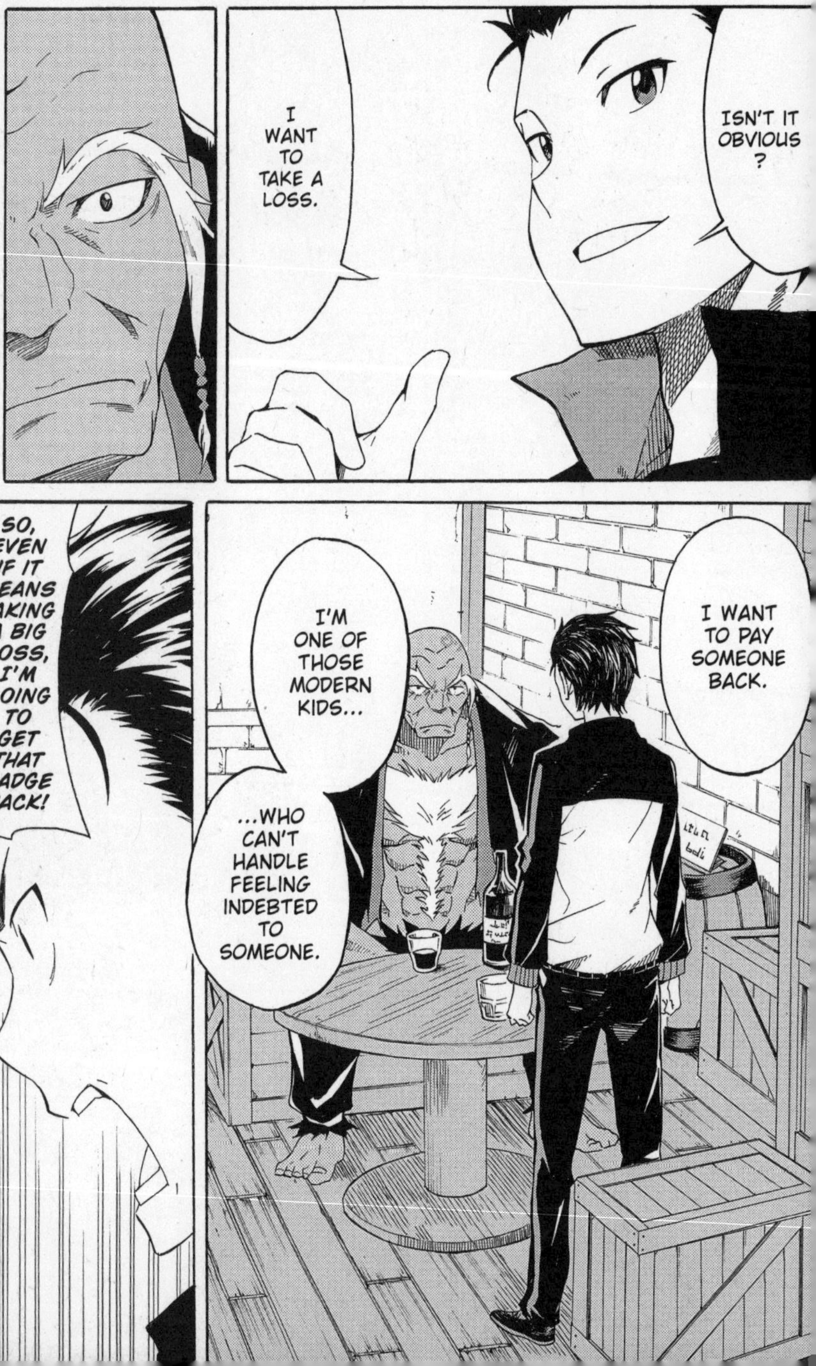
ISN'T IT OBVIOUS?
I WANT TO TAKE A LOSS.
I WANT TO PAY SOMEONE BACK.
I'M ONE OF THOSE MODERN KIDS...
...WHO CAN'T HANDLE FEELING INDEBTED TO SOMEONE.
SO, EVEN IF IT MEANS TAKING A BIG LOSS, I'M GOING TO GET THAT BADGE BACK!

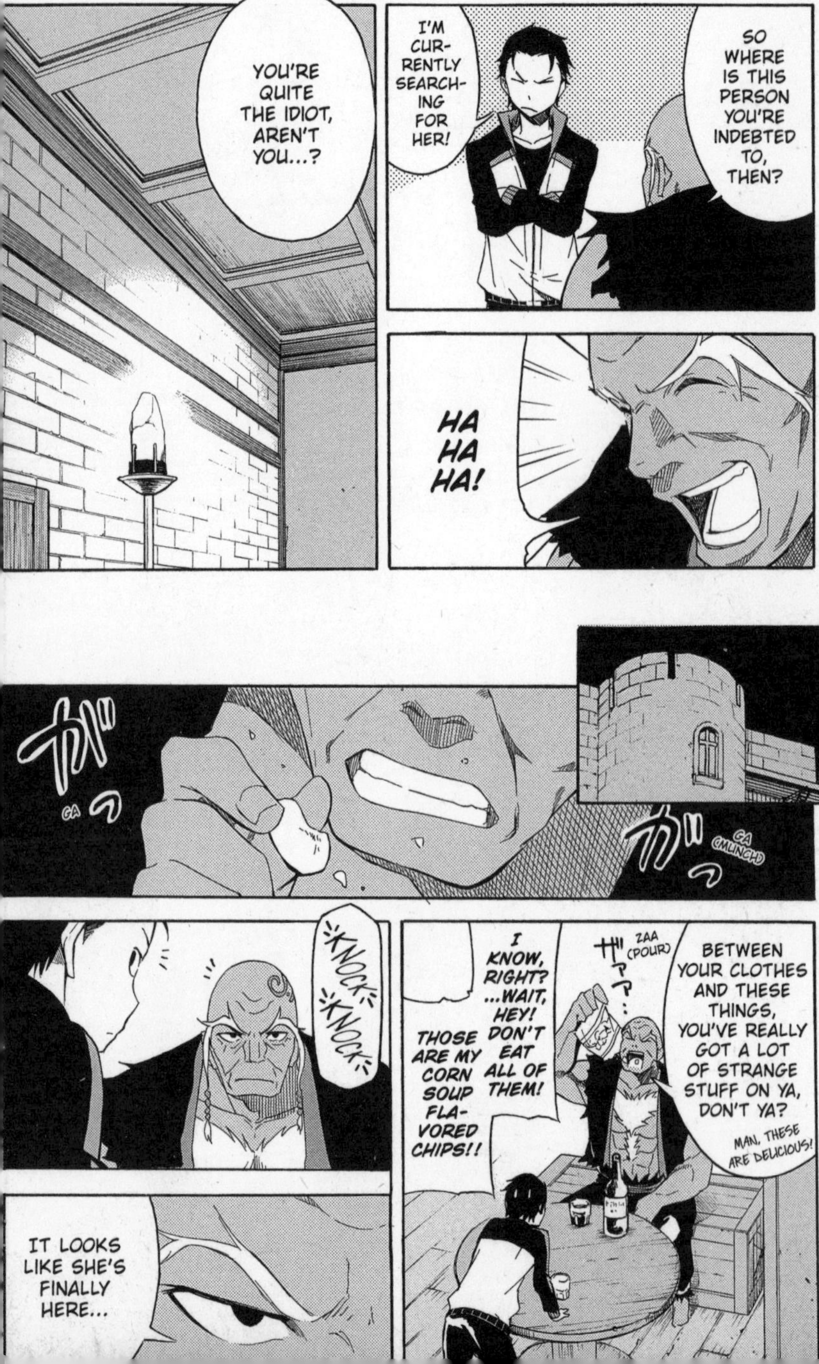
SO WHERE IS THIS PERSON YOU'RE INDEBTED TO, THEN?
I'M CUR-RENTLY SEARCH-ING FOR HER!
HA HA HA!
YOU'RE QUITE THE IDIOT, AREN'T YOU...?
ガッ
GA (MUNCH)
ガッ
GA
BETWEEN YOUR CLOTHES AND THESE THINGS, YOU'VE REALLY GOT A LOT OF STRANGE STUFF ON YA, DON'T YA?
ザァ
ZAA (POUR)
MAN, THESE ARE DELICIOUS!
I KNOW, RIGHT? ...WAIT, HEY! DON'T EAT ALL OF THEM!
THOSE ARE MY CORN SOUP FLA-VORED CHIPS!!
KNOCK KNOCK
IT LOOKS LIKE SHE'S FINALLY HERE...

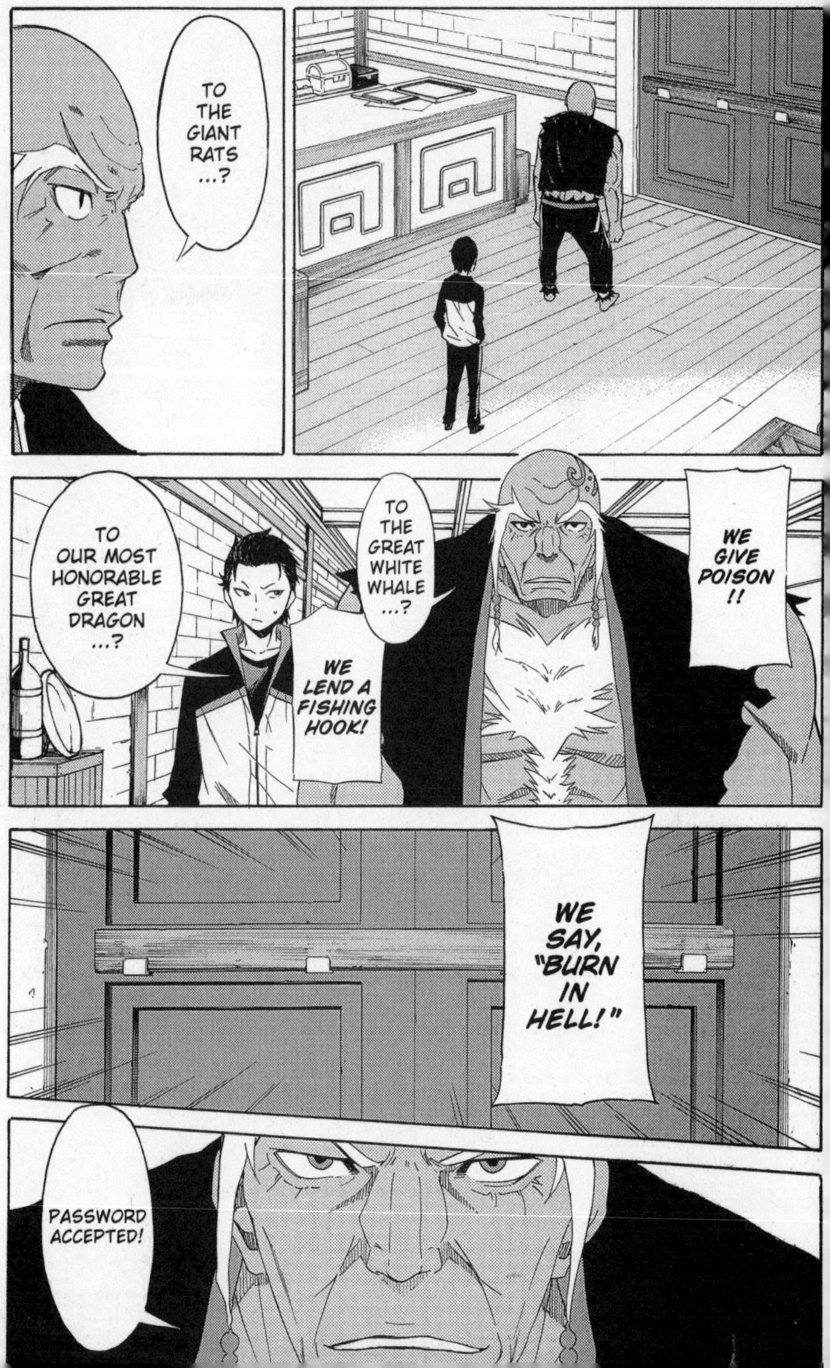
TO THE GIANT RATS ...?
WE GIVE POISON!!
TO THE GREAT WHITE WHALE ...?
WE LEND A FISHING HOOK!
TO OUR MOST HONORABLE GREAT DRAGON ...?
WE SAY, "BURN IN HELL!"
PASSWORD ACCEPTED!

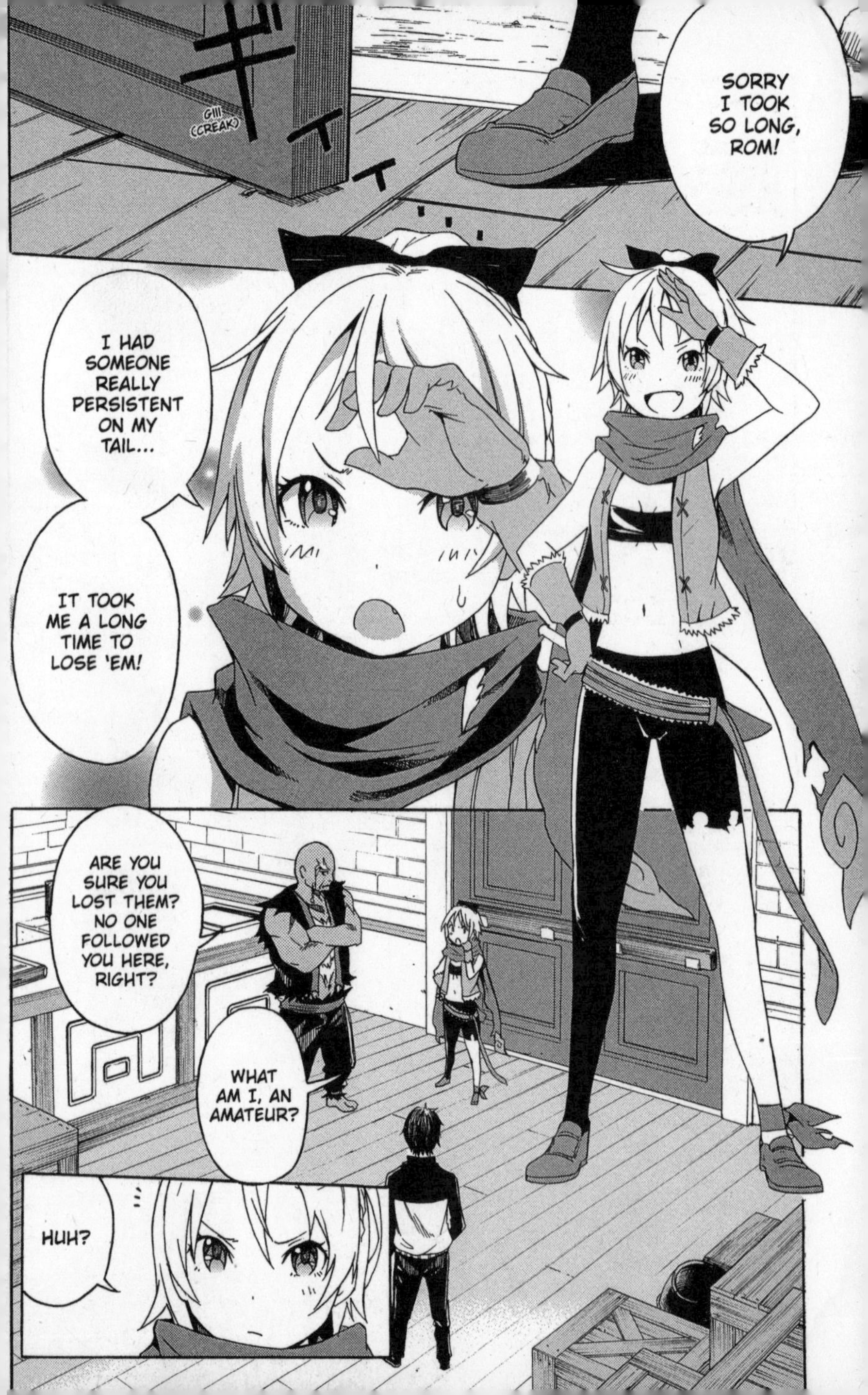
SORRY I TOOK SO LONG, ROM!
GIII (CREAK)
I HAD SOMEONE REALLY PERSISTENT ON MY TAIL...
IT TOOK ME A LONG TIME TO LOSE 'EM!
ARE YOU SURE YOU LOST THEM? NO ONE FOLLOWED YOU HERE, RIGHT?
WHAT AM I, AN AMATEUR?
HUH?

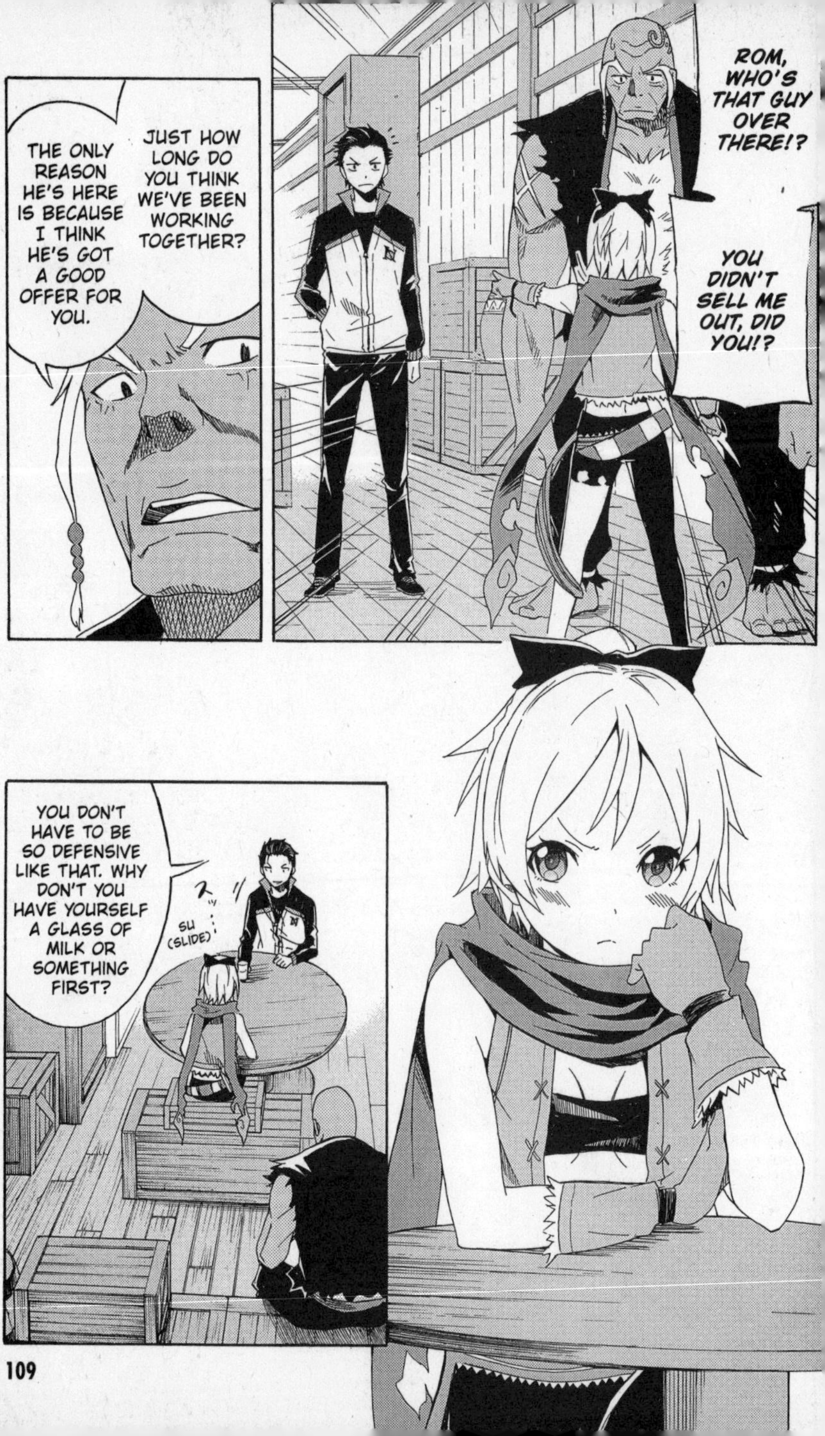
ROM, WHO'S THAT GUY OVER THERE!?
YOU DIDN'T SELL ME OUT, DID YOU!?
JUST HOW LONG DO YOU THINK WE'VE BEEN WORKING TOGETHER?
THE ONLY REASON HE'S HERE IS BECAUSE I THINK HE'S GOT A GOOD OFFER FOR YOU.
YOU DON'T HAVE TO BE SO DEFENSIVE LIKE THAT. WHY DON'T YOU HAVE YOURSELF A GLASS OF MILK OR SOMETHING FIRST?
SU (SLIDE)

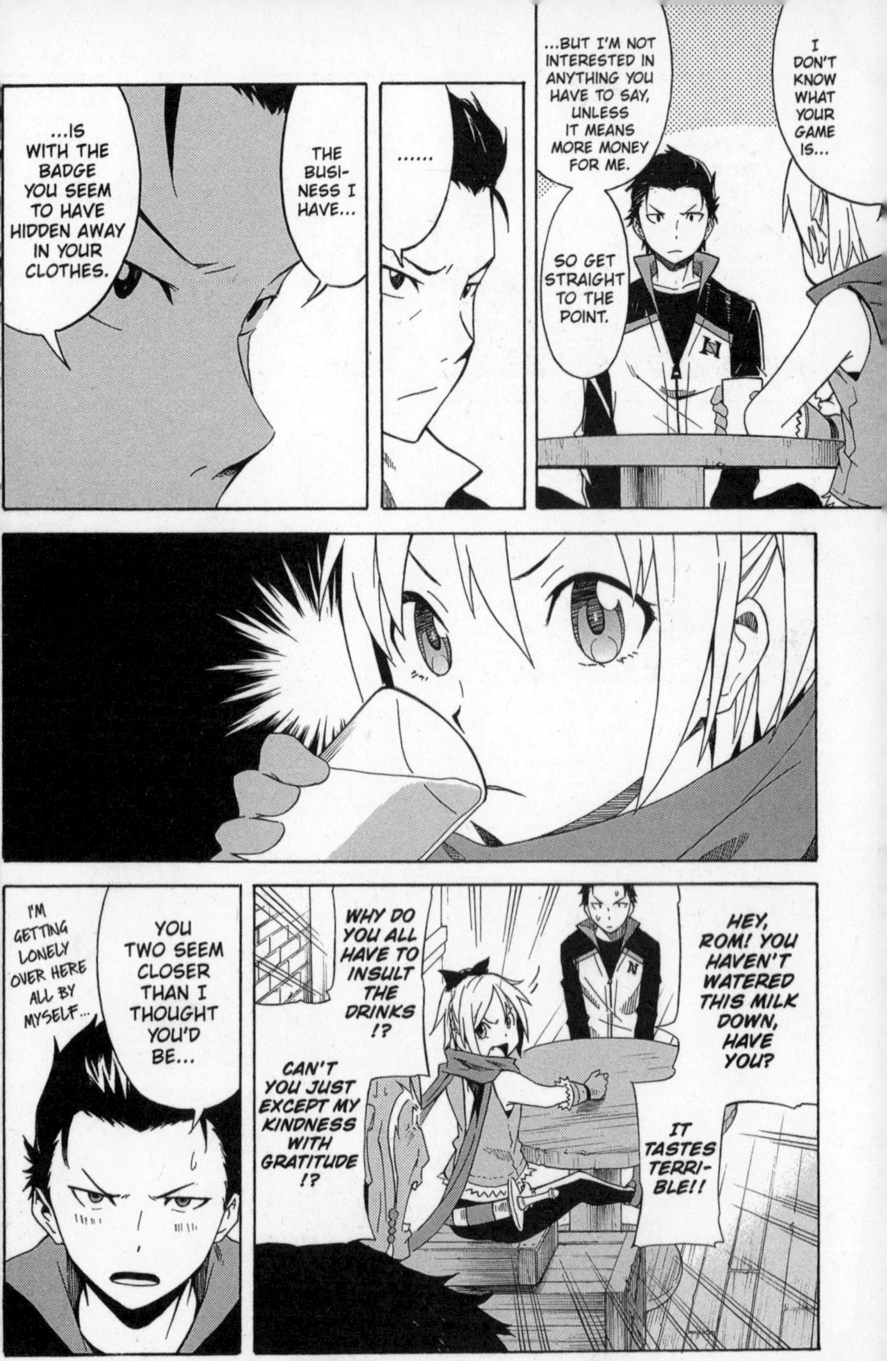
I DON'T KNOW WHAT YOUR GAME IS...
...BUT I'M NOT INTERESTED IN ANYTHING YOU HAVE TO SAY, UNLESS IT MEANS MORE MONEY FOR ME.
SO GET STRAIGHT TO THE POINT.
......
THE BUSINESS I HAVE...
...IS WITH THE BADGE YOU SEEM TO HAVE HIDDEN AWAY IN YOUR CLOTHES.
HEY, ROM! YOU HAVEN'T WATERED THIS MILK DOWN, HAVE YOU?
IT TASTES TERRIBLE!!
WHY DO YOU ALL HAVE TO INSULT THE DRINKS!?
CAN'T YOU JUST EXCEPT MY KINDNESS WITH GRATITUDE!?
YOU TWO SEEM CLOSER THAN I THOUGHT YOU'D BE...
I'M GETTING LONELY OVER HERE ALL BY MYSELF...

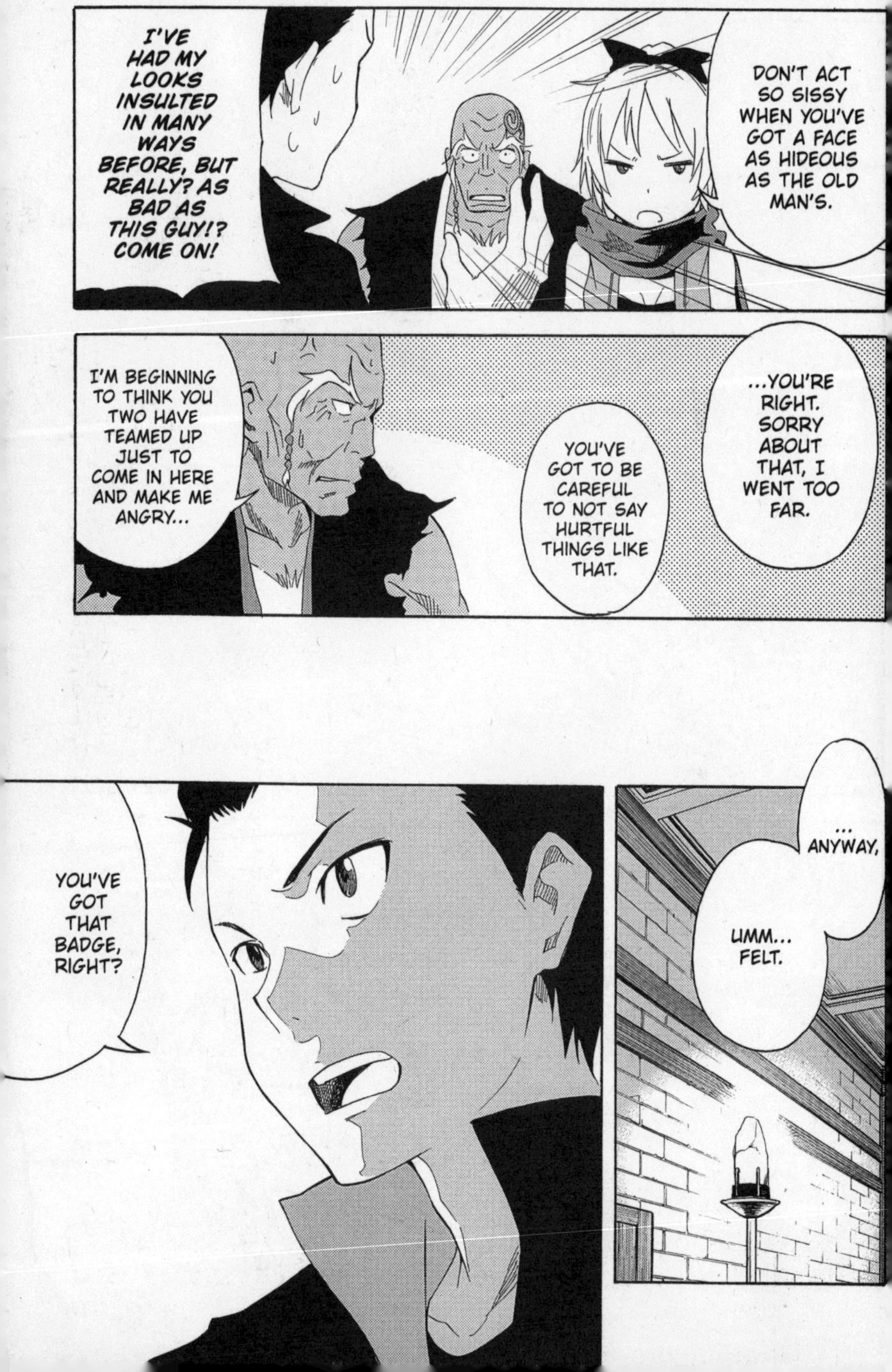
DON'T ACT SO SISSY WHEN YOU'VE GOT A FACE AS HIDEOUS AS THE OLD MAN'S.
I'VE HAD MY LOOKS INSULTED IN MANY WAYS BEFORE, BUT REALLY? AS BAD AS THIS GUY!? COME ON!
...YOU'RE RIGHT. SORRY ABOUT THAT, I WENT TOO FAR.
YOU'VE GOT TO BE CAREFUL TO NOT SAY HURTFUL THINGS LIKE THAT.
I'M BEGINNING TO THINK YOU TWO HAVE TEAMED UP JUST TO COME IN HERE AND MAKE ME ANGRY...
...ANYWAY,
UMM... FELT.
YOU'VE GOT THAT BADGE, RIGHT?

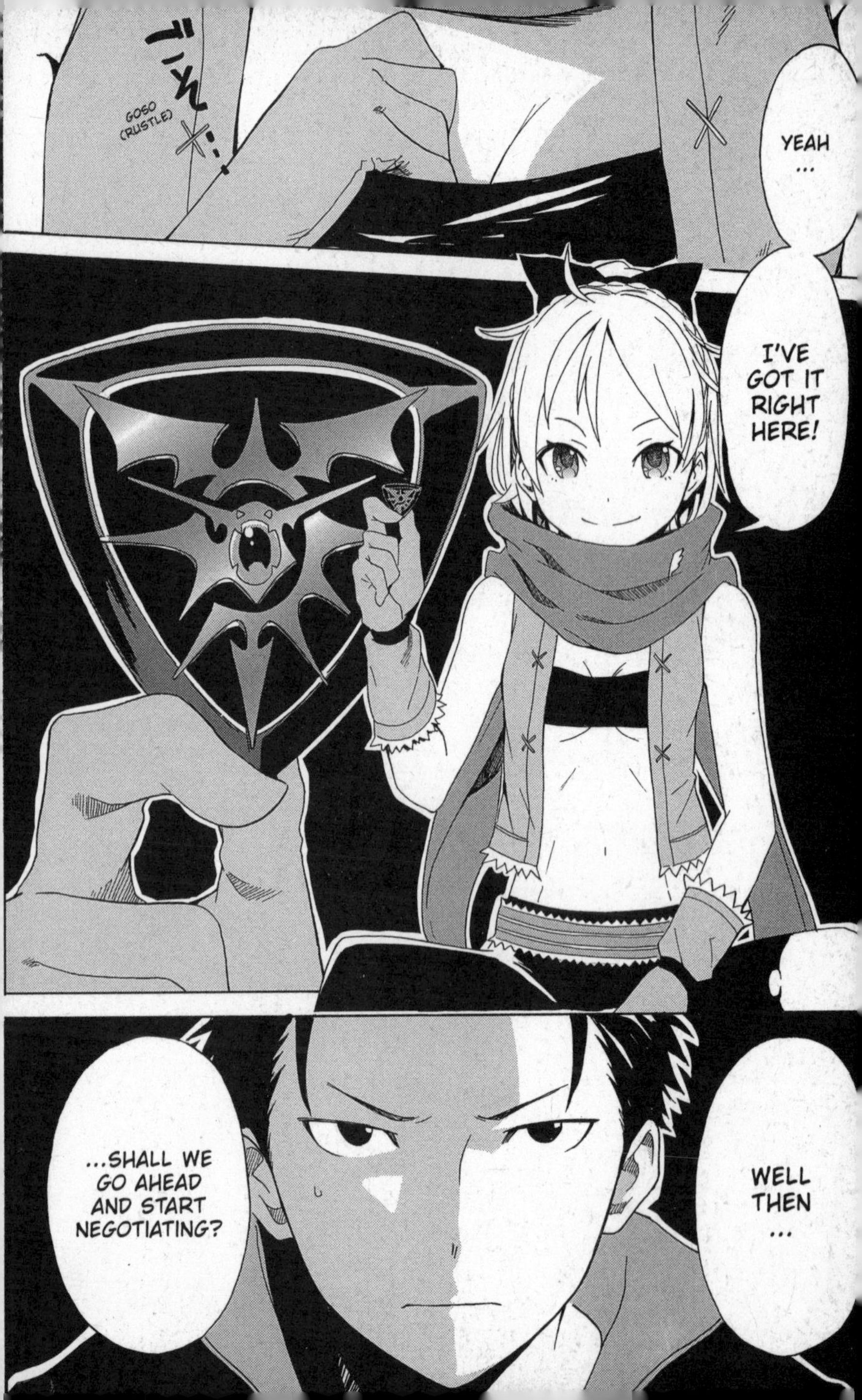
YEAH ...
ゴソ…
GOSO (RUSTLE)
I'VE GOT IT RIGHT HERE!
WELL THEN ...
...SHALL WE GO AHEAD AND START NEGOTIATING?

Re:ZERO -Starting Life in Another World-

Chapter 1: A Day in the Capital

The only ability Subaru Natsuki gets when
he's summoned to another world is time
travel via his own death. But to save her,
he'll die as many times as it takes.

Re:ZeRo

-Starting Life in Another World-

Chapter 1: A Day in the Capital

The only ability Subaru Natsuki gets when he's summoned to another world is time travel via his own death. But to save her, he'll die as many times as it takes.

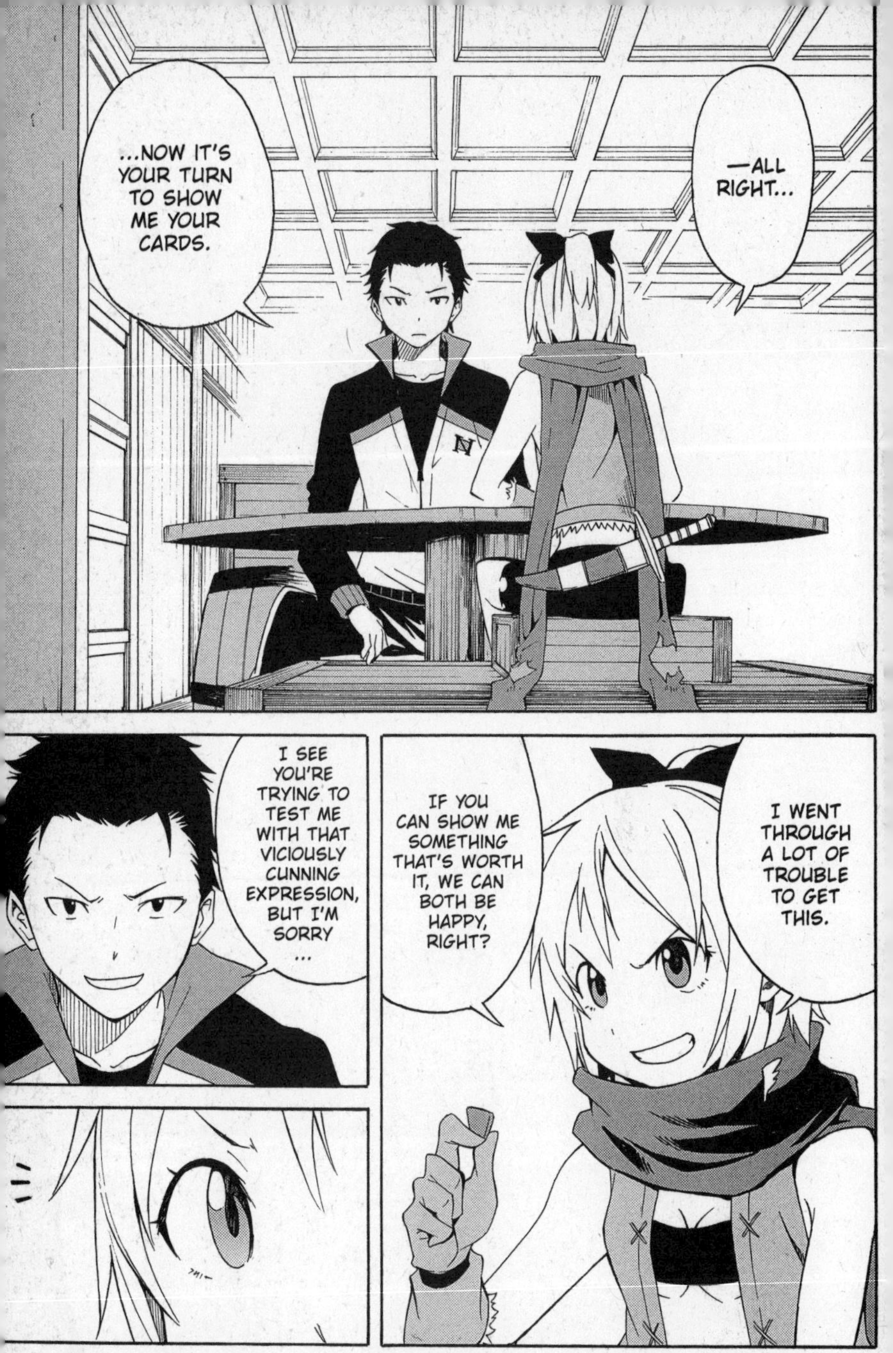
—ALL RIGHT...
...NOW IT'S YOUR TURN TO SHOW ME YOUR CARDS.
I WENT THROUGH A LOT OF TROUBLE TO GET THIS.
IF YOU CAN SHOW ME SOMETHING THAT'S WORTH IT, WE CAN BOTH BE HAPPY, RIGHT?
I SEE YOU'RE TRYING TO TEST ME WITH THAT VICIOUSLY CUNNING EXPRESSION, BUT I'M SORRY ...

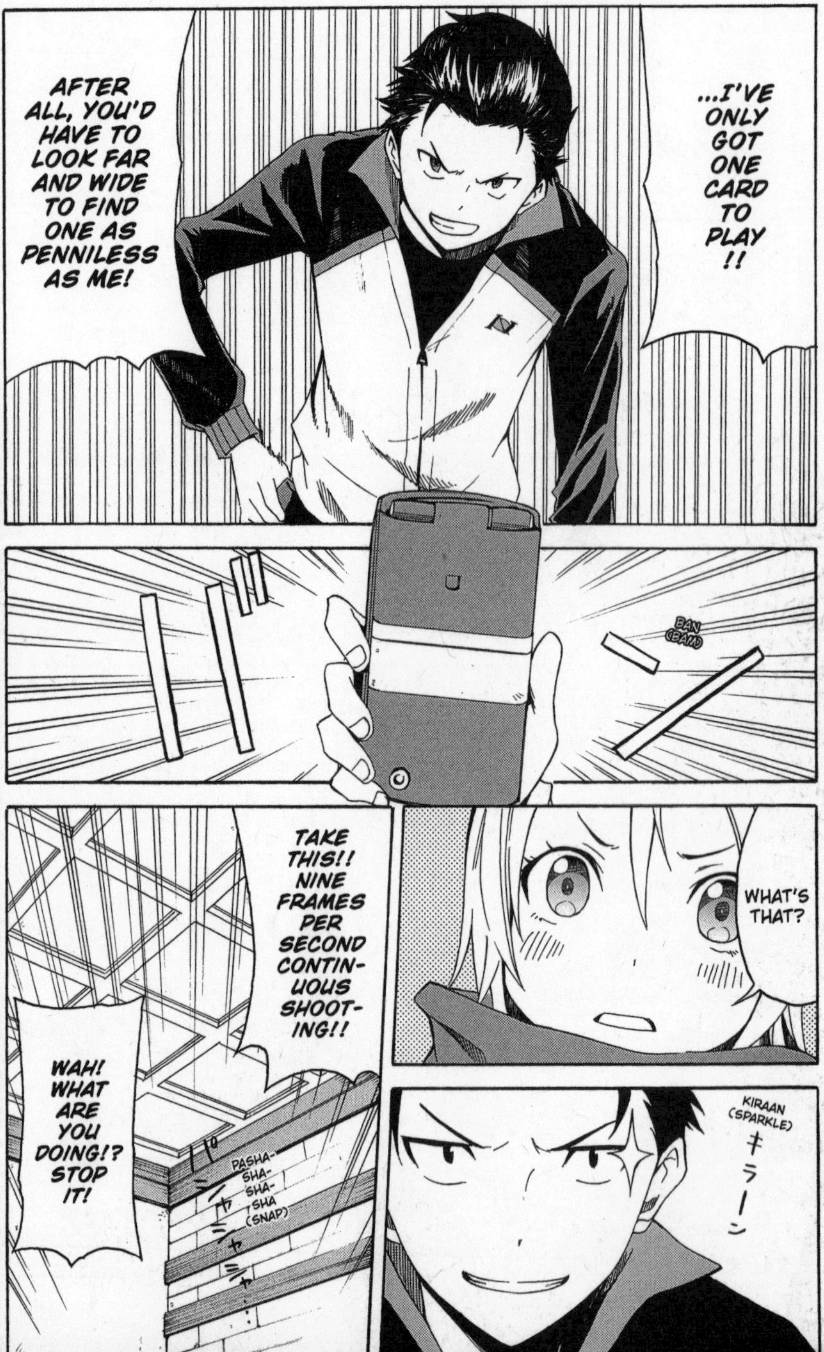
...I'VE ONLY GOT ONE CARD TO PLAY!!
AFTER ALL, YOU'D HAVE TO LOOK FAR AND WIDE TO FIND ONE AS PENNILESS AS ME!
BAN (BAM)
WHAT'S THAT?
KIRAAN (SPARKLE)
キラーン
TAKE THIS!! NINE FRAMES PER SECOND CONTIN-UOUS SHOOT-ING!!
WAH! WHAT ARE YOU DOING!? STOP IT!
PASHA-SHA-SHA-SHA (SNAP)

Episode 5: A Struggle Far Too Late

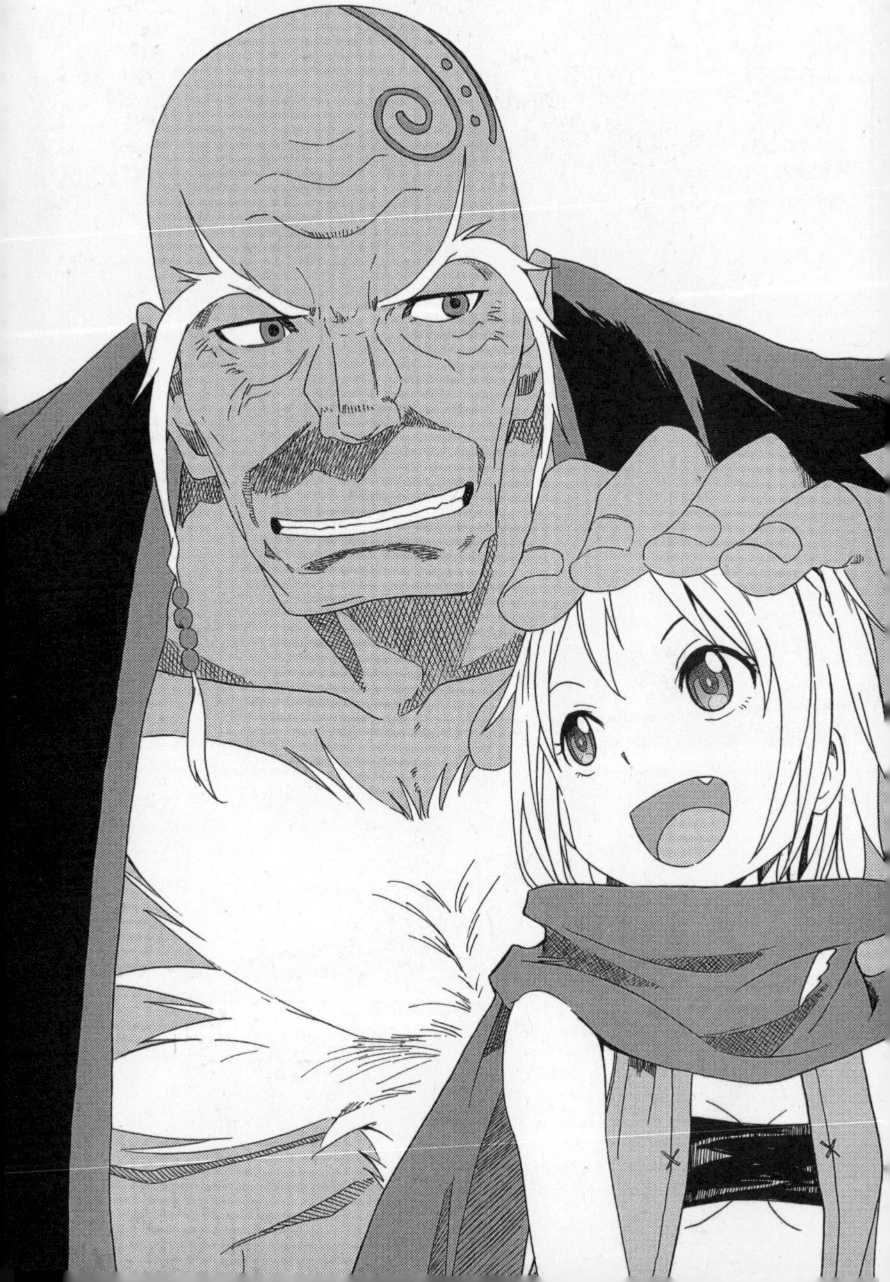

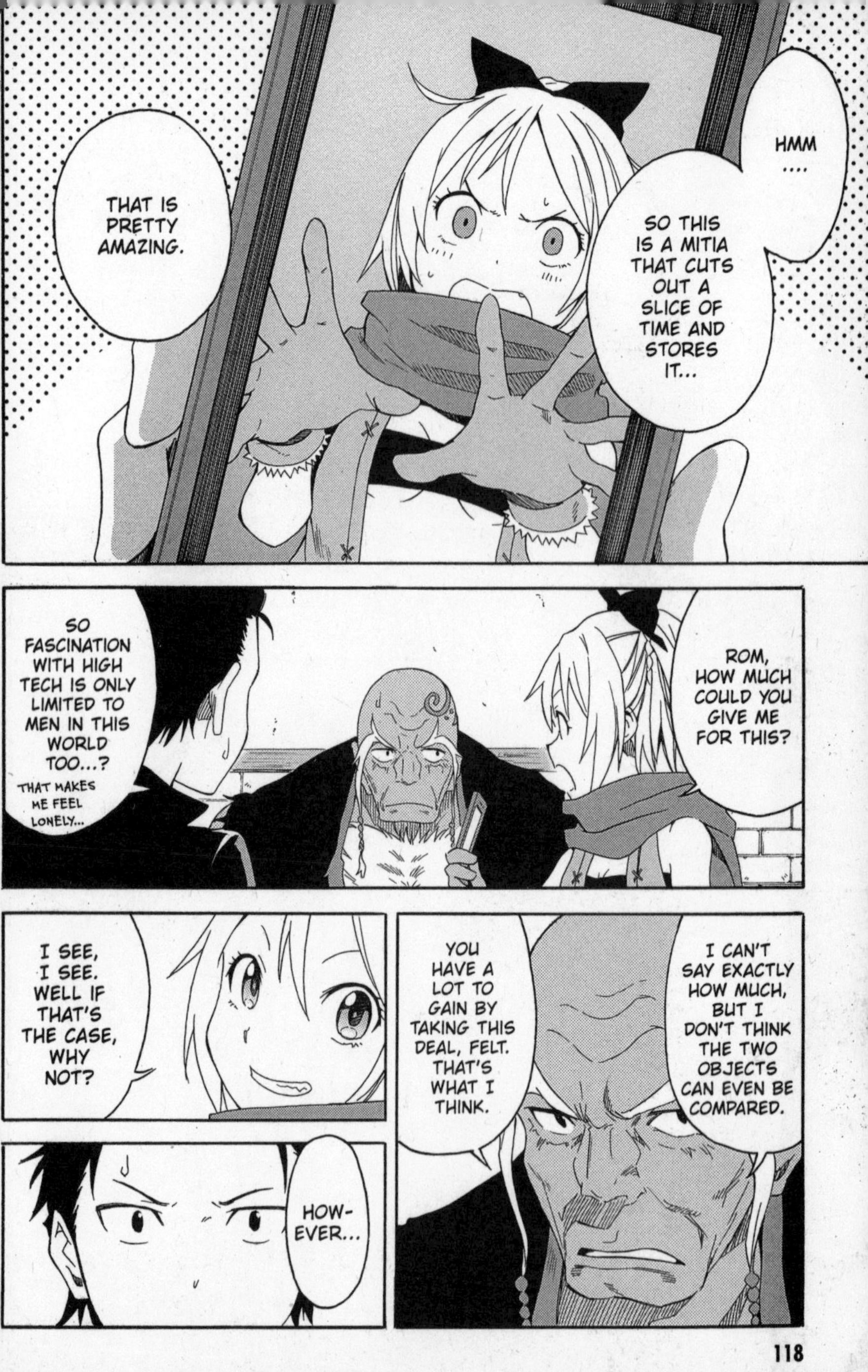
HMM ....
SO THIS IS A MITIA THAT CUTS OUT A SLICE OF TIME AND STORES IT...
THAT IS PRETTY AMAZING.
ROM, HOW MUCH COULD YOU GIVE ME FOR THIS?
SO FASCINATION WITH HIGH TECH IS ONLY LIMITED TO MEN IN THIS WORLD TOO...?
THAT MAKES ME FEEL LONELY...
I CAN'T SAY EXACTLY HOW MUCH, BUT I DON'T THINK THE TWO OBJECTS CAN EVEN BE COMPARED.
YOU HAVE A LOT TO GAIN BY TAKING THIS DEAL, FELT. THAT'S WHAT I THINK.
I SEE, I SEE. WELL IF THAT'S THE CASE, WHY NOT?
HOW-EVER...

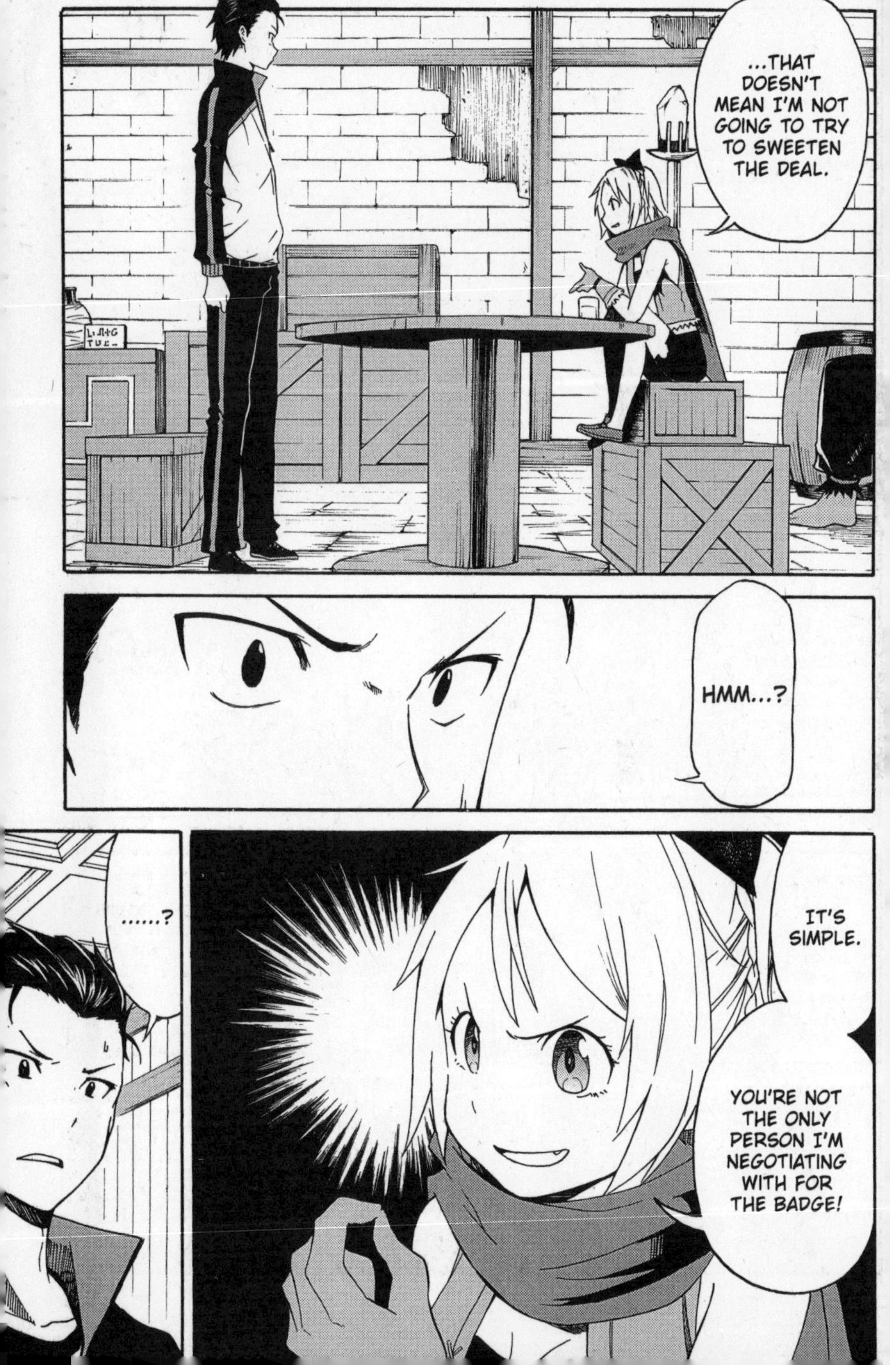
...THAT DOESN'T MEAN I'M NOT GOING TO TRY TO SWEETEN THE DEAL.
HMM...?
IT'S SIMPLE.
YOU'RE NOT THE ONLY PERSON I'M NEGOTIATING WITH FOR THE BADGE!
......?

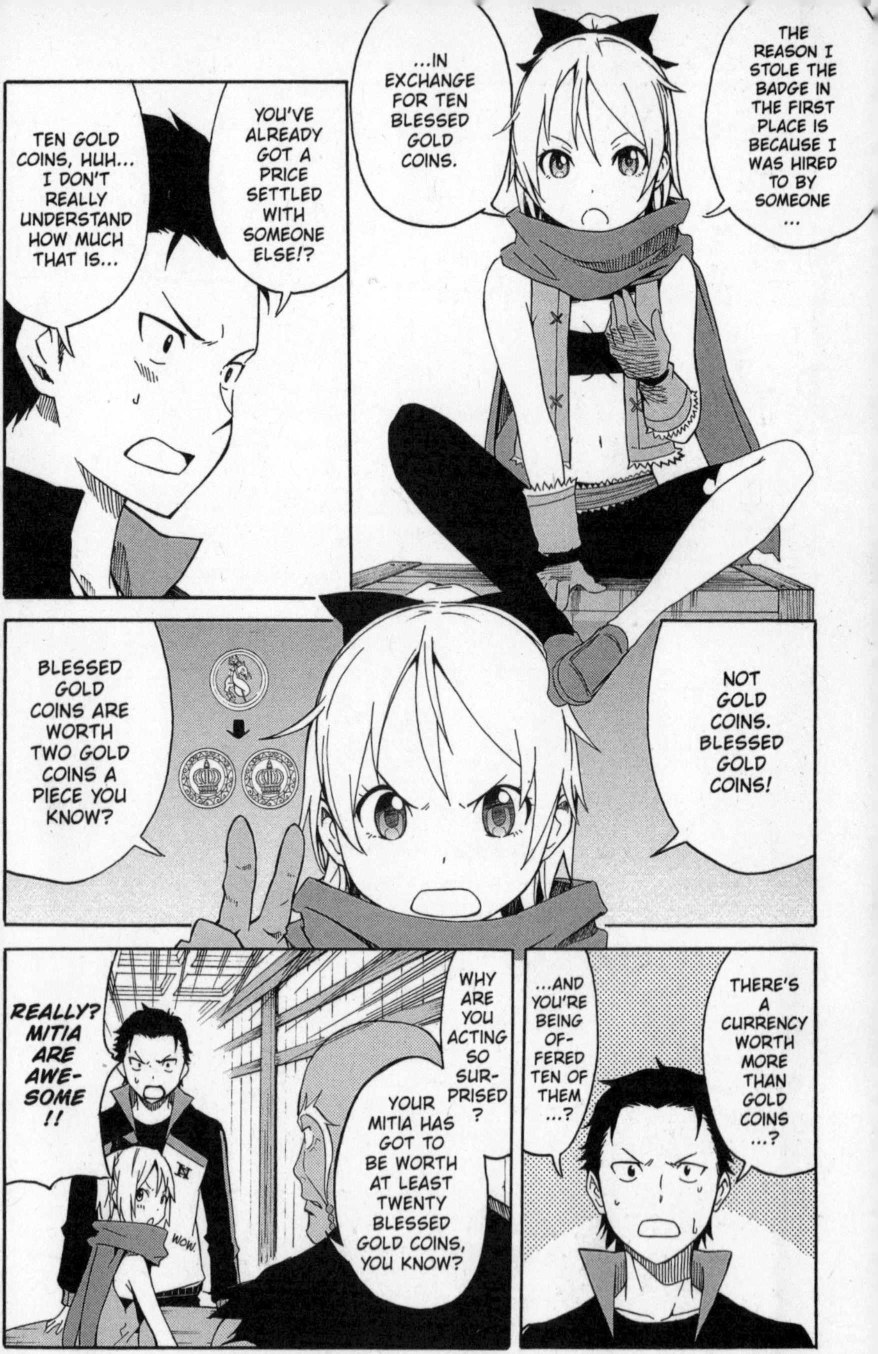
THE REASON I STOLE THE BADGE IN THE FIRST PLACE IS BECAUSE I WAS HIRED TO BY SOMEONE ...
...IN EXCHANGE FOR TEN BLESSED GOLD COINS.
YOU'VE ALREADY GOT A PRICE SETTLED WITH SOMEONE ELSE!?
TEN GOLD COINS, HUH... I DON'T REALLY UNDERSTAND HOW MUCH THAT IS...
NOT GOLD COINS. BLESSED GOLD COINS!
BLESSED GOLD COINS ARE WORTH TWO GOLD COINS A PIECE YOU KNOW?
THERE'S A CURRENCY WORTH MORE THAN GOLD COINS ...?
...AND YOU'RE BEING OF-FERED TEN OF THEM ...?
WHY ARE YOU ACTING SO SUR-PRISED ?
YOUR MITIA HAS GOT TO BE WORTH AT LEAST TWENTY BLESSED GOLD COINS, YOU KNOW?
REALLY? MITIA ARE AWE-SOME !!
WOW!

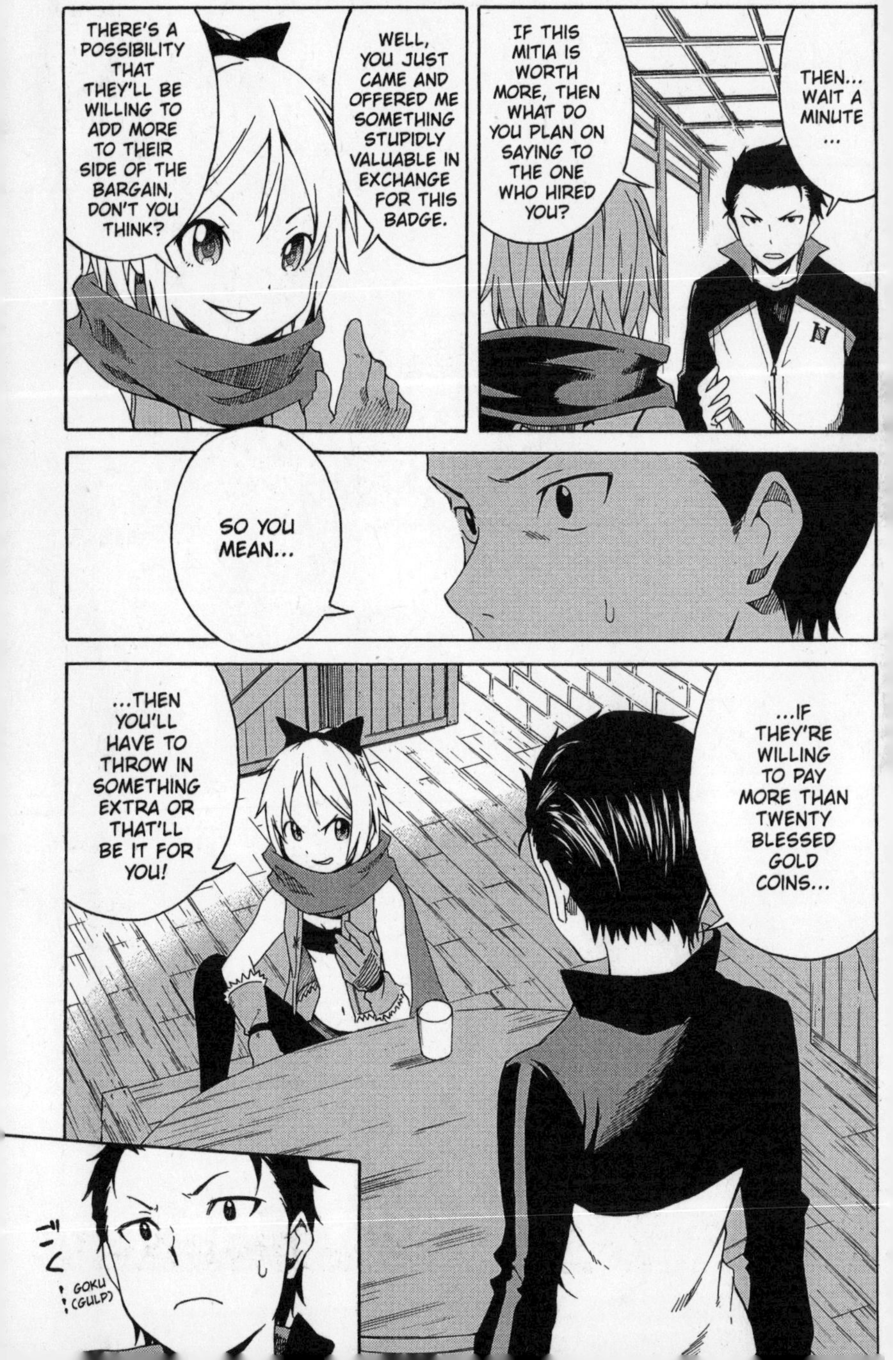
THEN... WAIT A MINUTE...
IF THIS MITIA IS WORTH MORE, THEN WHAT DO YOU PLAN ON SAYING TO THE ONE WHO HIRED YOU?
WELL, YOU JUST CAME AND OFFERED ME SOMETHING STUPIDLY VALUABLE IN EXCHANGE FOR THIS BADGE.
THERE'S A POSSIBILITY THAT THEY'LL BE WILLING TO ADD MORE TO THEIR SIDE OF THE BARGAIN, DON'T YOU THINK?
SO YOU MEAN...
...IF THEY'RE WILLING TO PAY MORE THAN TWENTY BLESSED GOLD COINS...
...THEN YOU'LL HAVE TO THROW IN SOMETHING EXTRA OR THAT'LL BE IT FOR YOU!
GOKU (GULP)

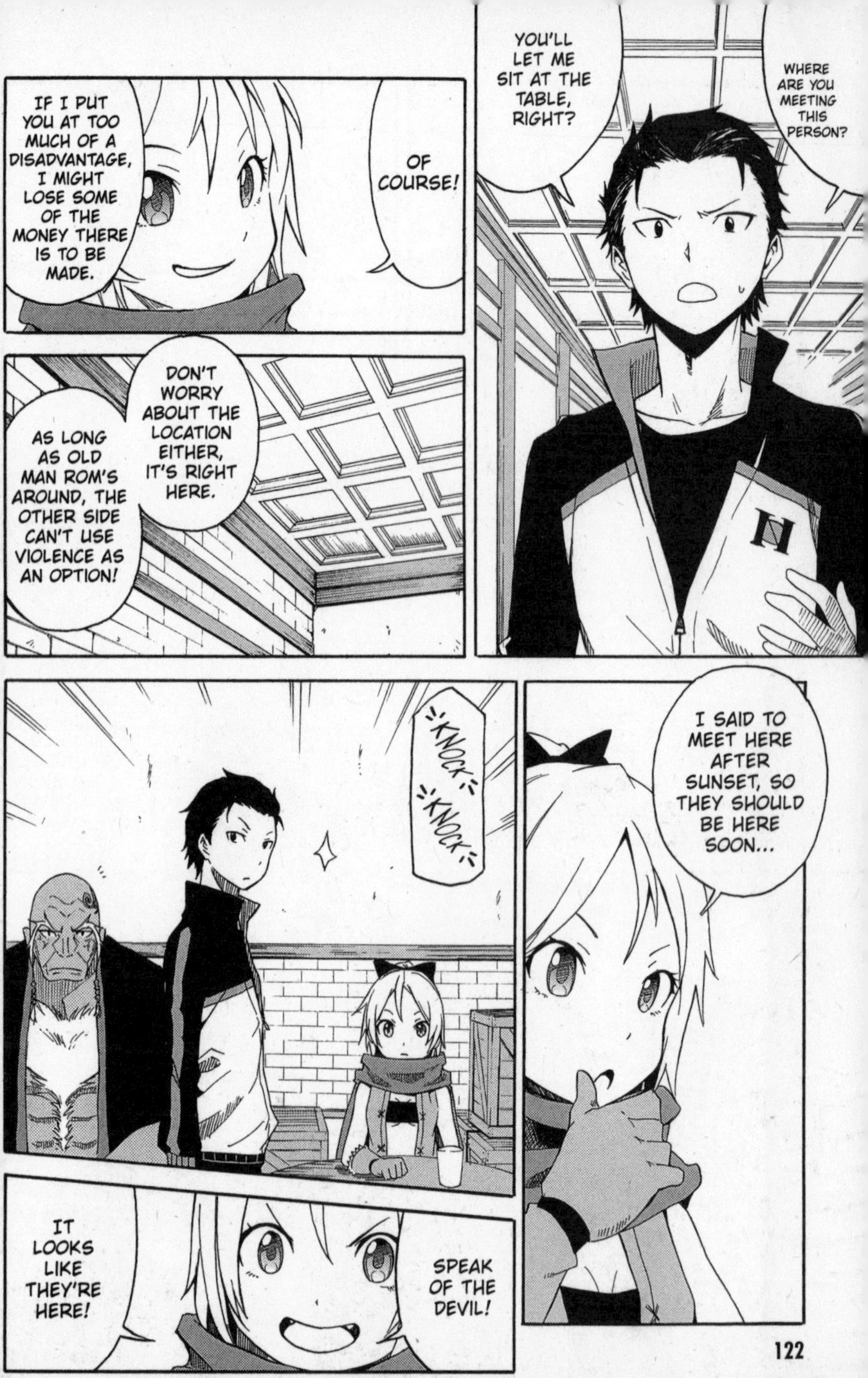
YOU'LL LET ME SIT AT THE TABLE, RIGHT?
WHERE ARE YOU MEETING THIS PERSON?
OF COURSE!
IF I PUT YOU AT TOO MUCH OF A DISADVANTAGE, I MIGHT LOSE SOME OF THE MONEY THERE IS TO BE MADE.
DON'T WORRY ABOUT THE LOCATION EITHER, IT'S RIGHT HERE.
AS LONG AS OLD MAN ROM'S AROUND, THE OTHER SIDE CAN'T USE VIOLENCE AS AN OPTION!
I SAID TO MEET HERE AFTER SUNSET, SO THEY SHOULD BE HERE SOON...
KNOCK KNOCK
SPEAK OF THE DEVIL!
IT LOOKS LIKE THEY'RE HERE!

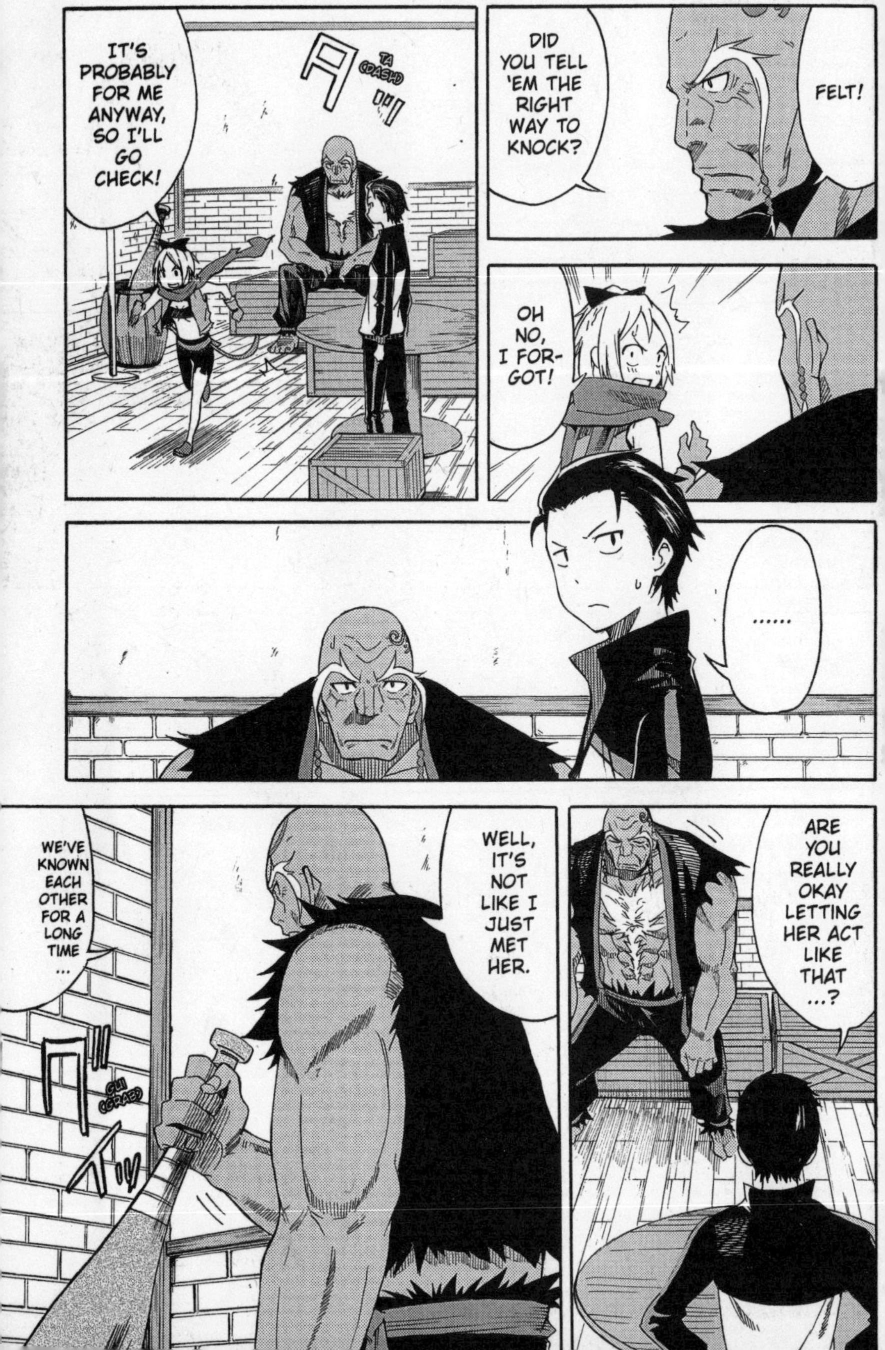
FELT!
DID YOU TELL 'EM THE RIGHT WAY TO KNOCK?
OH NO, I FOR-GOT!
TA (DASH)
IT'S PROBABLY FOR ME ANYWAY, SO I'LL GO CHECK!
......
ARE YOU REALLY OKAY LETTING HER ACT LIKE THAT ...?
WELL, IT'S NOT LIKE I JUST MET HER.
WE'VE KNOWN EACH OTHER FOR A LONG TIME ...
GUI (GRAB)

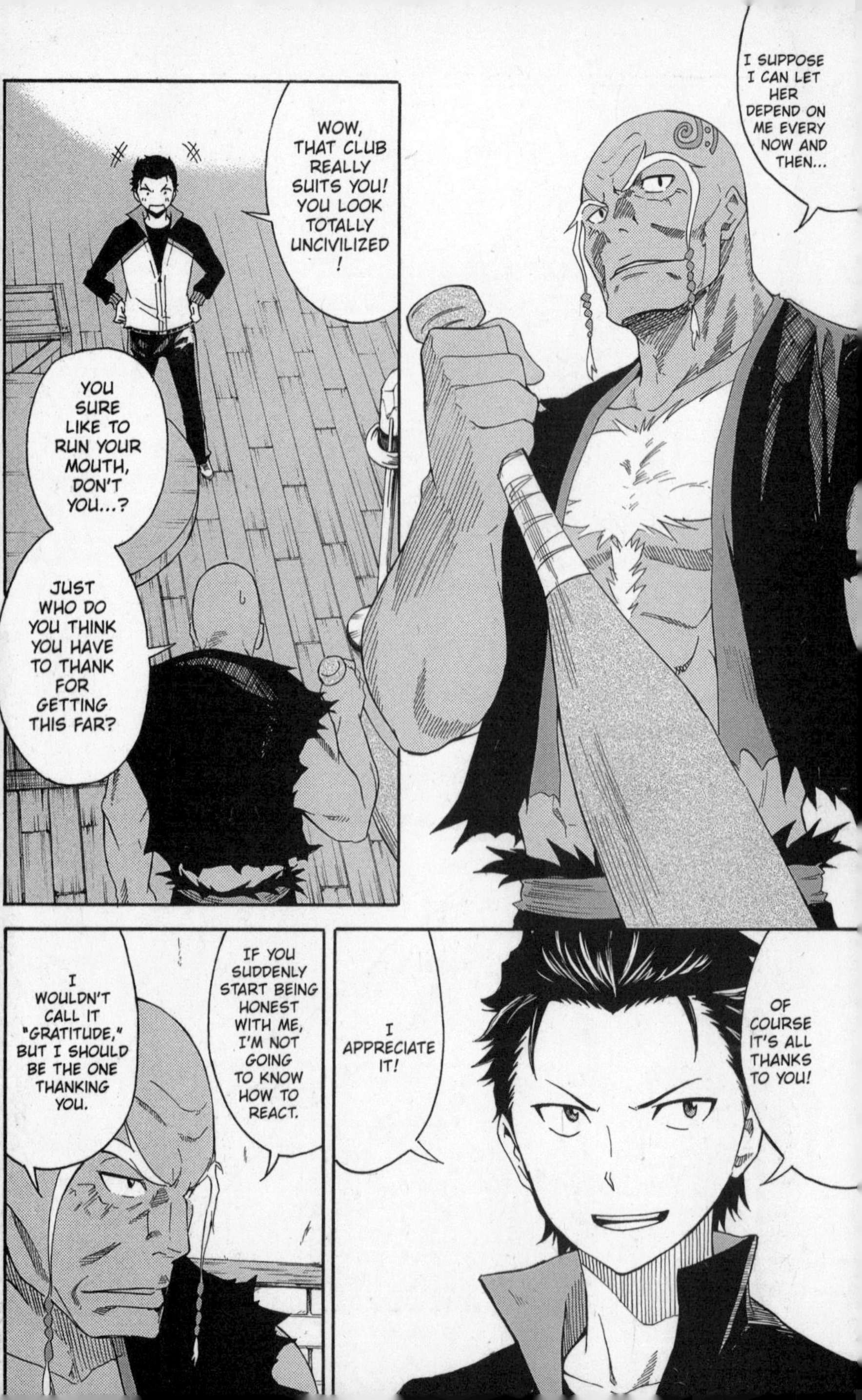
I SUPPOSE I CAN LET HER DEPEND ON ME EVERY NOW AND THEN...
WOW, THAT CLUB REALLY SUITS YOU! YOU LOOK TOTALLY UNCIVILIZED!
YOU SURE LIKE TO RUN YOUR MOUTH, DON'T YOU...?
JUST WHO DO YOU THINK YOU HAVE TO THANK FOR GETTING THIS FAR?
OF COURSE IT'S ALL THANKS TO YOU!
I APPRECIATE IT!
IF YOU SUDDENLY START BEING HONEST WITH ME, I'M NOT GOING TO KNOW HOW TO REACT.
I WOULDN'T CALL IT "GRATITUDE," BUT I SHOULD BE THE ONE THANKING YOU.

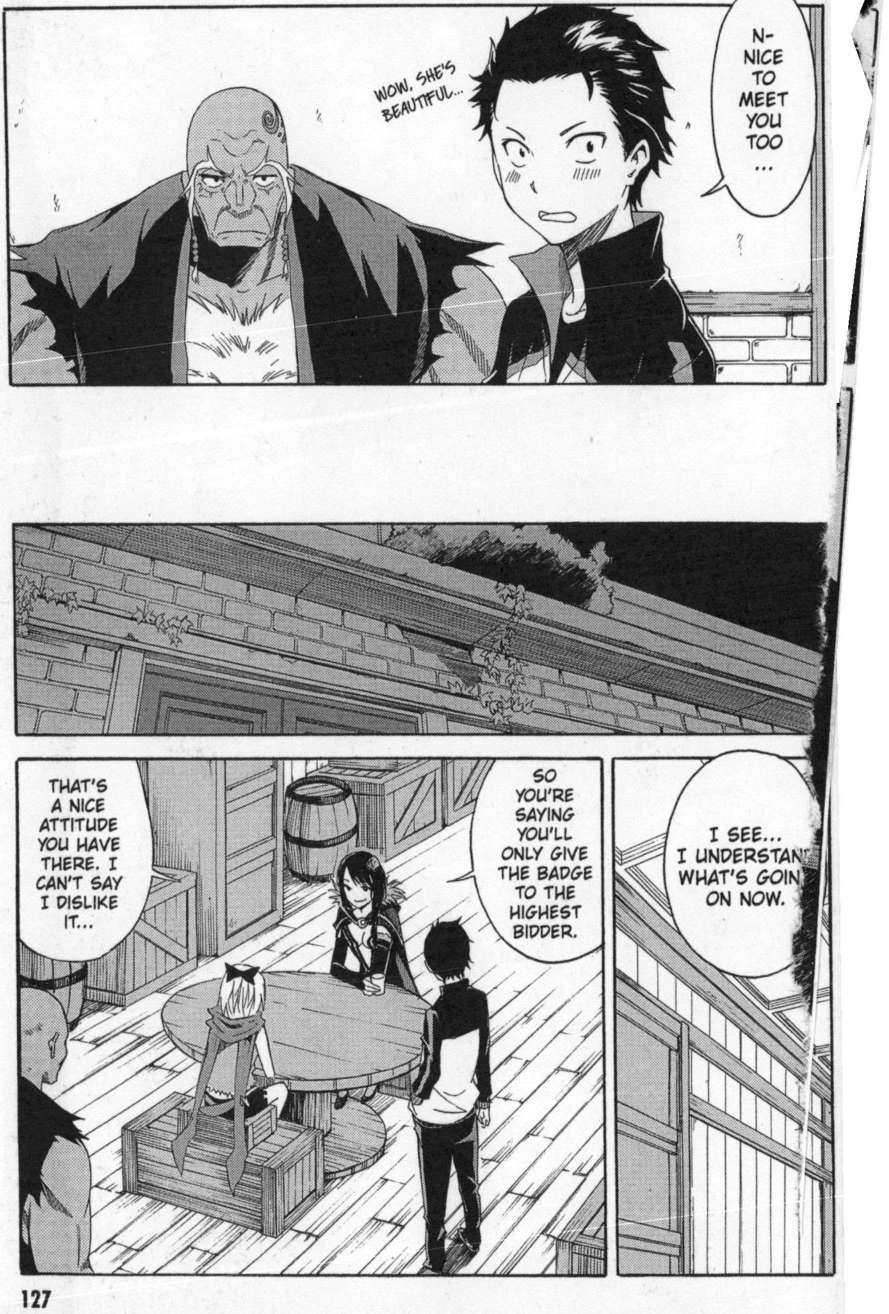
N-NICE TO MEET YOU TOO...
WOW, SHE'S BEAUTIFUL...
I SEE... I UNDERSTAN WHAT'S GOIN ON NOW.
SO YOU'RE SAYING YOU'LL ONLY GIVE THE BADGE TO THE HIGHEST BIDDER.
THAT'S A NICE ATTITUDE YOU HAVE THERE. I CAN'T SAY I DISLIKE IT...

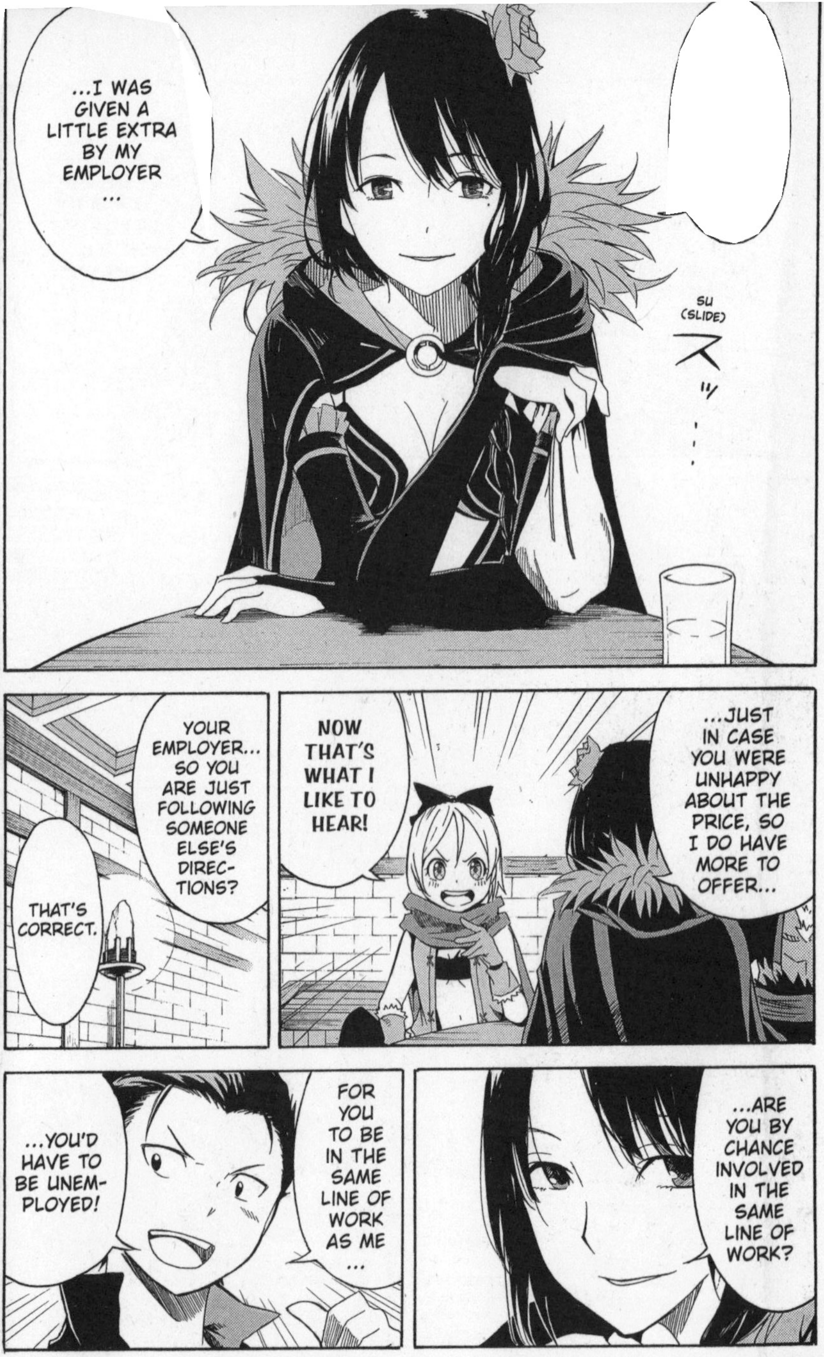
...I WAS GIVEN A LITTLE EXTRA BY MY EMPLOYER ...
SU (SLIDE)
スッ...
...JUST IN CASE YOU WERE UNHAPPY ABOUT THE PRICE, SO I DO HAVE MORE TO OFFER...
NOW THAT'S WHAT I LIKE TO HEAR!
YOUR EMPLOYER... SO YOU ARE JUST FOLLOWING SOMEONE ELSE'S DIREC-TIONS?
THAT'S CORRECT.
...ARE YOU BY CHANCE INVOLVED IN THE SAME LINE OF WORK?
FOR YOU TO BE IN THE SAME LINE OF WORK AS ME ...
...YOU'D HAVE TO BE UNEM-PLOYED!

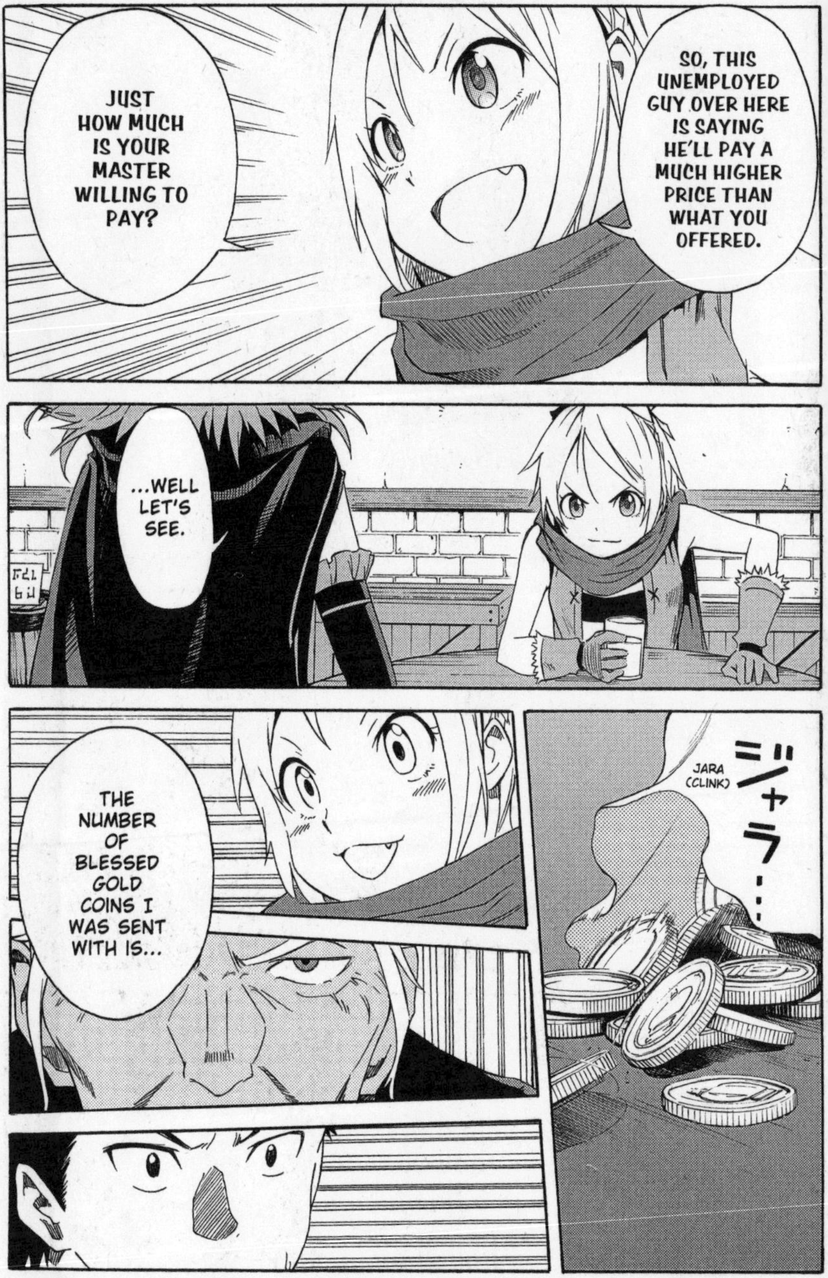
SO, THIS UNEMPLOYED GUY OVER HERE IS SAYING HE'LL PAY A MUCH HIGHER PRICE THAN WHAT YOU OFFERED.
JUST HOW MUCH IS YOUR MASTER WILLING TO PAY?
...WELL LET'S SEE.
ジャラ…
JARA (CLINK)
THE NUMBER OF BLESSED GOLD COINS I WAS SENT WITH IS...

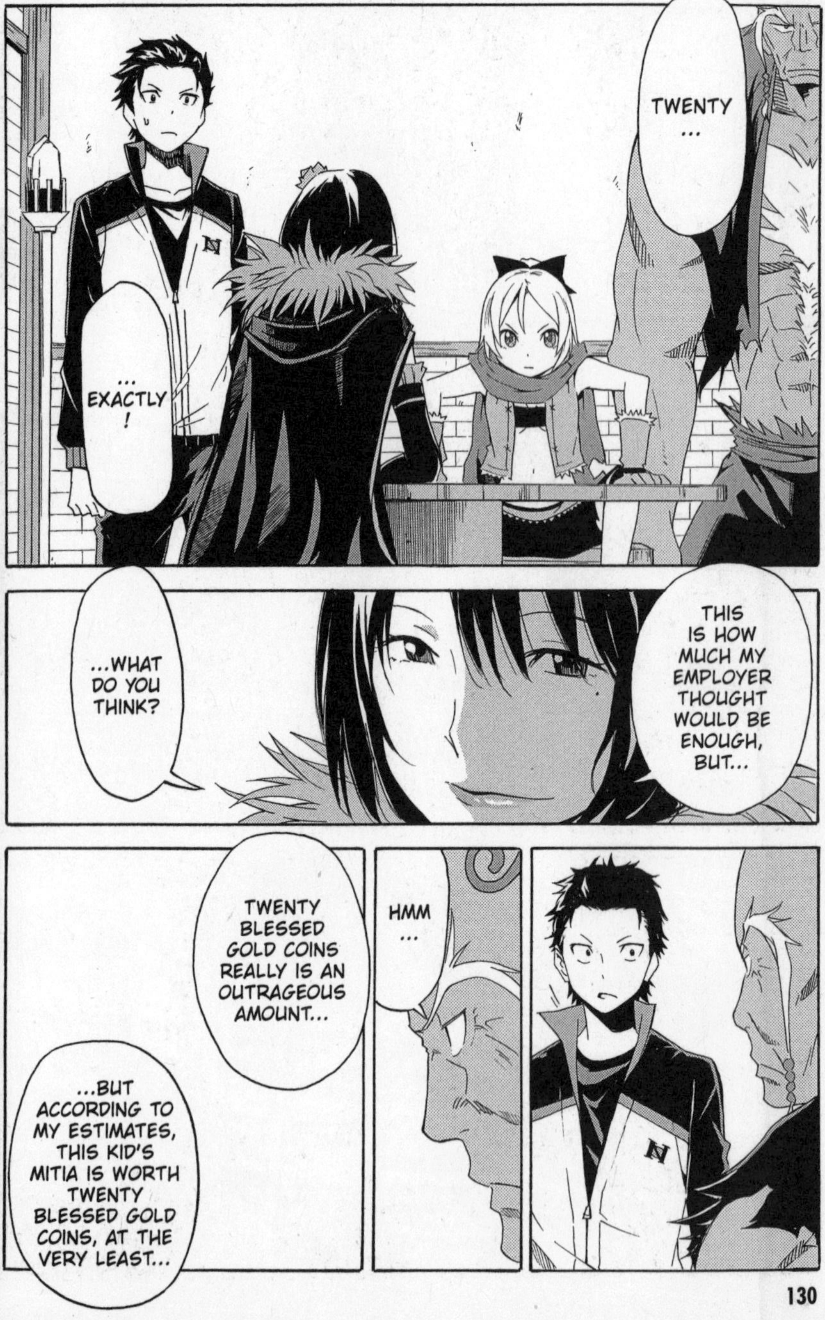
TWENTY ...
... EXACTLY !
THIS IS HOW MUCH MY EMPLOYER THOUGHT WOULD BE ENOUGH, BUT...
...WHAT DO YOU THINK?
HMM ...
TWENTY BLESSED GOLD COINS REALLY IS AN OUTRAGEOUS AMOUNT...
...BUT ACCORDING TO MY ESTIMATES, THIS KID'S MITIA IS WORTH TWENTY BLESSED GOLD COINS, AT THE VERY LEAST...

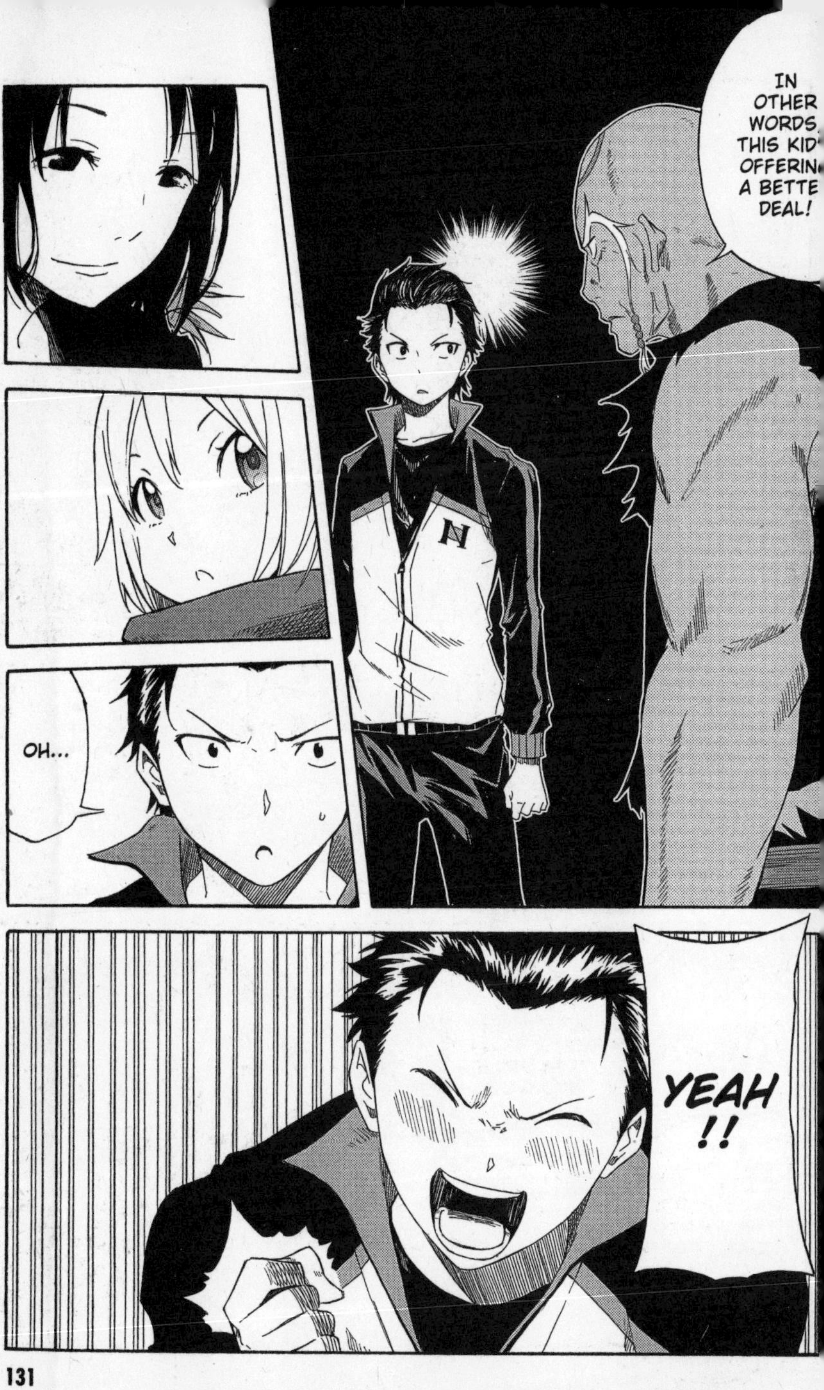
IN OTHER WORDS, THIS KID OFFERIN A BETTE DEAL!
OH...
YEAH!!

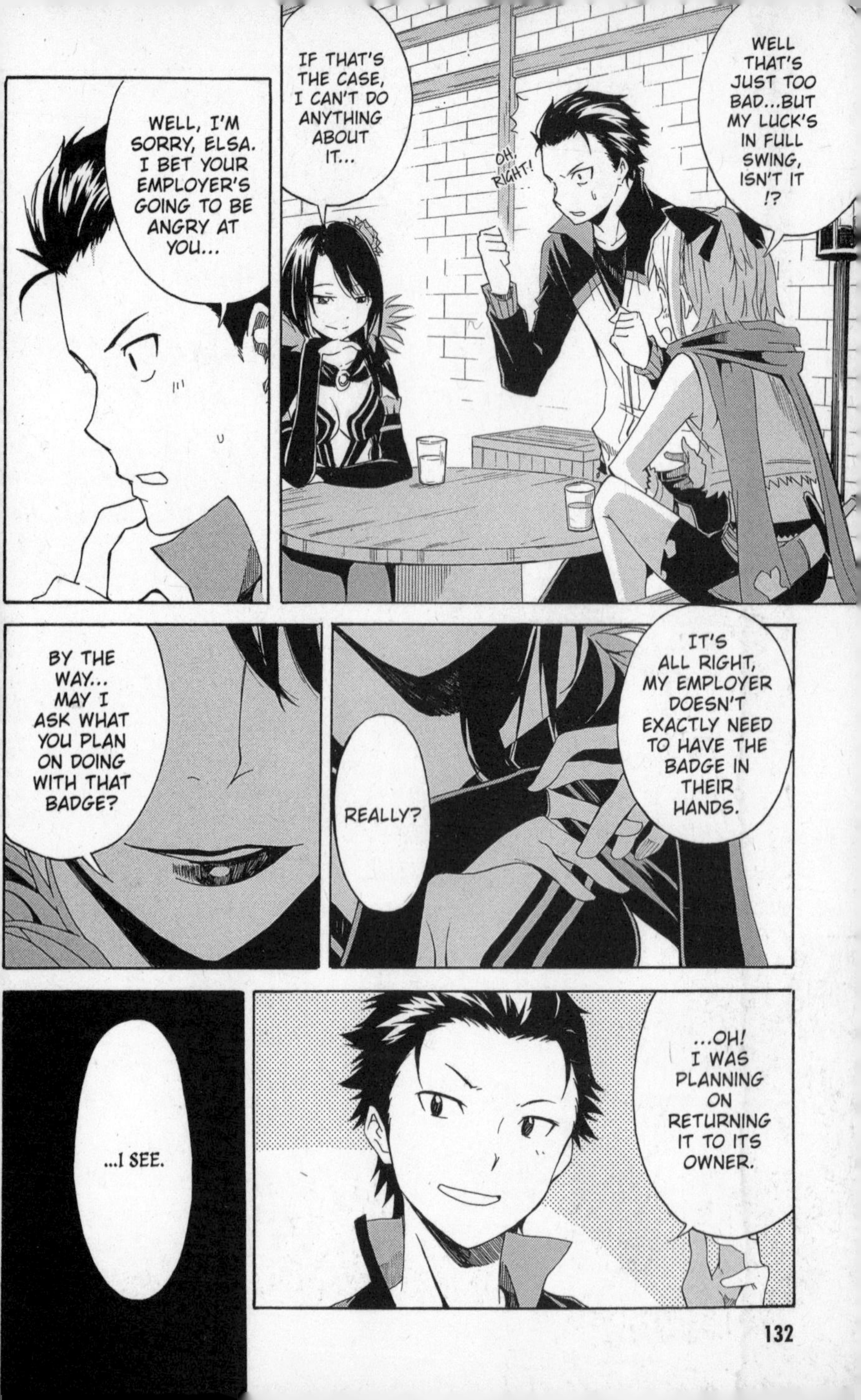
WELL THAT'S JUST TOO BAD...BUT MY LUCK'S IN FULL SWING, ISN'T IT !?
OH, RIGHT!
IF THAT'S THE CASE, I CAN'T DO ANYTHING ABOUT IT...
WELL, I'M SORRY, ELSA. I BET YOUR EMPLOYER'S GOING TO BE ANGRY AT YOU...
IT'S ALL RIGHT, MY EMPLOYER DOESN'T EXACTLY NEED TO HAVE THE BADGE IN THEIR HANDS.
REALLY?
BY THE WAY... MAY I ASK WHAT YOU PLAN ON DOING WITH THAT BADGE?
...OH! I WAS PLANNING ON RETURNING IT TO ITS OWNER.
...I SEE.

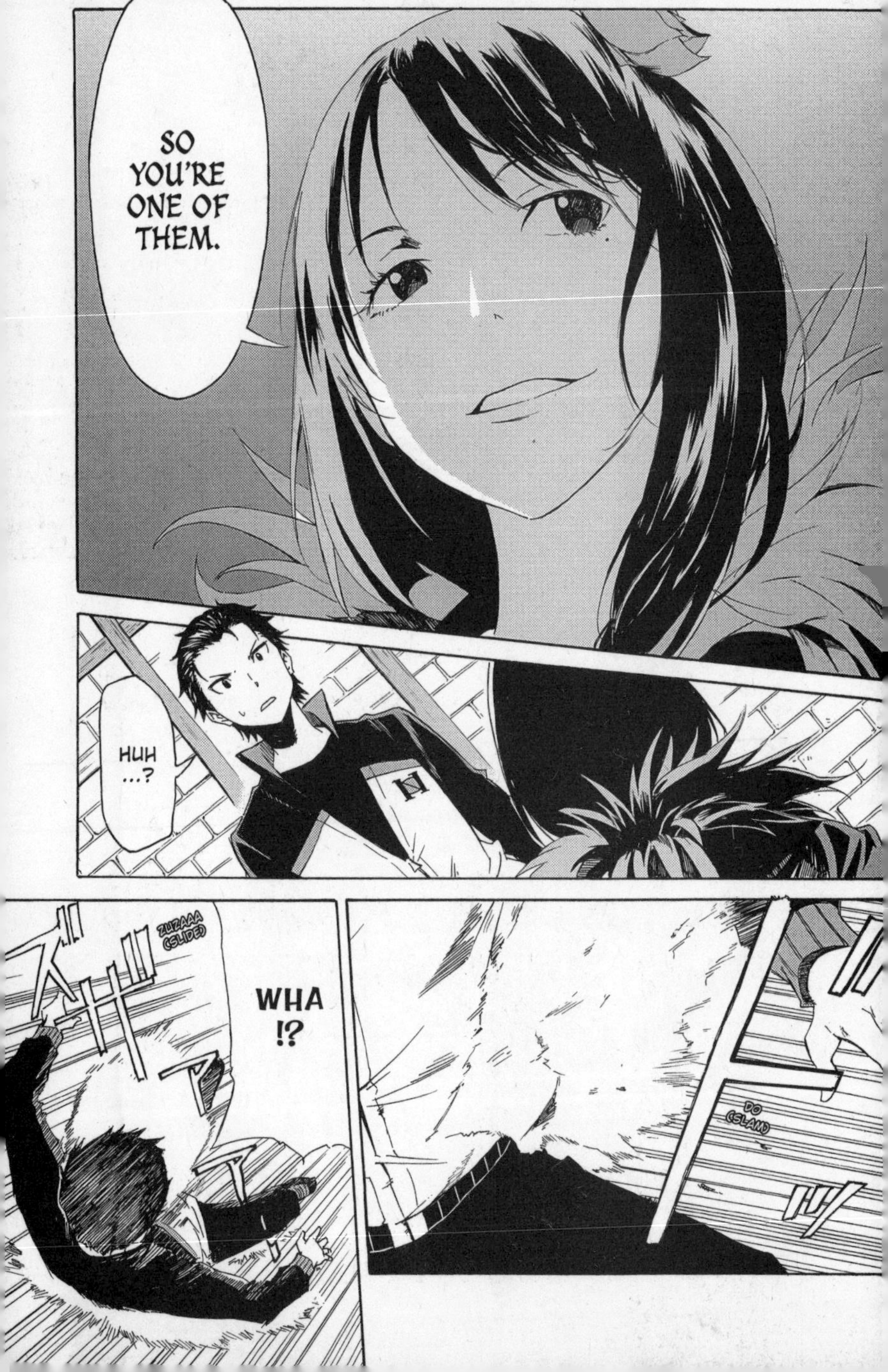
SO YOU'RE ONE OF THEM.
HUH ...?
DO (SLAM)
ZUZAAA (SLIDE)
WHA !?

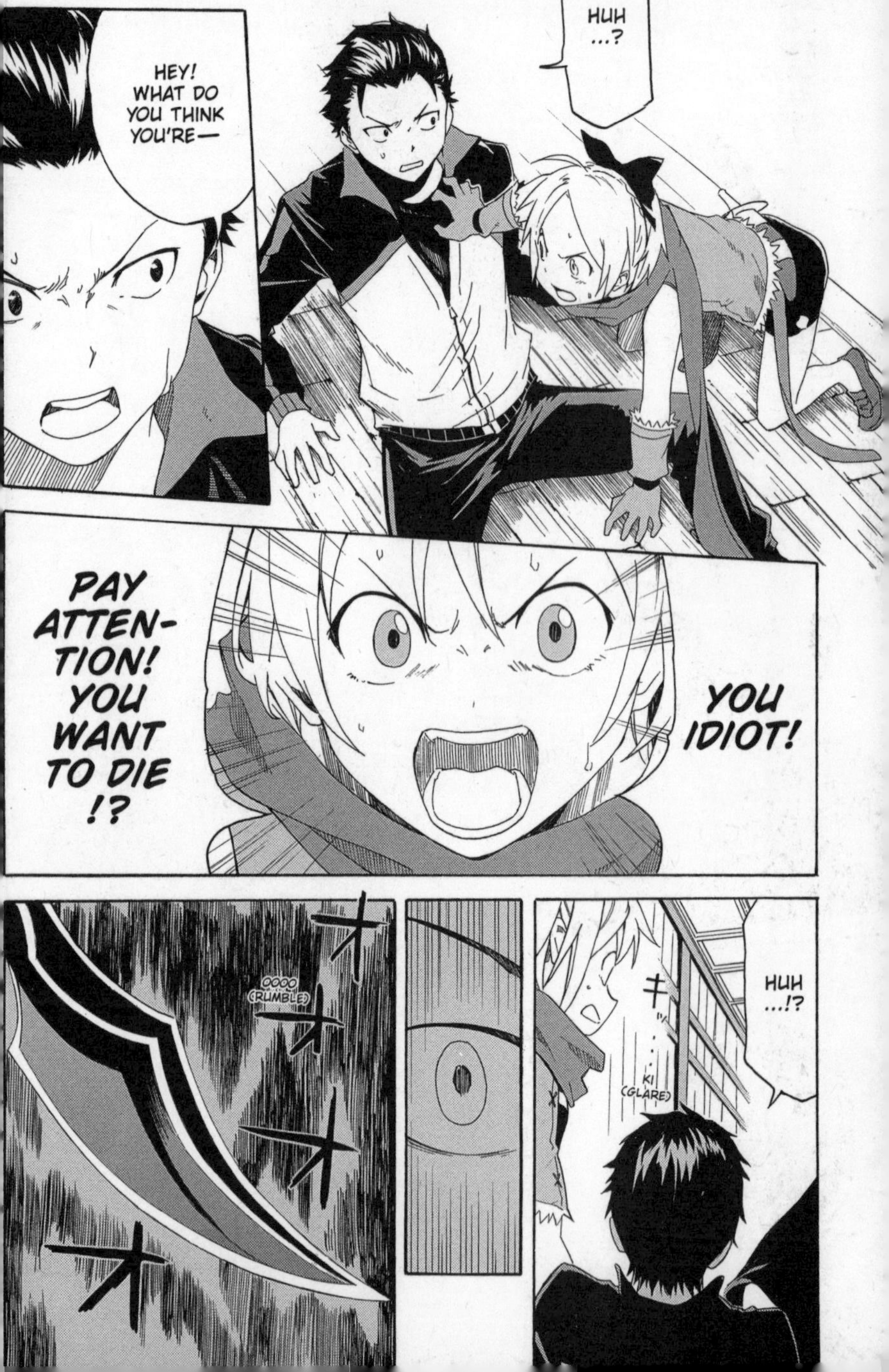
HUH ...?
HEY! WHAT DO YOU THINK YOU'RE—
YOU IDIOT!
PAY ATTEN-TION! YOU WANT TO DIE !?
HUH ...!?
KI (GLARE)
OOOO (RUMBLE)

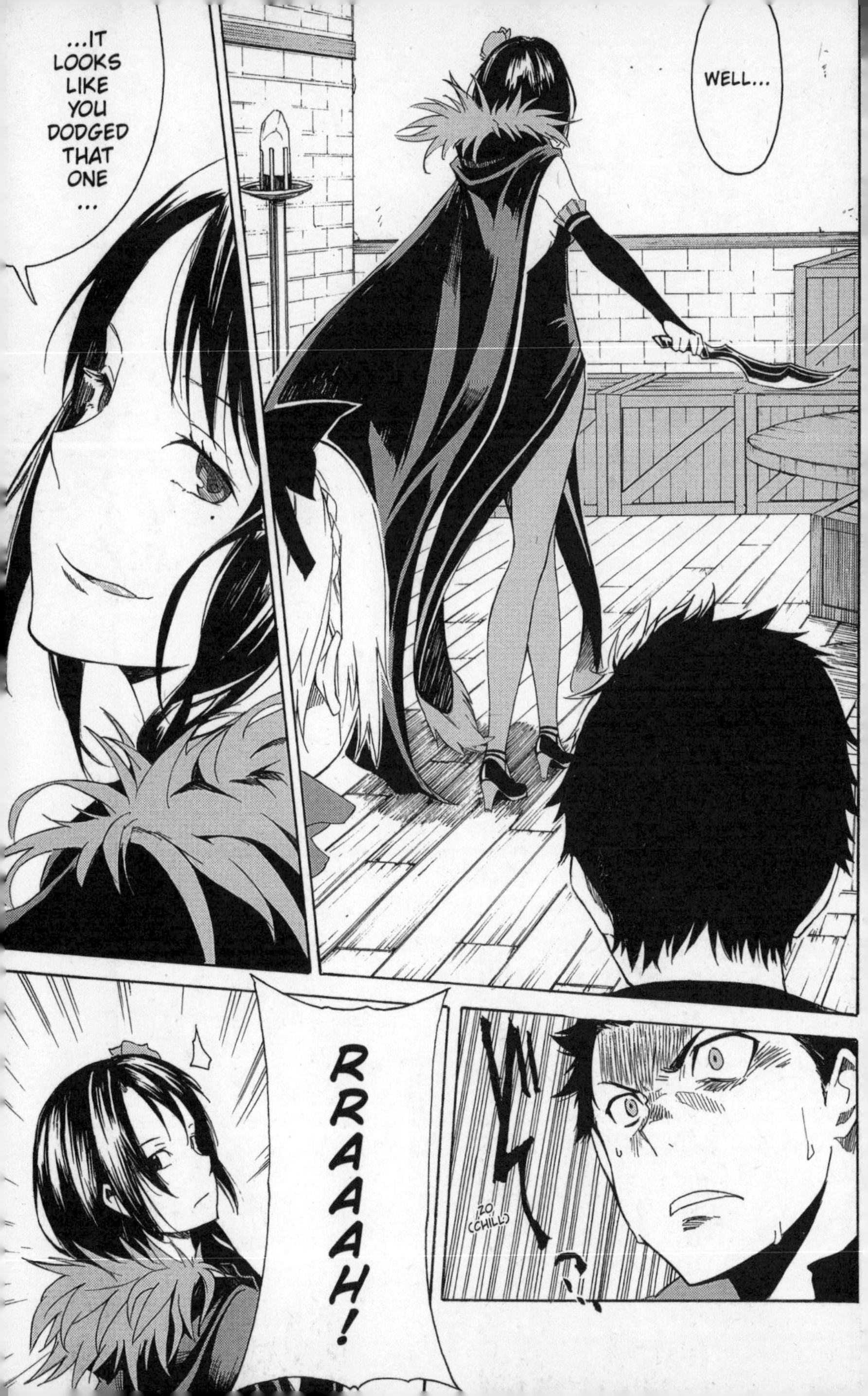
WELL...
...IT LOOKS LIKE YOU DODGED THAT ONE...
ZO (CHILL)
RRAAAAH!

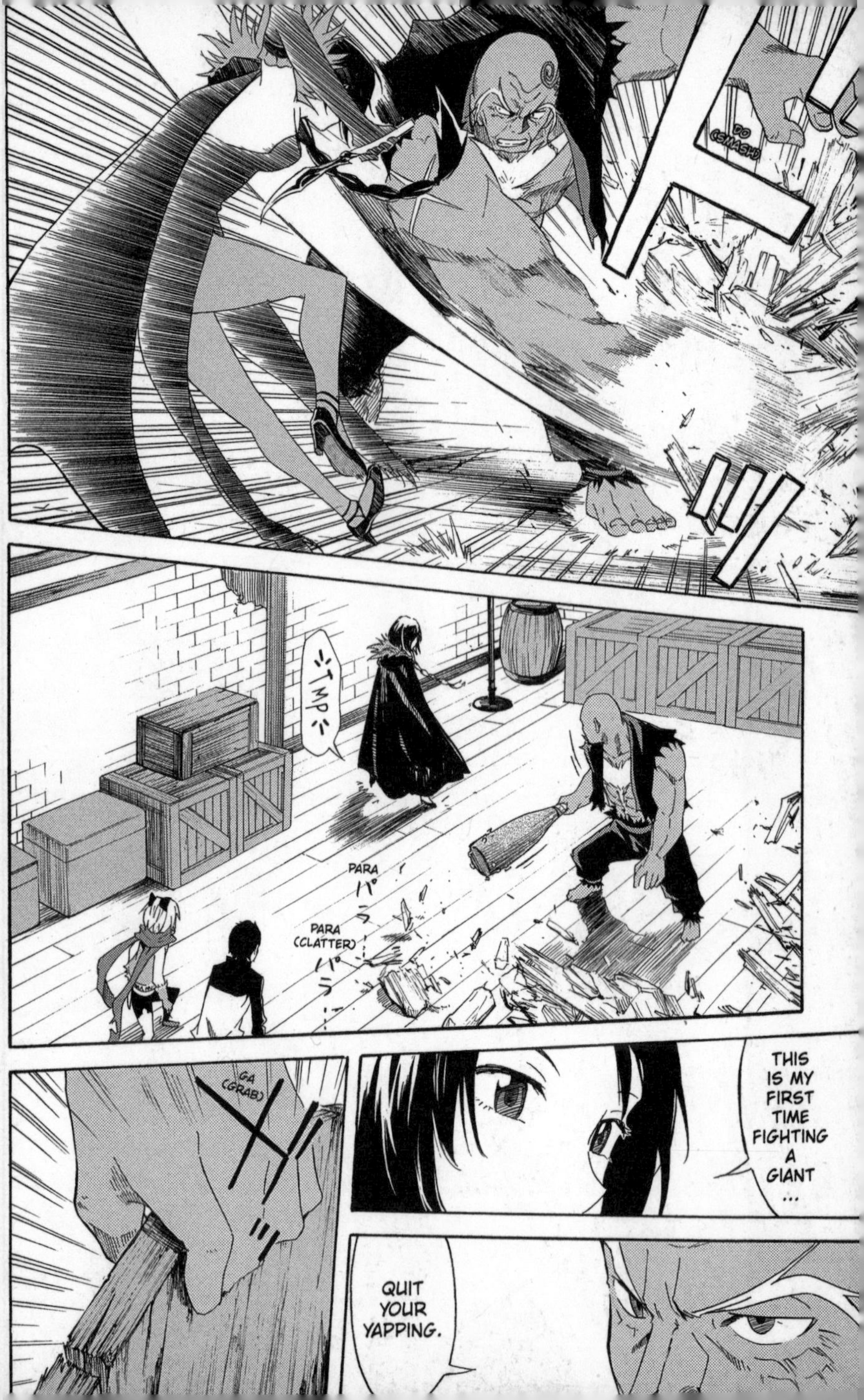
DO (SMASH)
TMP
PARA
パラ
PARA (CLATTER)
パラ…
THIS IS MY FIRST TIME FIGHTING A GIANT...
QUIT YOUR YAPPING.
GA (GRAB)

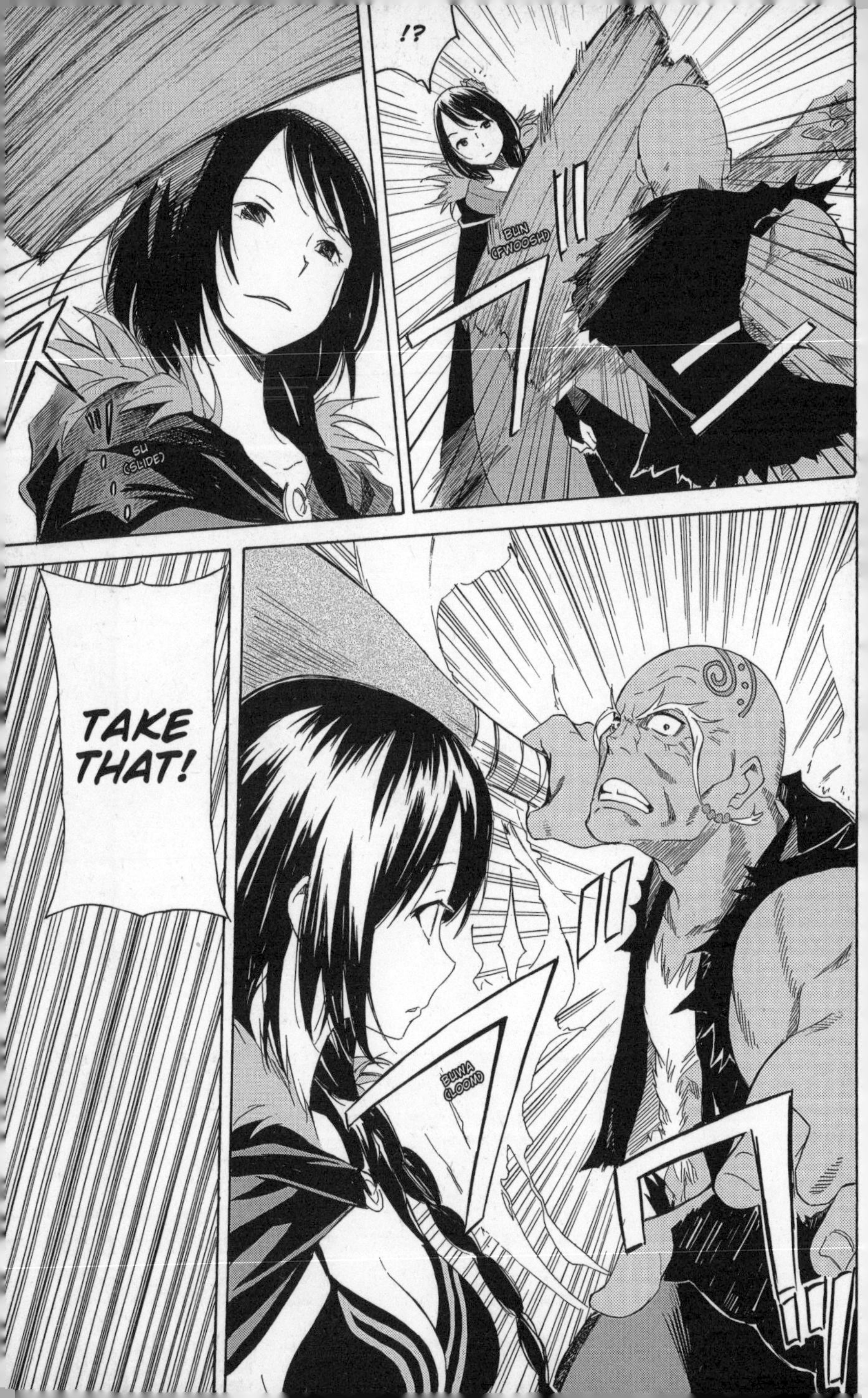
!?
BUN (FWOOSH)
SU (SLIDE)
BUWA (LOOM)
TAKE THAT!

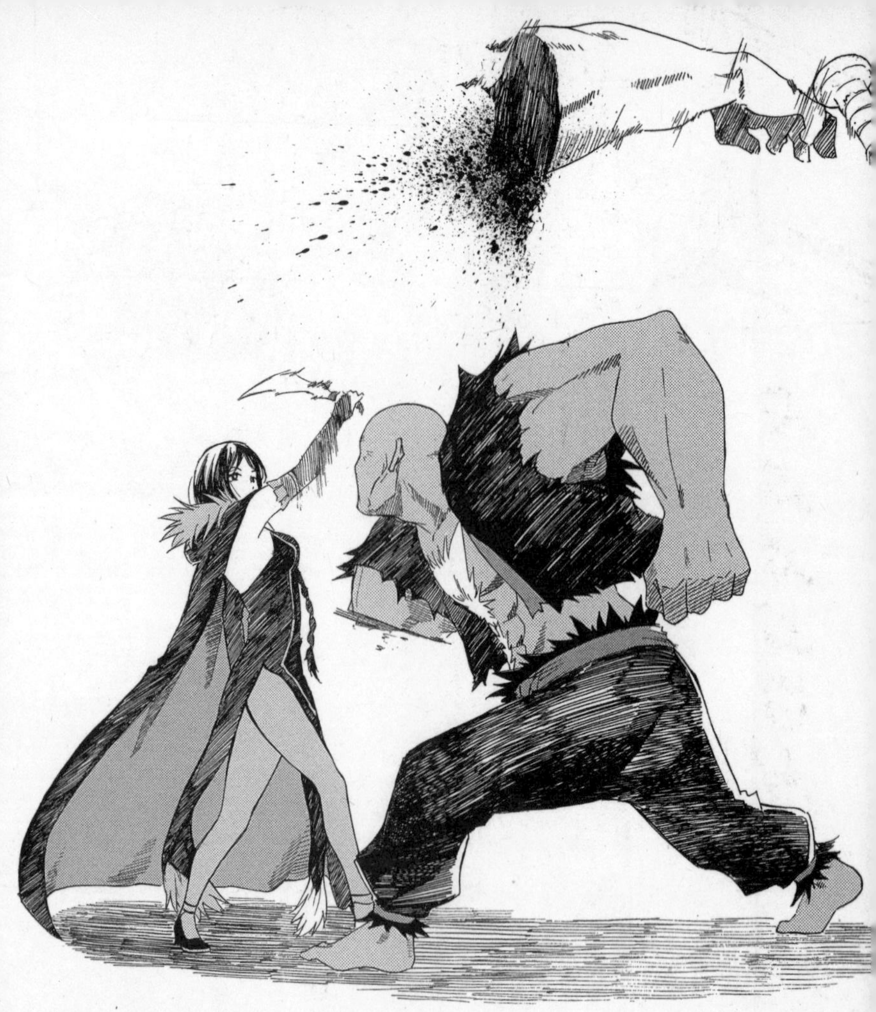

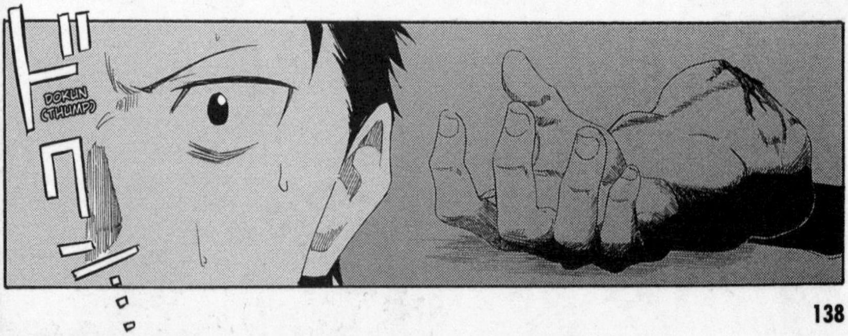
ドクン
DOKUN (THUMP)

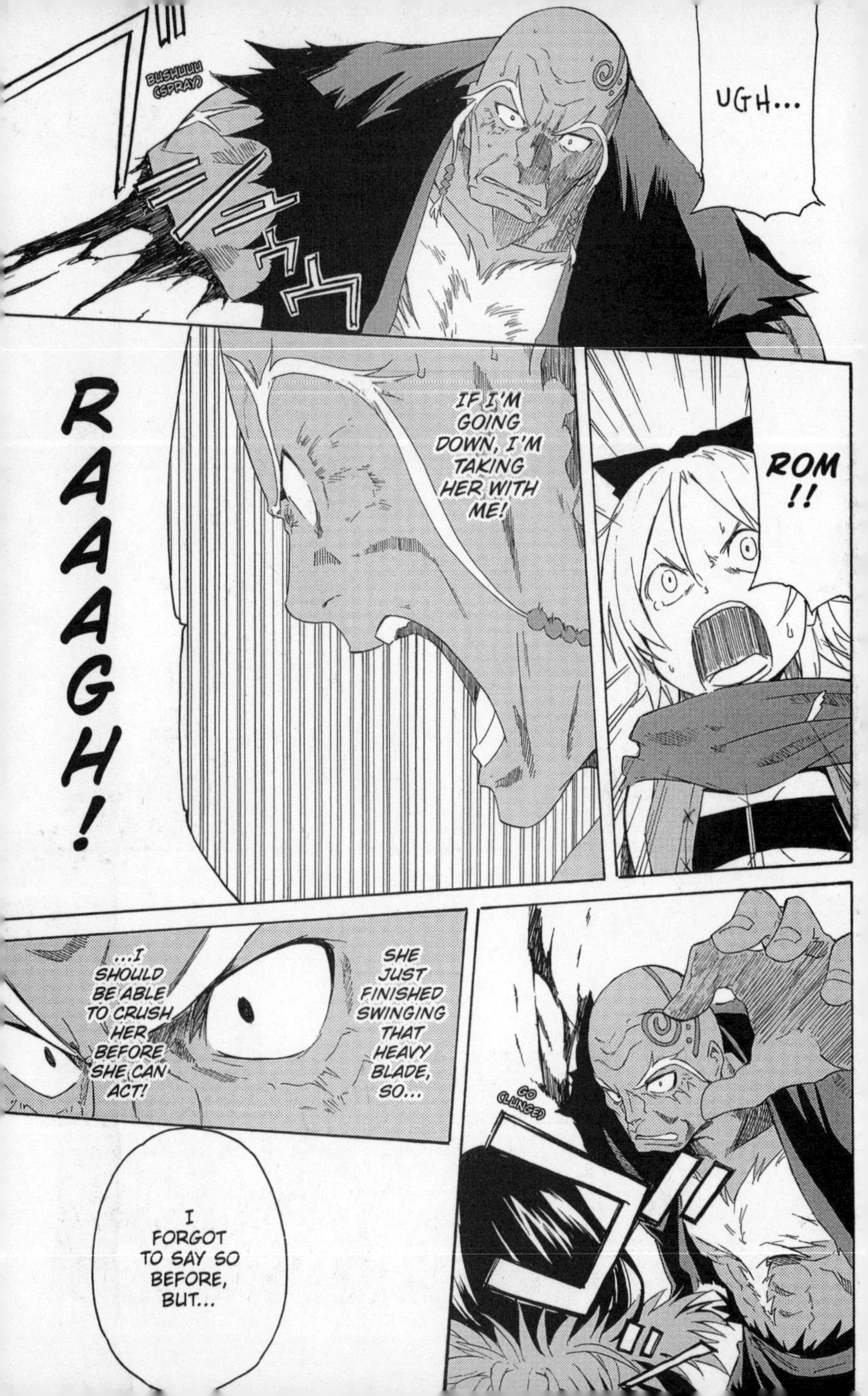
UGH...
BUSHUUU (SPRAY)
ROM !!
IF I'M GOING DOWN, I'M TAKING HER WITH ME!
RAAAGH!
GO (LUNGE)
SHE JUST FINISHED SWINGING THAT HEAVY BLADE, SO...
...I SHOULD BE ABLE TO CRUSH HER BEFORE SHE CAN ACT!
I FORGOT TO SAY SO BEFORE, BUT...

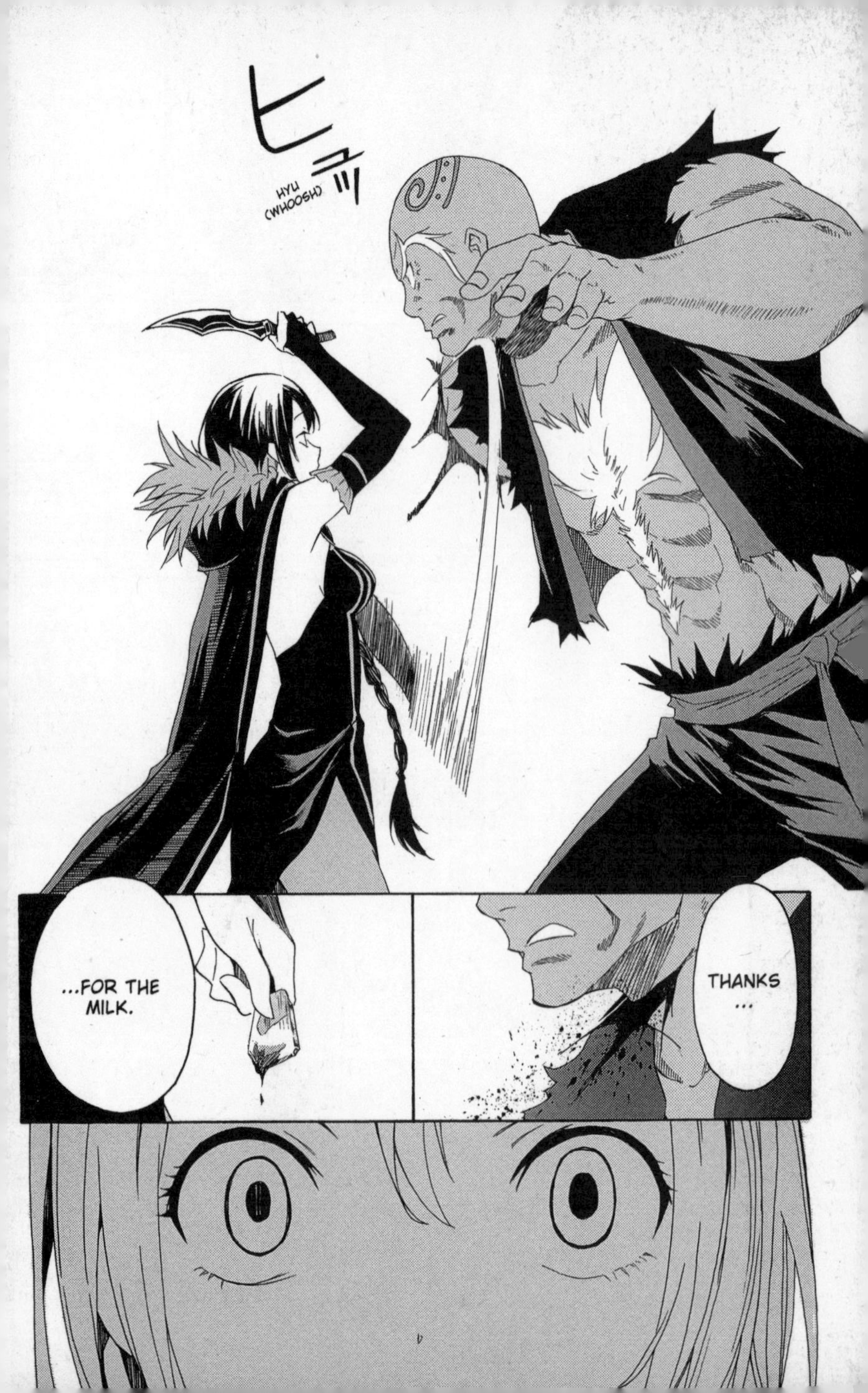
ヒュッ
HYU (WHOOSH)
THANKS ...
...FOR THE MILK.

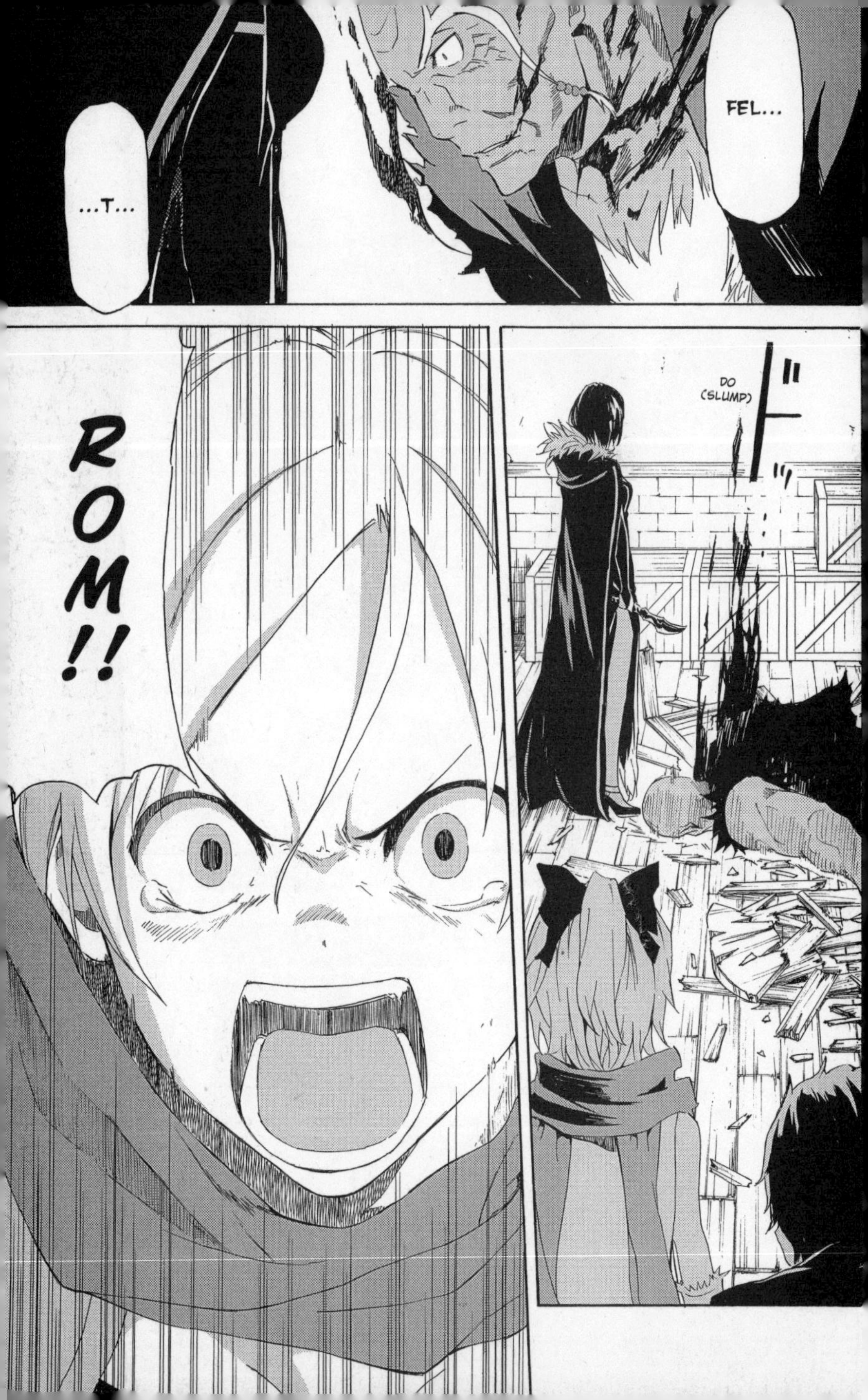
FEL...
...T...
DO (SLUMP)
ROM!!

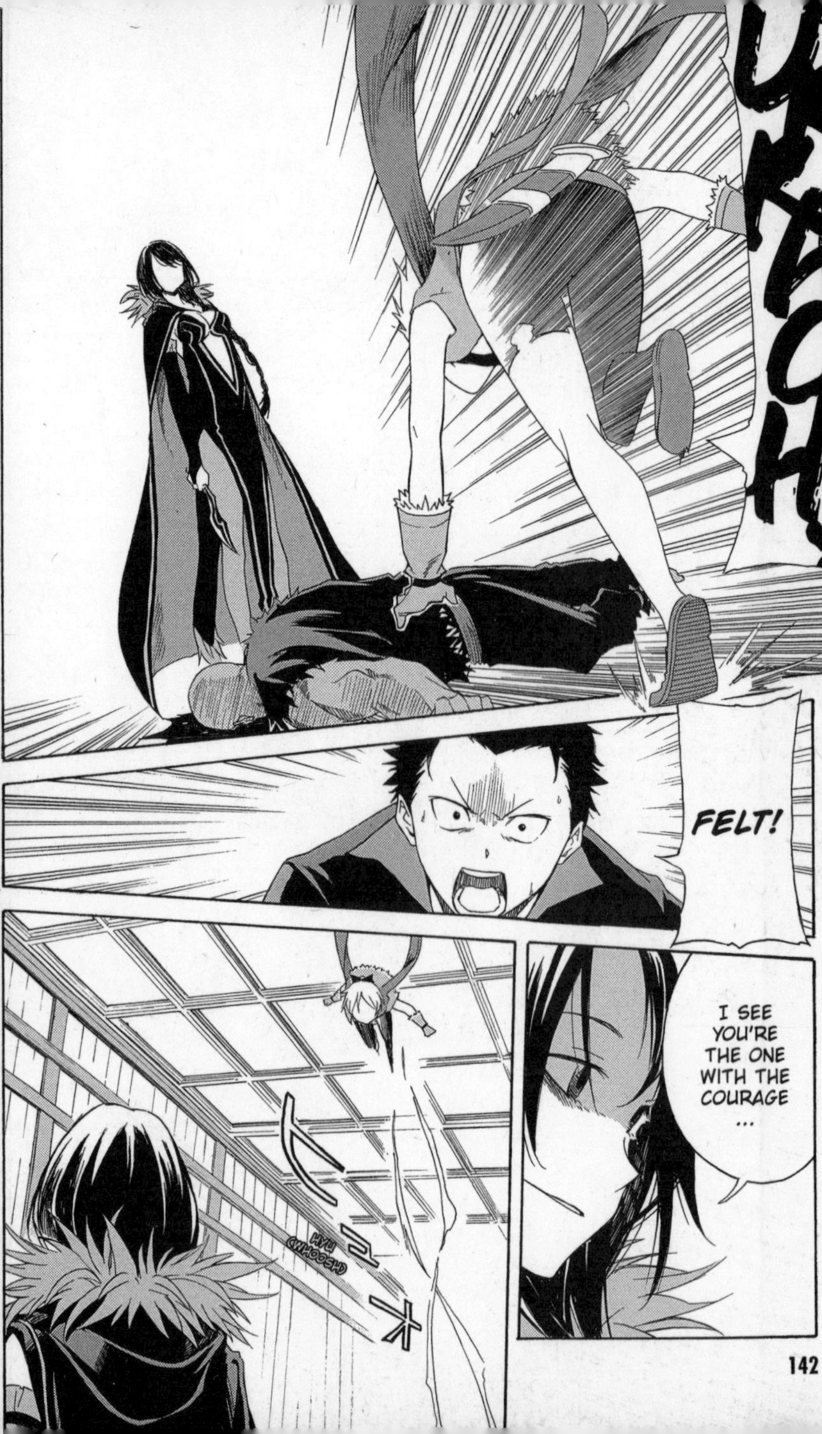
UKAGH!!
FELT!
I SEE YOU'RE THE ONE WITH THE COURAGE ...
HYU (WHOOSH)

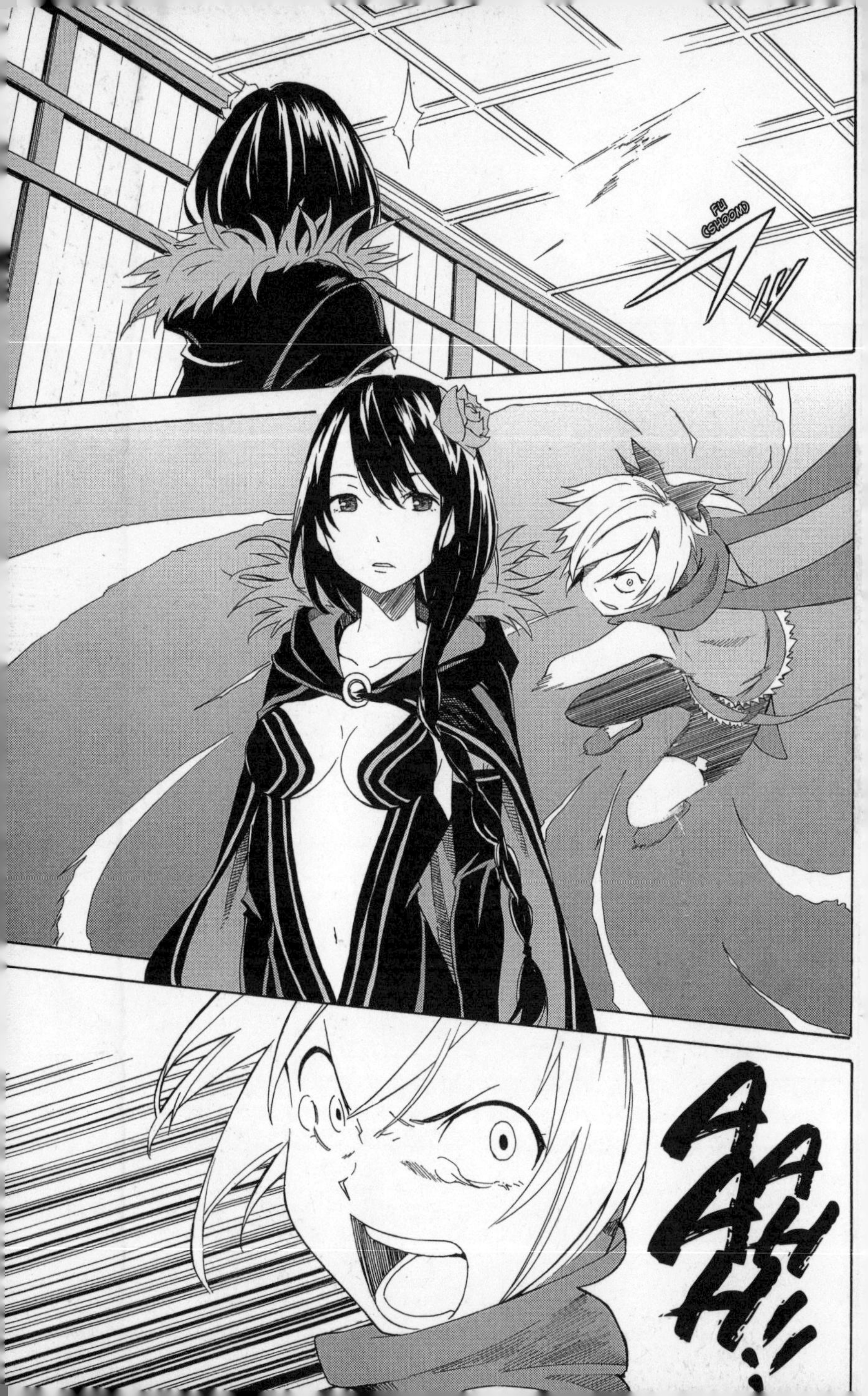
FU
(SHOOM)
AAAAH!!

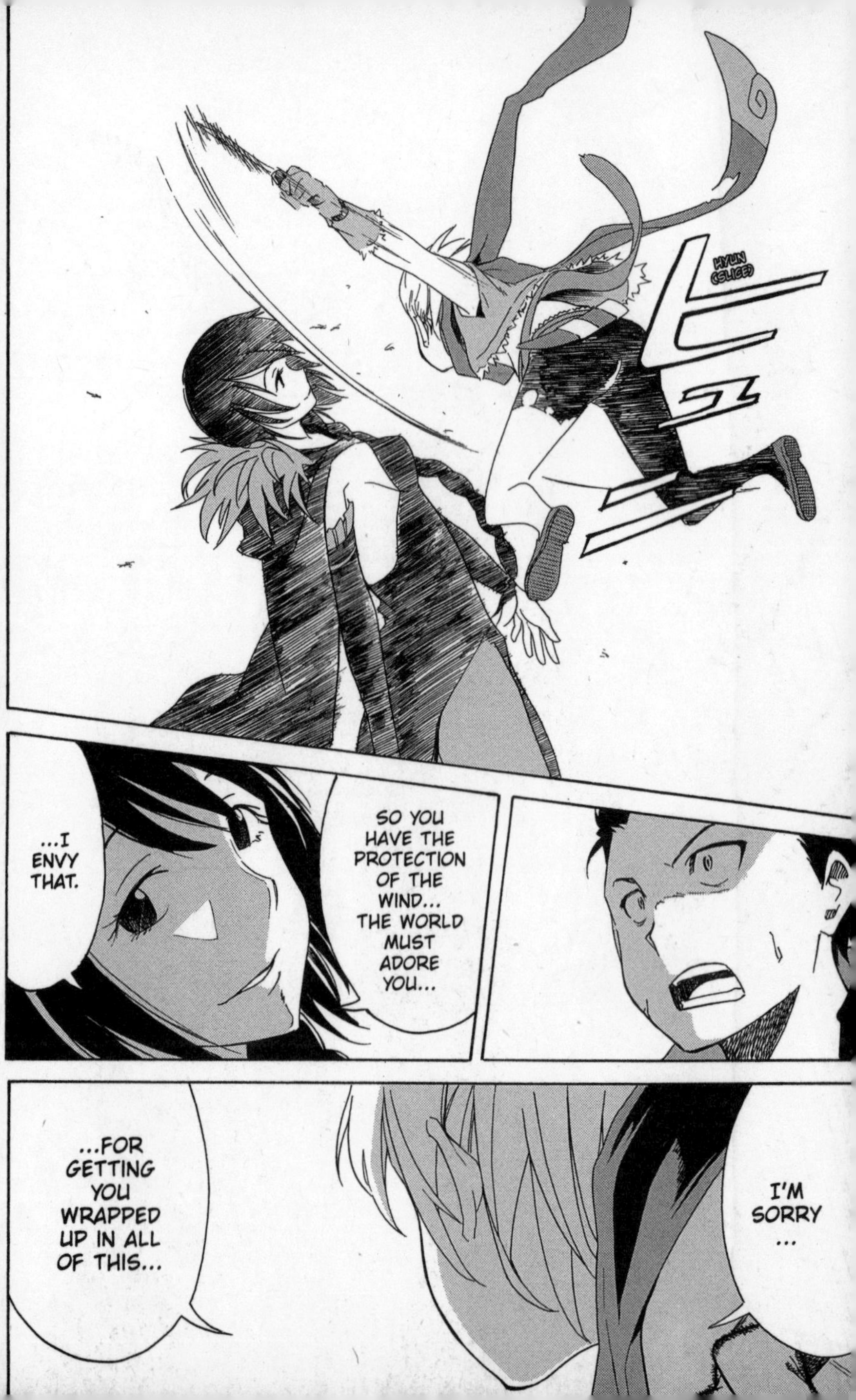
HYUN (SLICE)
SO YOU HAVE THE PROTECTION OF THE WIND... THE WORLD MUST ADORE YOU...
...I ENVY THAT.
I'M SORRY...
...FOR GETTING YOU WRAPPED UP IN ALL OF THIS...

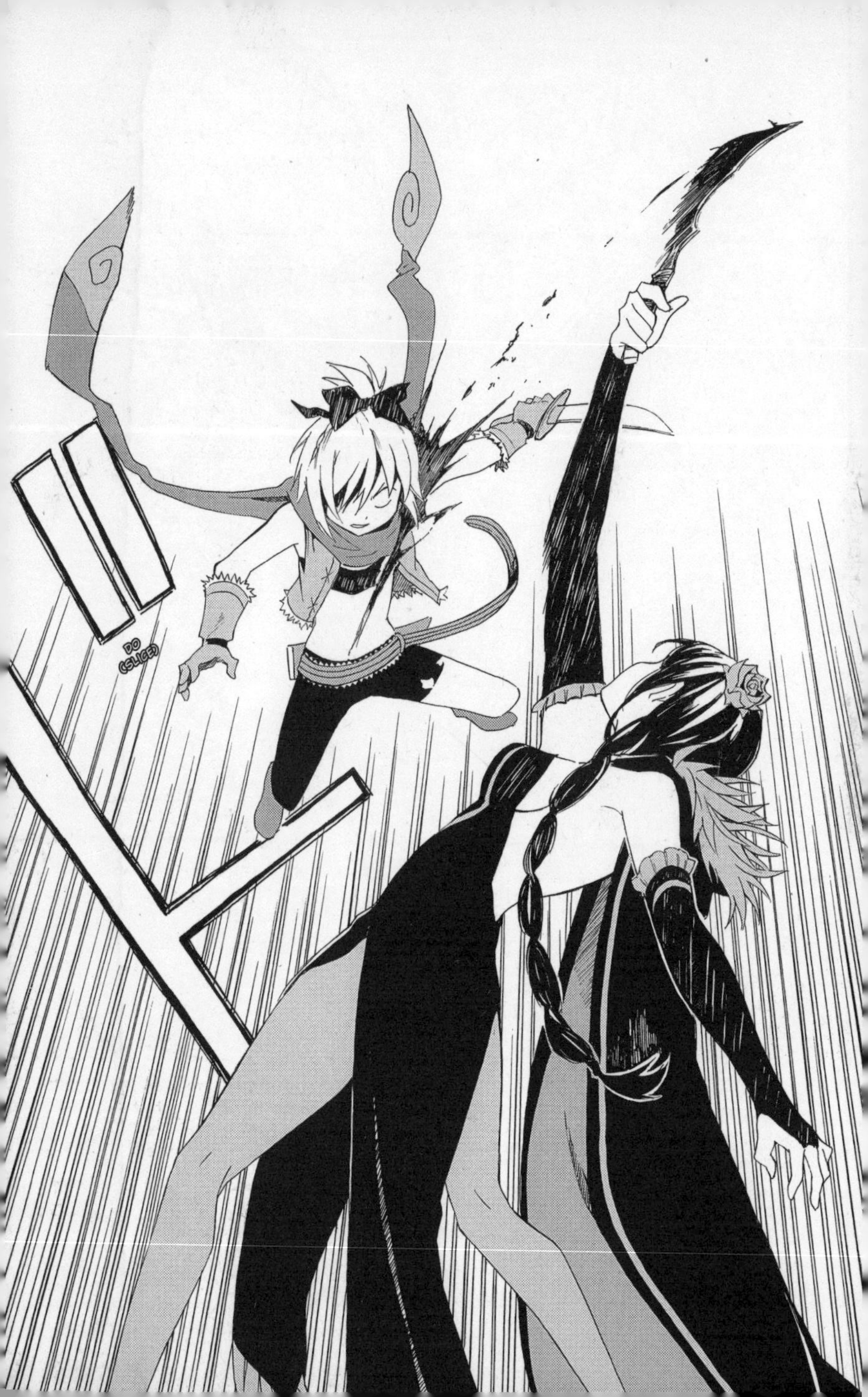
DO
(SLICE)

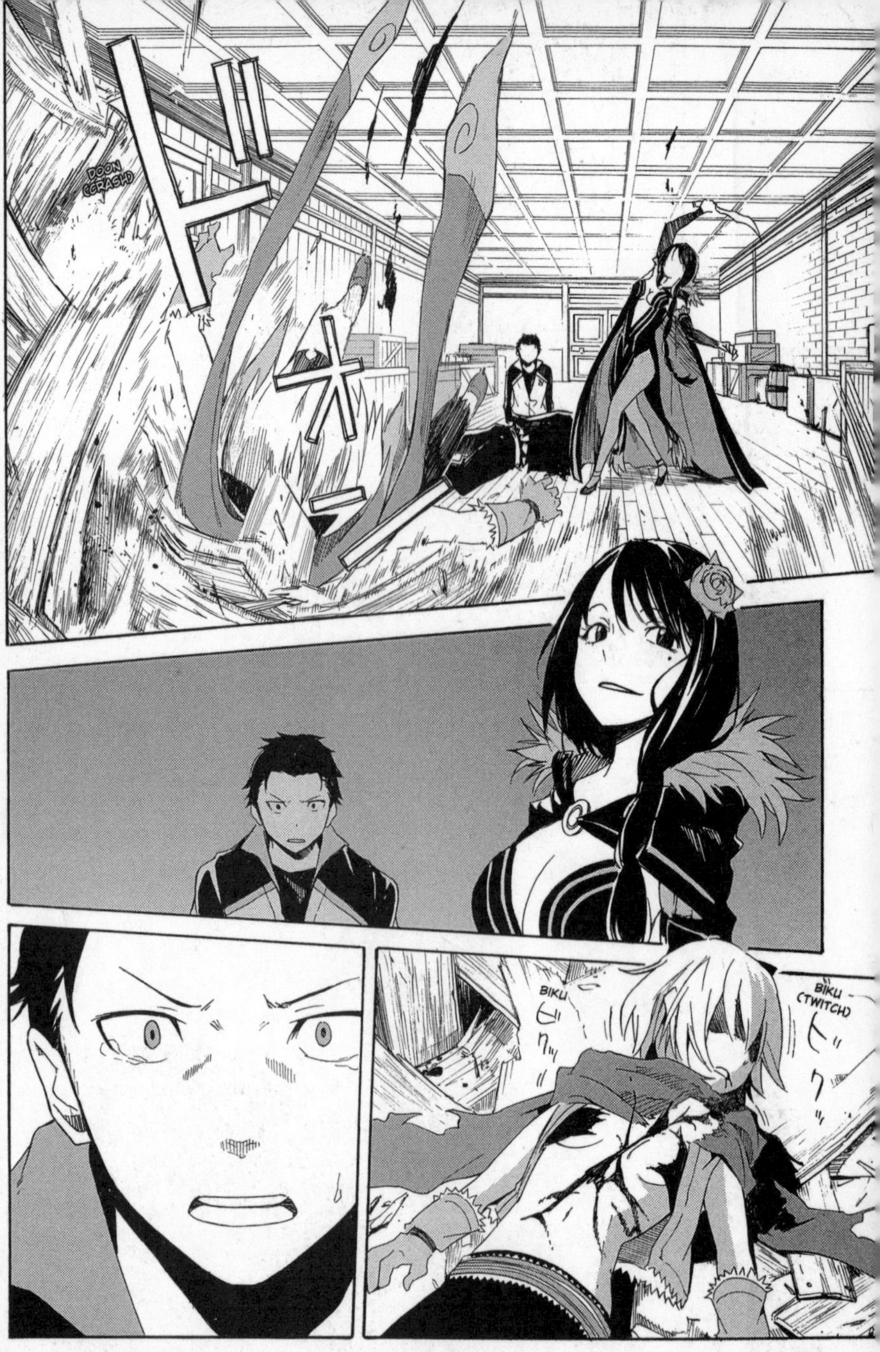
DOON (CRASH)
BIKU (TWITCH)
BIKU

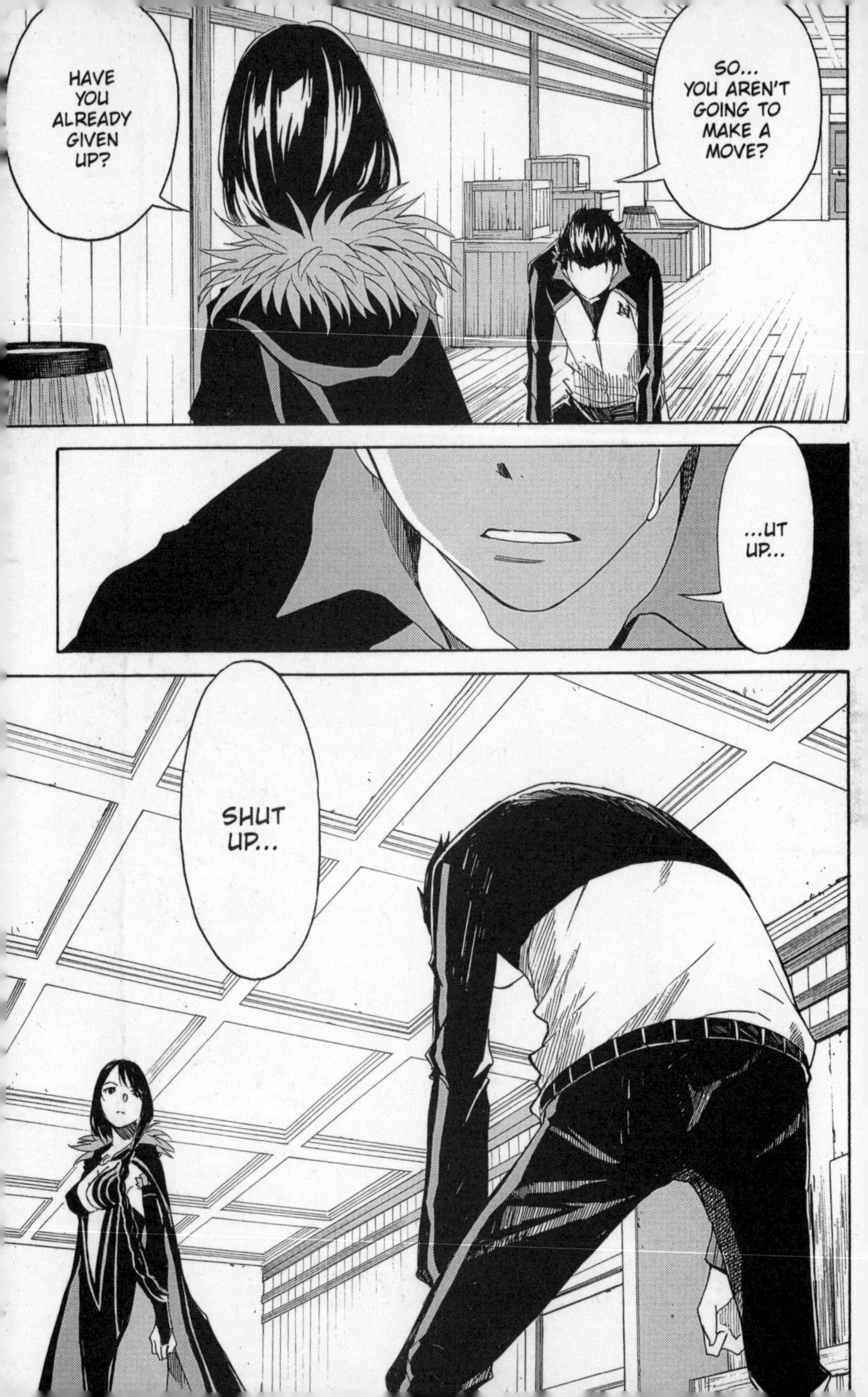
SO... YOU AREN'T GOING TO MAKE A MOVE?
HAVE YOU ALREADY GIVEN UP?
...UT UP...
SHUT UP...

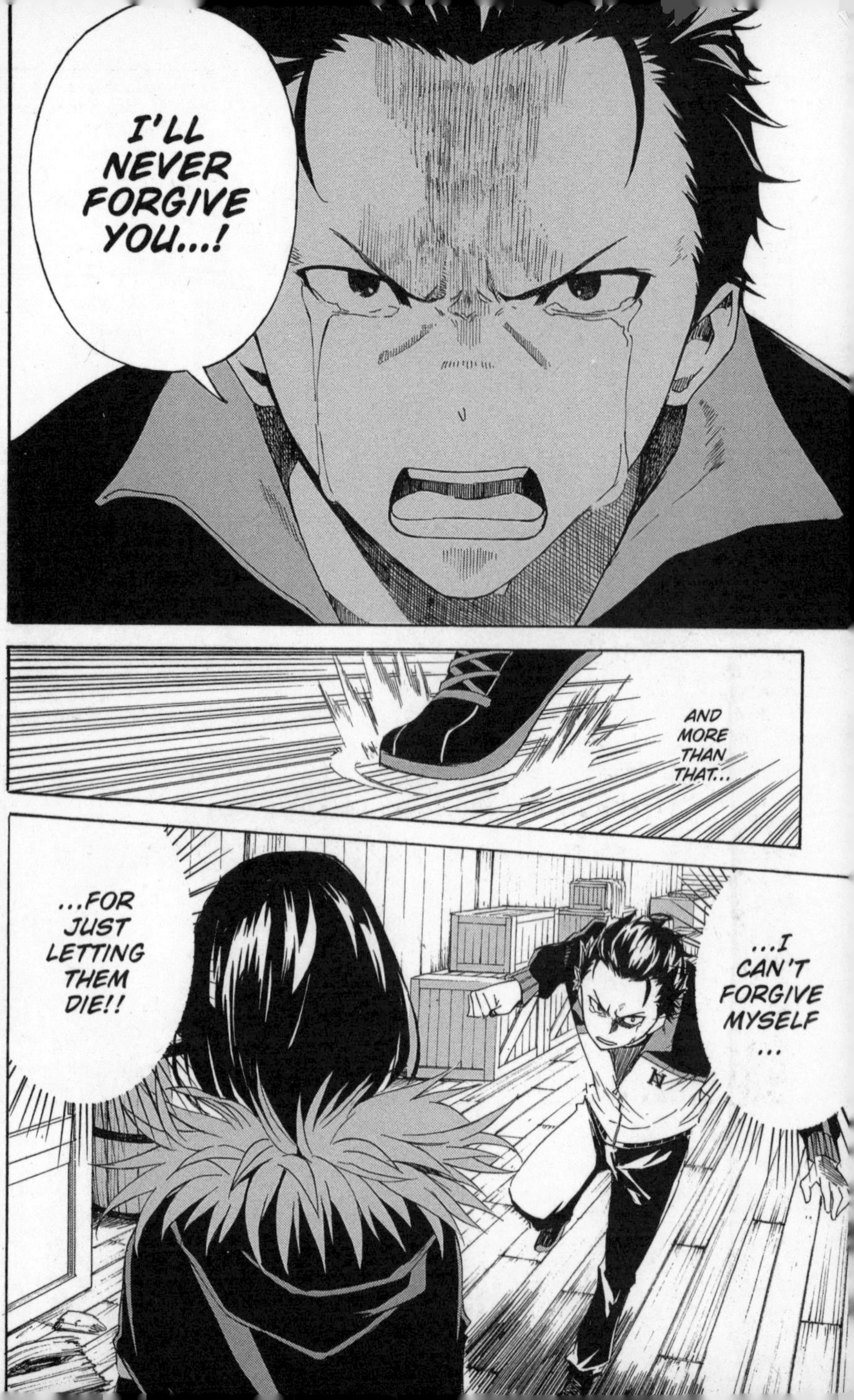
I'LL NEVER FORGIVE YOU...!
AND MORE THAN THAT...
...I CAN'T FORGIVE MYSELF...
...FOR JUST LETTING THEM DIE!!

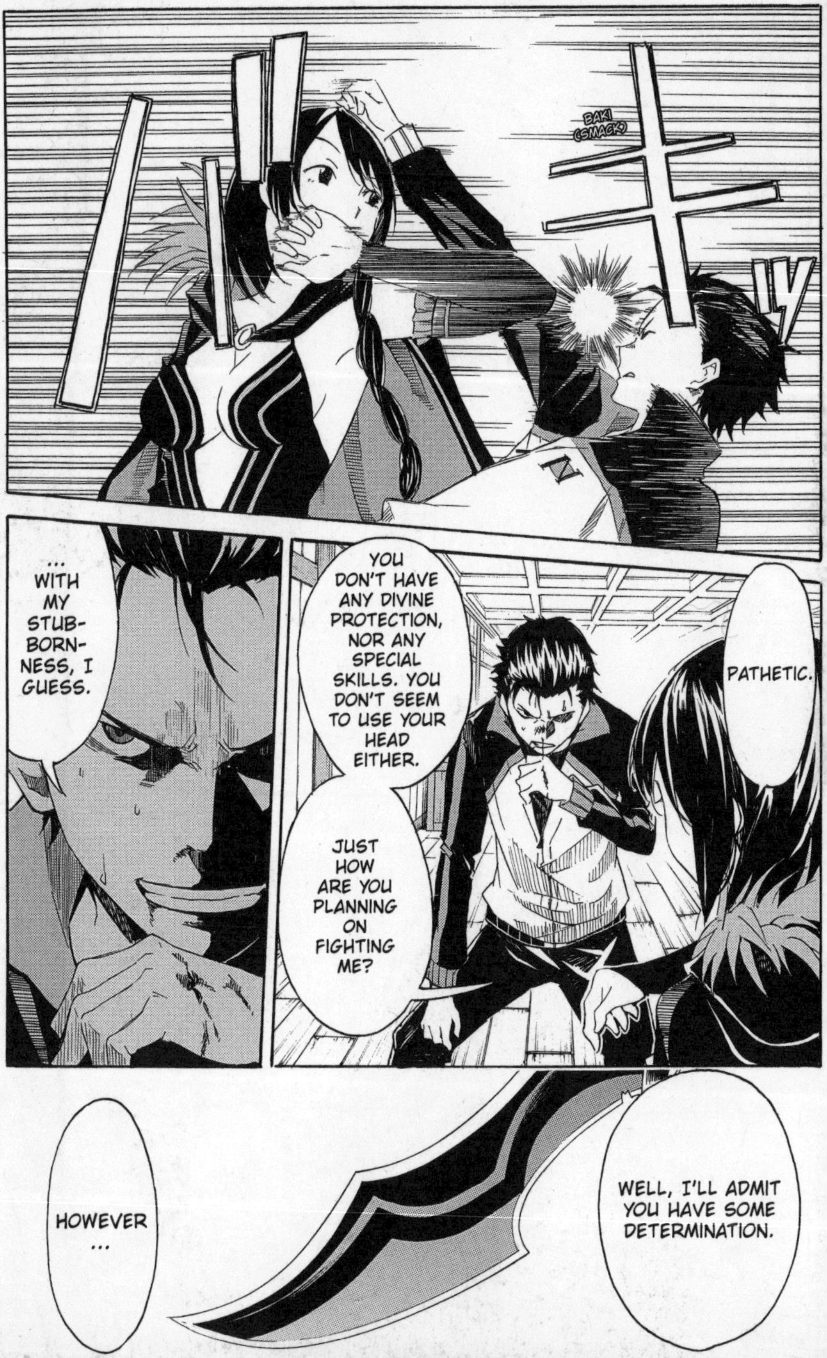
BAKI (SMACK)
PATHETIC.
YOU DON'T HAVE ANY DIVINE PROTECTION, NOR ANY SPECIAL SKILLS. YOU DON'T SEEM TO USE YOUR HEAD EITHER.
JUST HOW ARE YOU PLANNING ON FIGHTING ME?
... WITH MY STUBBORNNESS, I GUESS.
WELL, I'LL ADMIT YOU HAVE SOME DETERMINATION.
HOWEVER ...

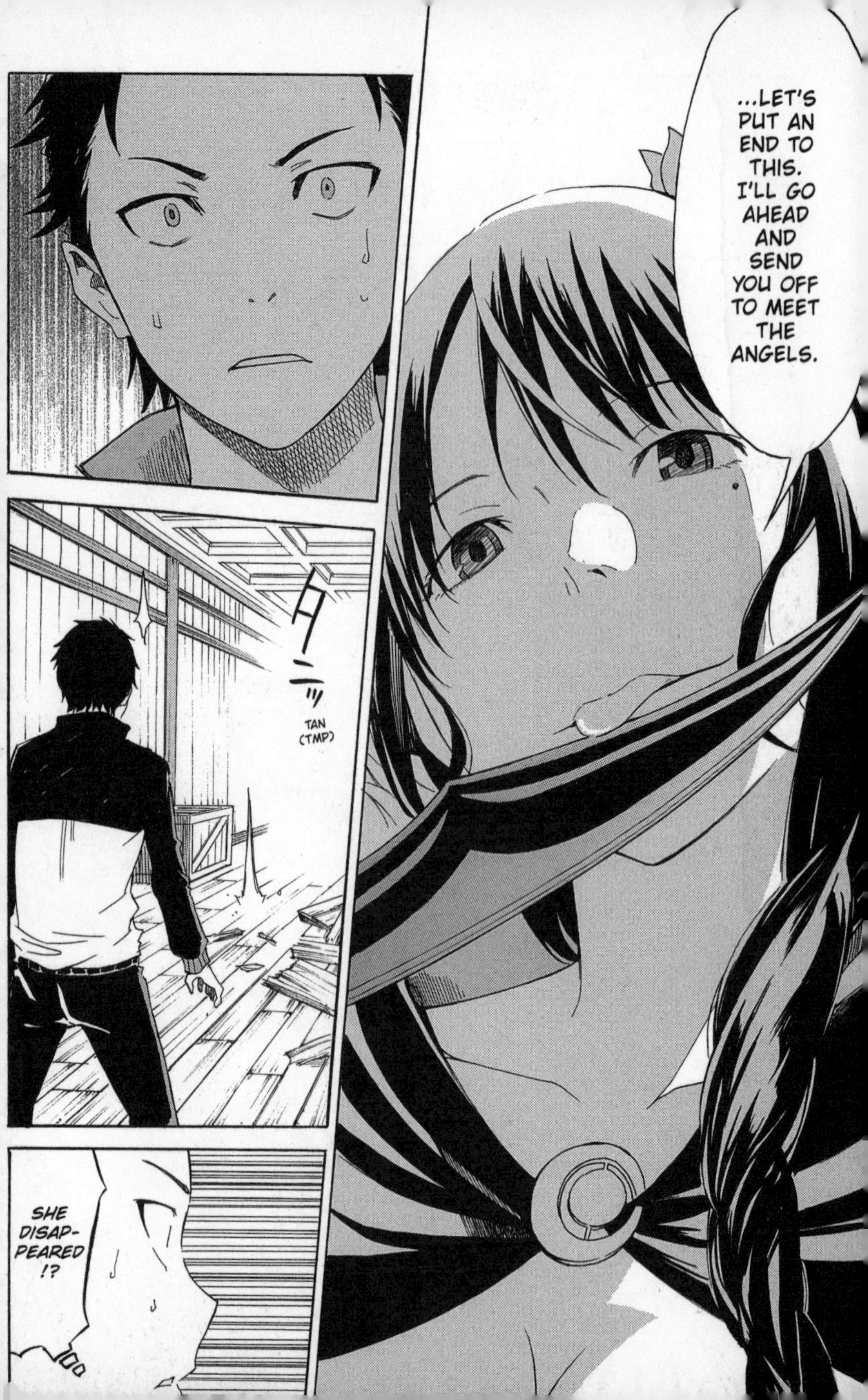
...LET'S PUT AN END TO THIS. I'LL GO AHEAD AND SEND YOU OFF TO MEET THE ANGELS.
タンッ
TAN (TMP)
SHE DISAP-PEARED !?

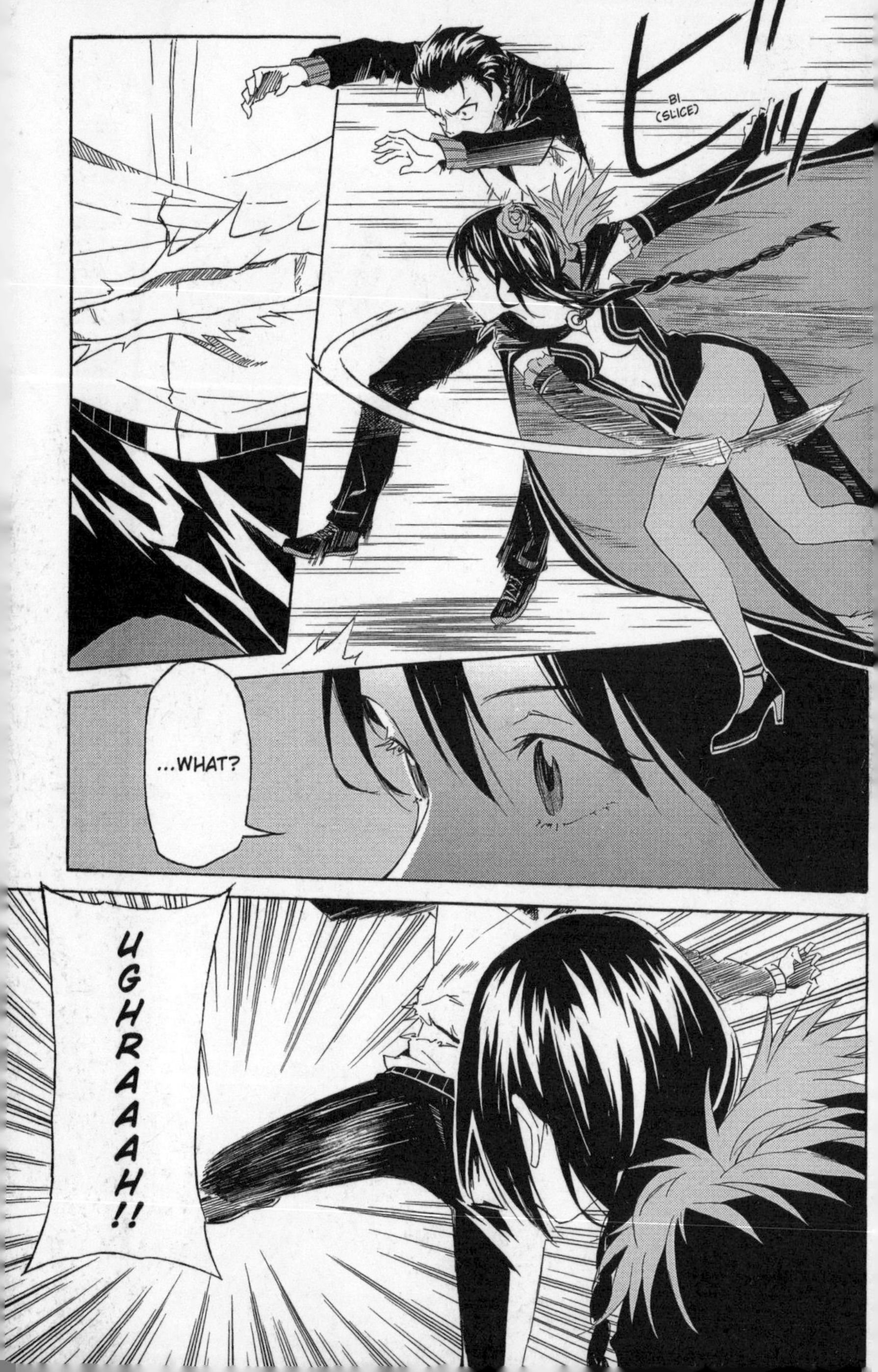
ビ
BI (SLICE)
...WHAT?
UGHRAAAAH!!

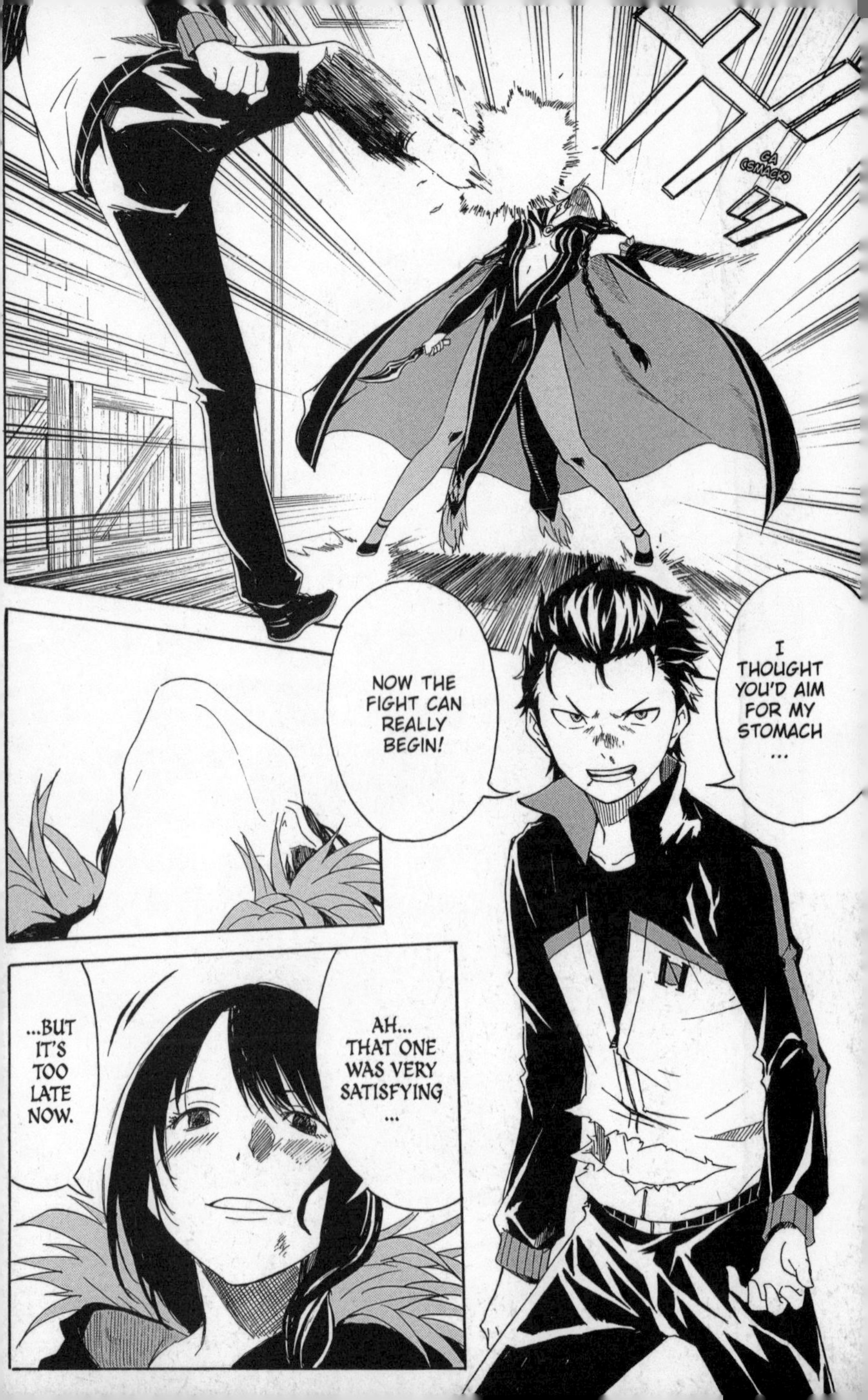
GA
(SMACK)
I THOUGHT YOU'D AIM FOR MY STOMACH ...
NOW THE FIGHT CAN REALLY BEGIN!
AH... THAT ONE WAS VERY SATISFYING ...
...BUT IT'S TOO LATE NOW.

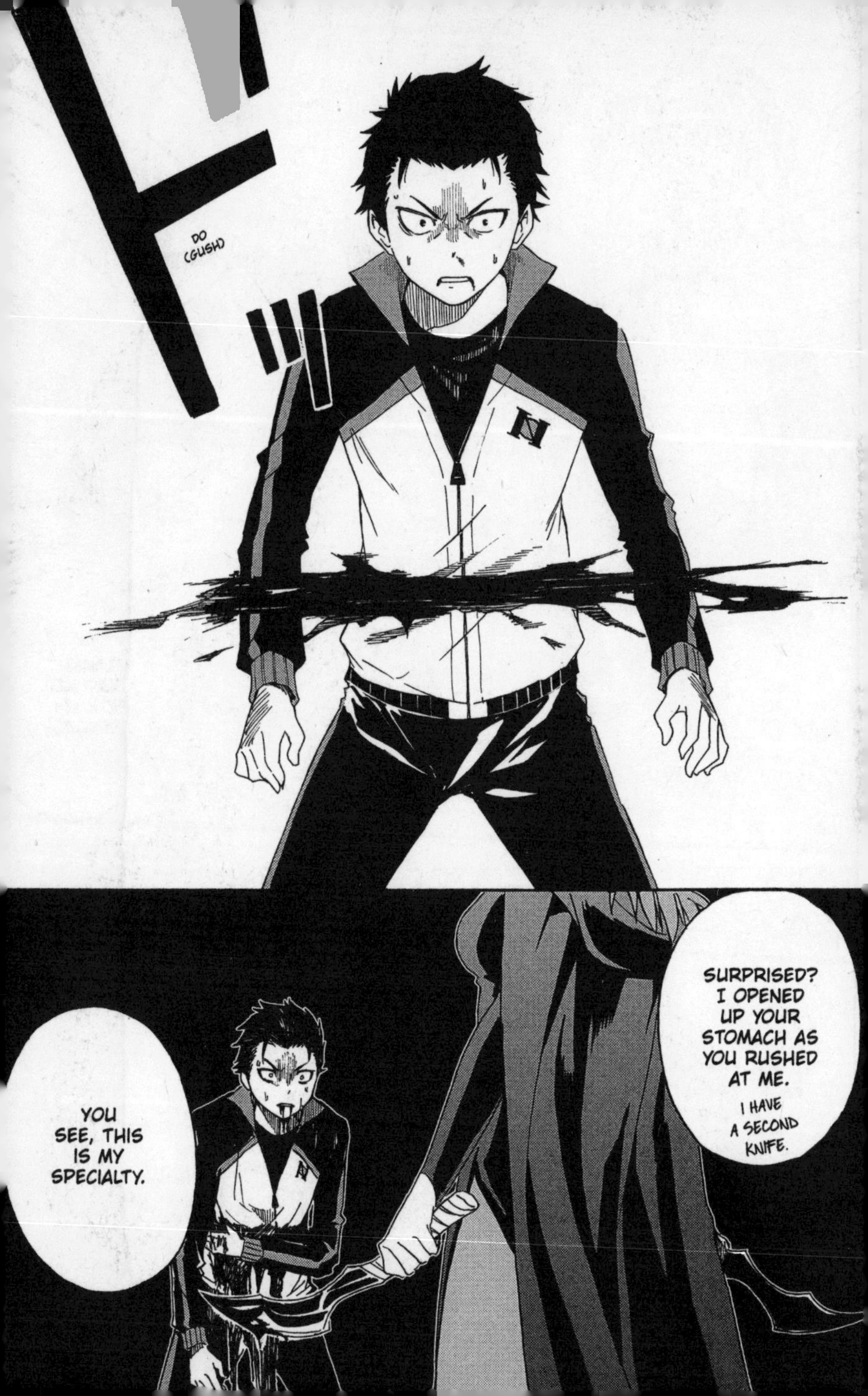
ドッ
DO (GUSH)
SURPRISED? I OPENED UP YOUR STOMACH AS YOU RUSHED AT ME.
I HAVE A SECOND KNIFE.
YOU SEE, THIS IS MY SPECIALTY.

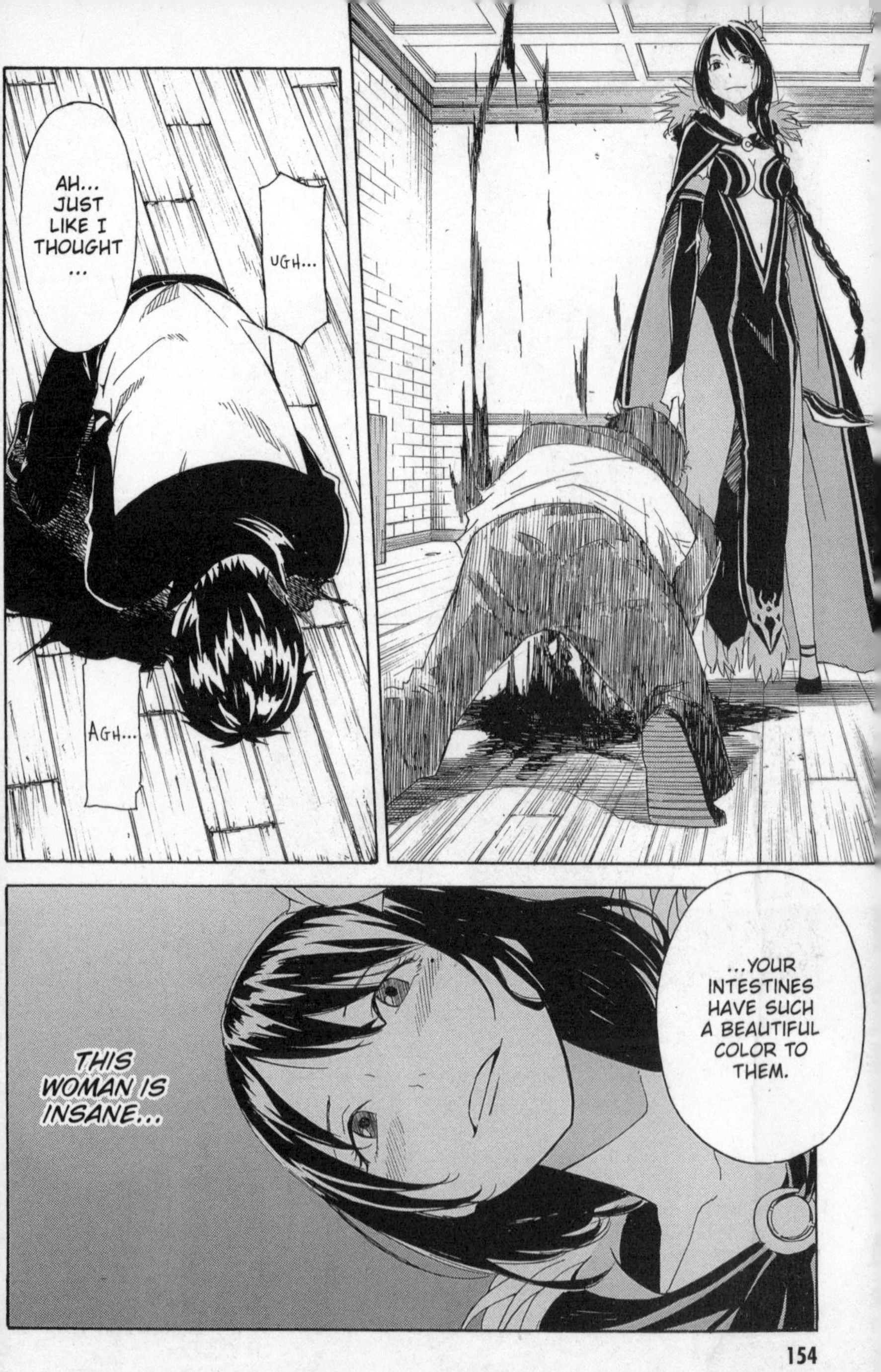
UGH...
AH... JUST LIKE I THOUGHT ...
AGH...
...YOUR INTESTINES HAVE SUCH A BEAUTIFUL COLOR TO THEM.
THIS WOMAN IS INSANE...

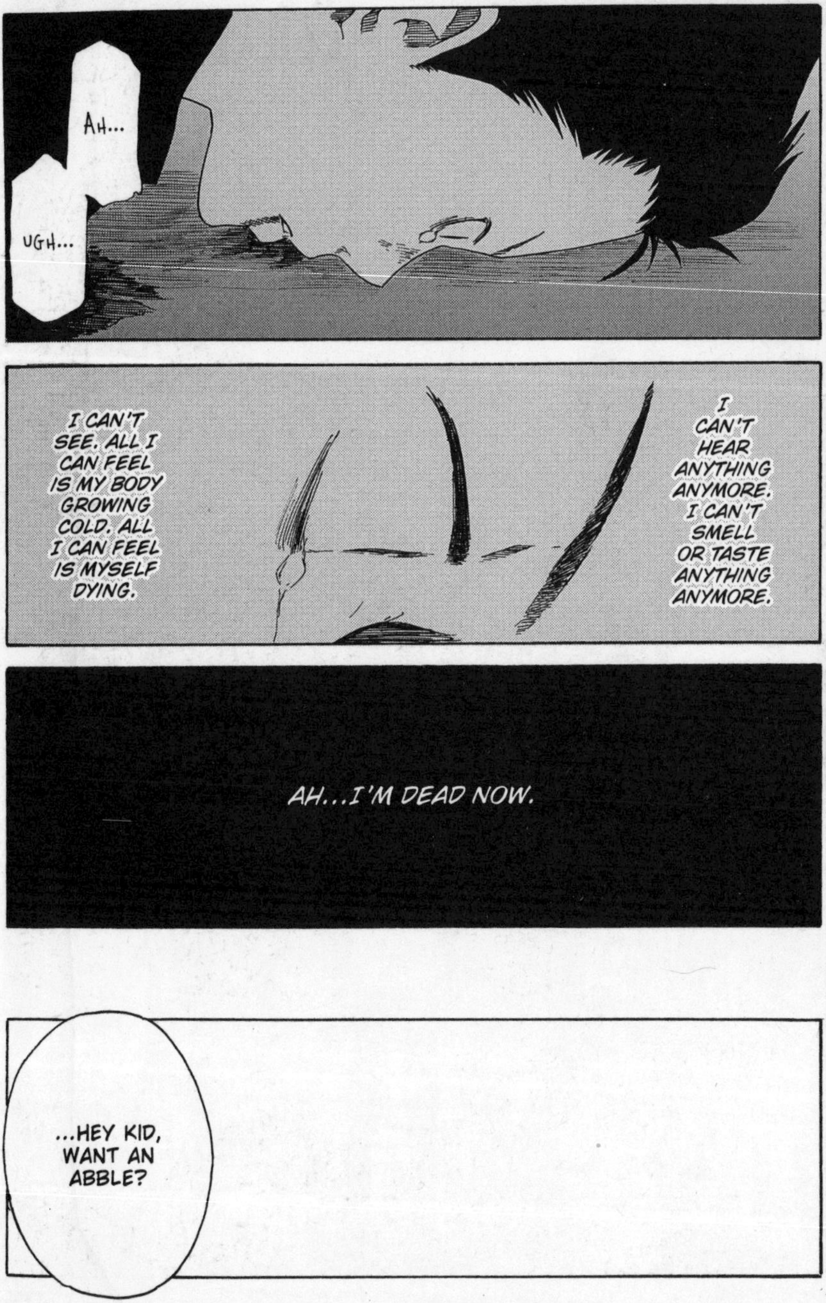
AH...
UGH...
I CAN'T HEAR ANYTHING ANYMORE. I CAN'T SMELL OR TASTE ANYTHING ANYMORE.
I CAN'T SEE. ALL I CAN FEEL IS MY BODY GROWING COLD. ALL I CAN FEEL IS MYSELF DYING.
AH...I'M DEAD NOW.
...HEY KID, WANT AN ABBLE?

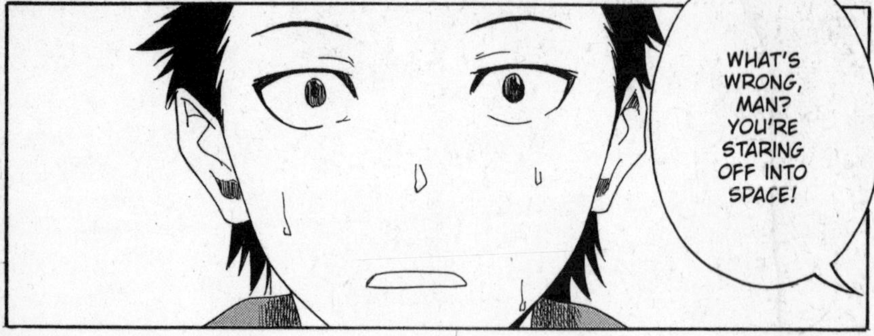
WHAT'S WRONG, MAN? YOU'RE STARING OFF INTO SPACE!

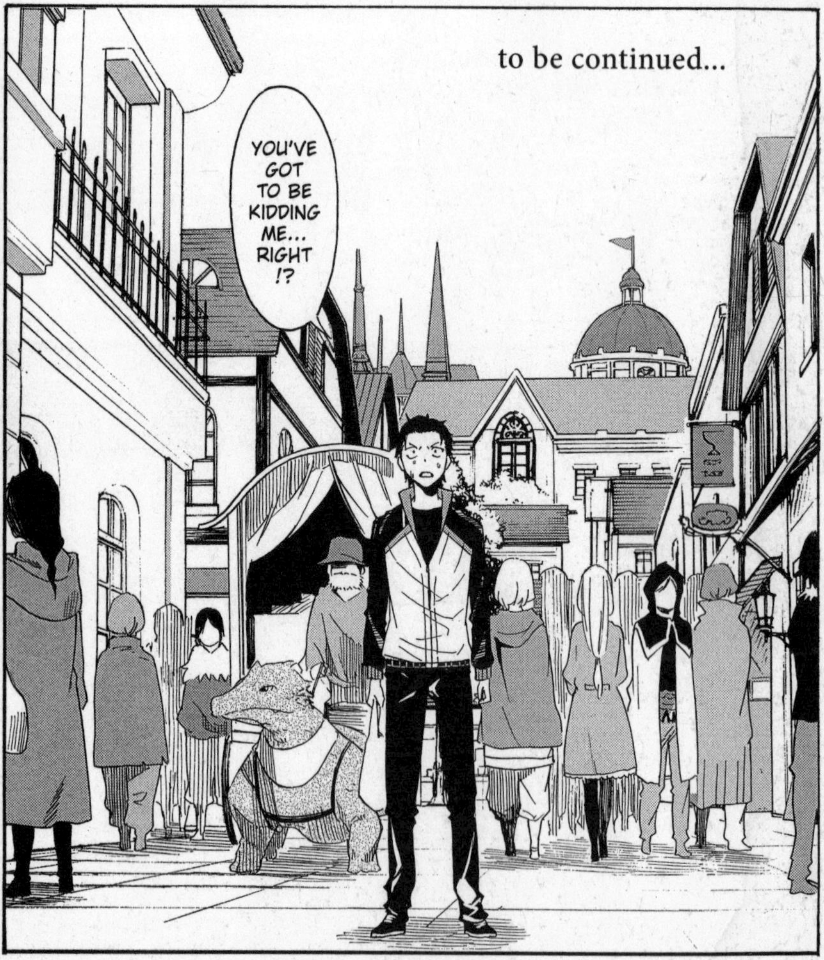
to be continued...
YOU'VE GOT TO BE KIDDING ME... RIGHT !?

Re:ZERO -Starting Life in Another World-

Chapter 1: A Day in the Capital

The only ability Subaru Natsuki gets when he's summoned to another world is time travel via his own death. But to save her, he'll die as many times as it takes.

Illustration by Shinichirou Otsuka
(Character Designer)

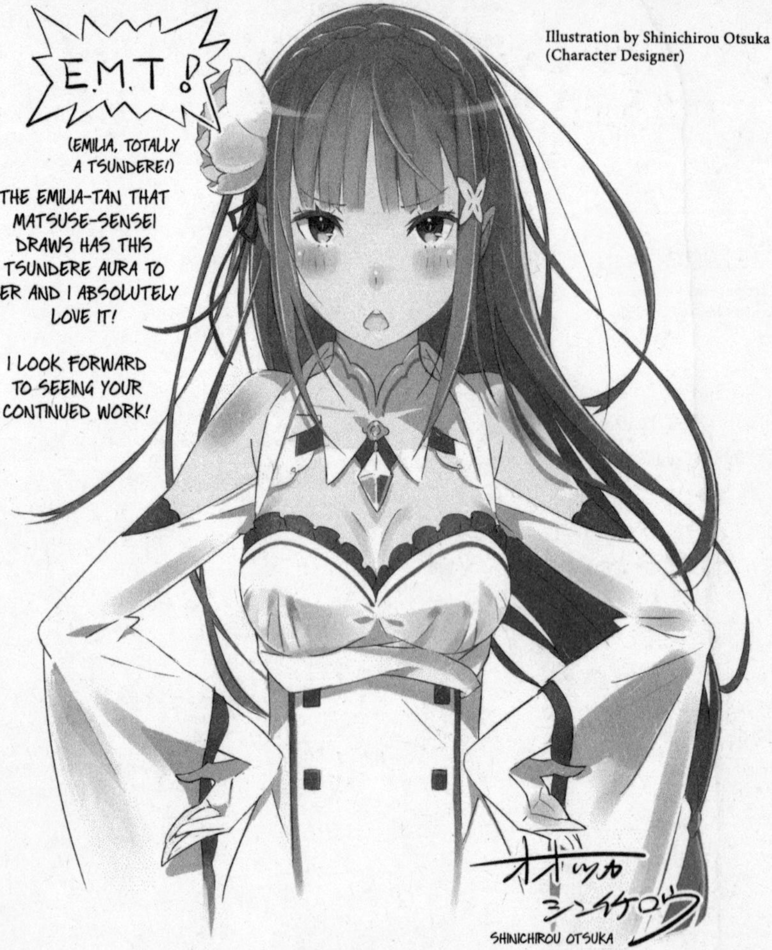
E.M.T!
(EMILIA, TOTALLY A TSUNDERE!)
THE EMILIA-TAN THAT MATSUSE-SENSEI DRAWS HAS THIS TSUNDERE AURA TO HER AND I ABSOLUTELY LOVE IT!
I LOOK FORWARD TO SEEING YOUR CONTINUED WORK!
SHINICHIROU OTSUKA

Re:ZERO -Starting Life in Another World-

Supporting Comments from the Author of the Original Work and the Character Designer

Congratulations, Daichi Matsuse-sensei on the release of Volume 1 of the *Re:ZERO* manga!
Also, thank you! Now, I wonder if it's okay to keep rambling on... (Ha-ha.)
Not only do I get to experience the joy of having my work published in print,
now my story's been made into a comic! I can't hold back my joy, especially when
someone who understands the work as well as Matsuse-sensei is doing the art!
It's amazing to see the characters moving around so cutely! Especially the energetic Felt—
and the intense scene with Rom and Elsa fighting it out was spectacular!
Subaru's death scene also had a lot of impact!
Along with all of the other readers, I'm really looking forward to how Matsuse-
sensei depicts the second half, when the story really starts rolling!
I hope you all are looking forward to the continuation of this death loop story too,
as well as how Matsuse-sensei will portray it!

Author of the Original Work: Tappei Nagatsuki

CONGRATULATIONS ON THE MANGA VERSION OF *RE:ZERO*!

Re:ZERO -Starting Life in Another World-

Supporting Comments
from Makoto Fuugetsu

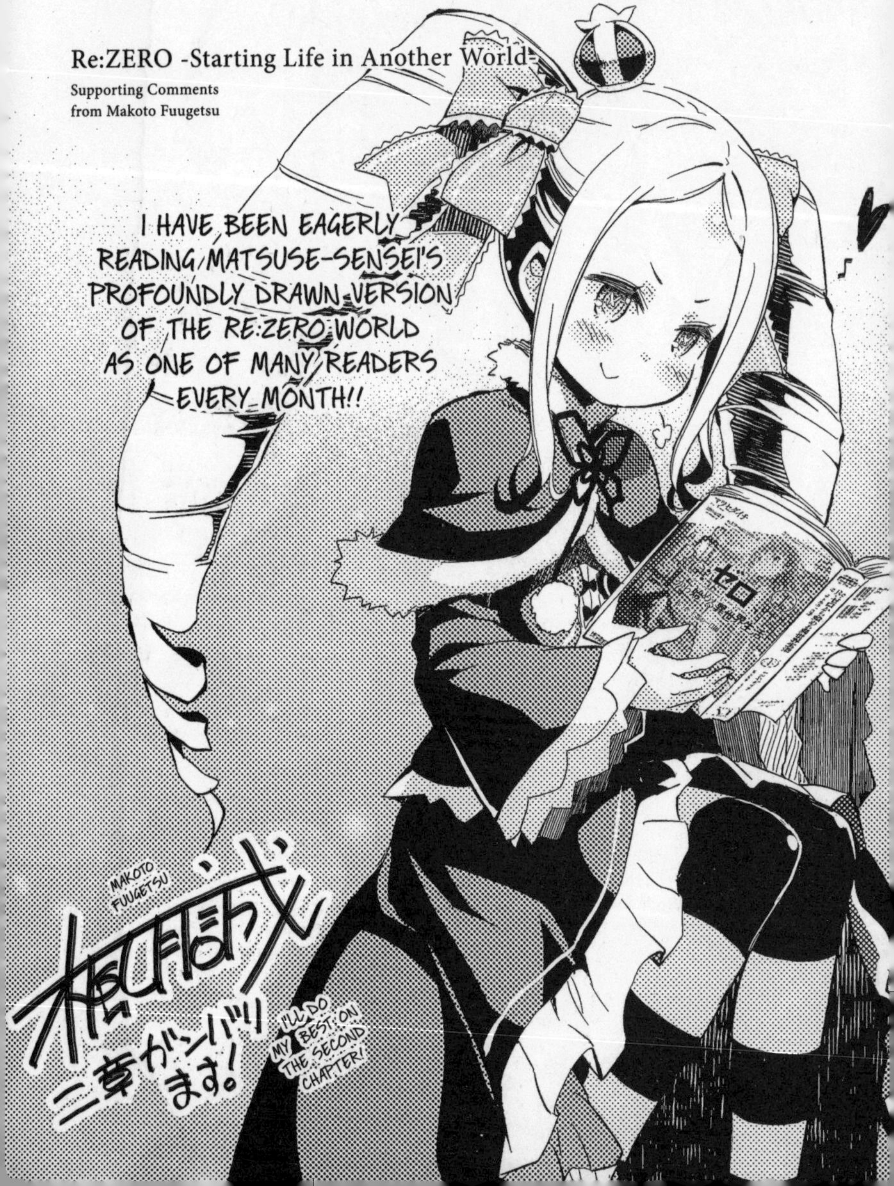
I HAVE BEEN EAGERLY READING MATSUSE-SENSEI'S PROFOUNDLY DRAWN VERSION OF THE RE:ZERO WORLD AS ONE OF MANY READERS EVERY MONTH!!
MAKOTO FUUGETSU
二章ガンバリます!
I'LL DO MY BEST ON THE SECOND CHAPTER!

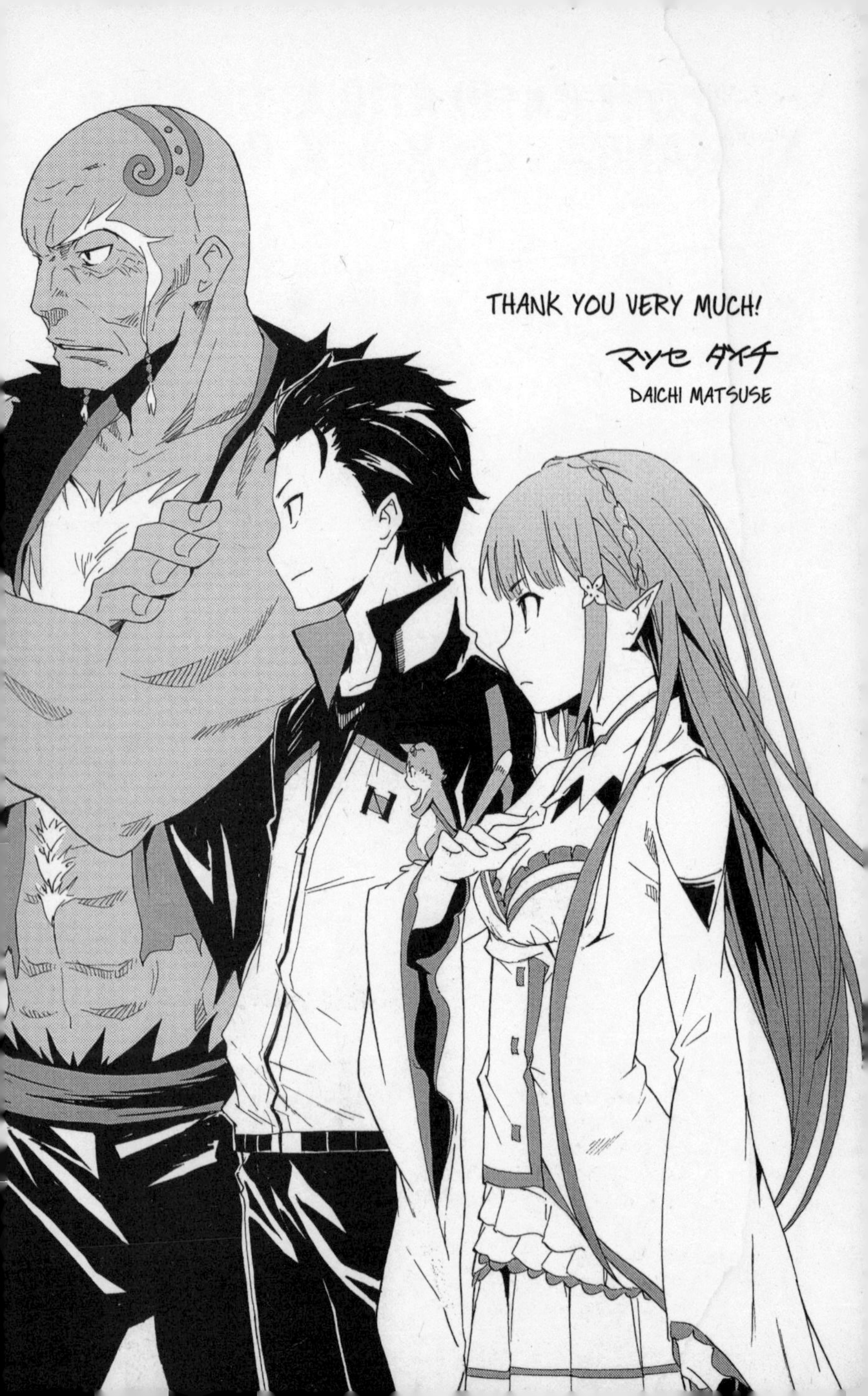
THANK YOU VERY MUCH!
マツセ ダイチ
DAICHI MATSUSE

Re:ZERO -Starting Life in Another World-

Afterword

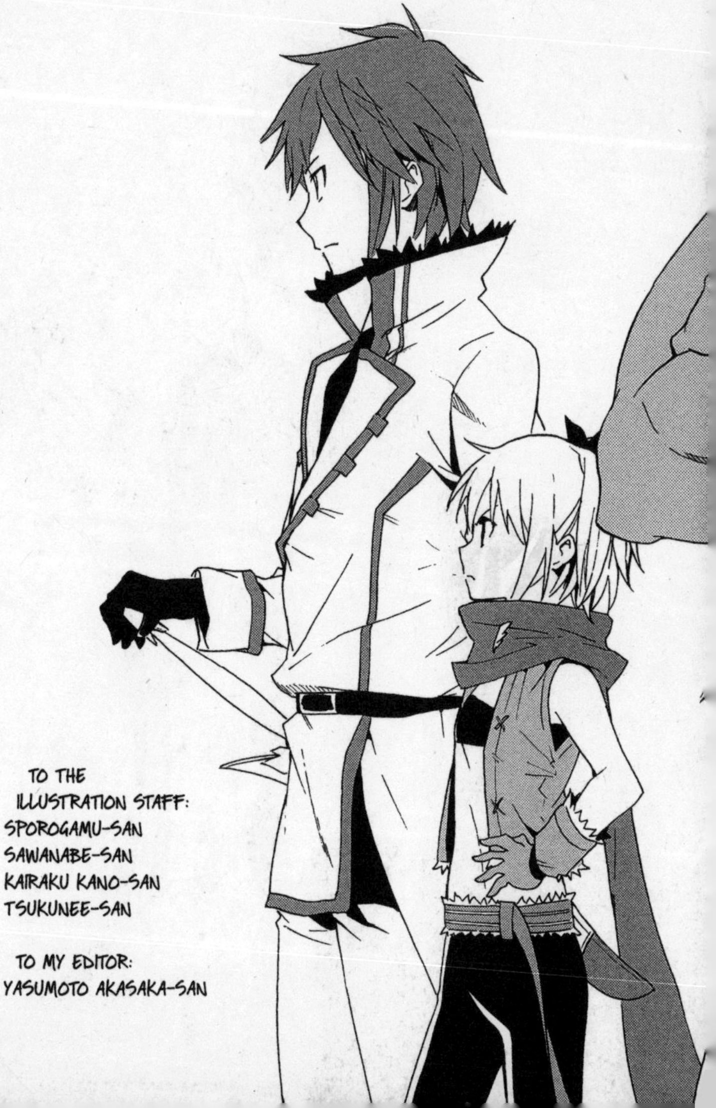
TO THE
ILLUSTRATION STAFF:
SPOROGAMU-SAN
SAWANABE-SAN
KAIRAKU KANO-SAN
TSUKUNEE-SAN
TO MY EDITOR:
YASUMOTO AKASAKA-SAN

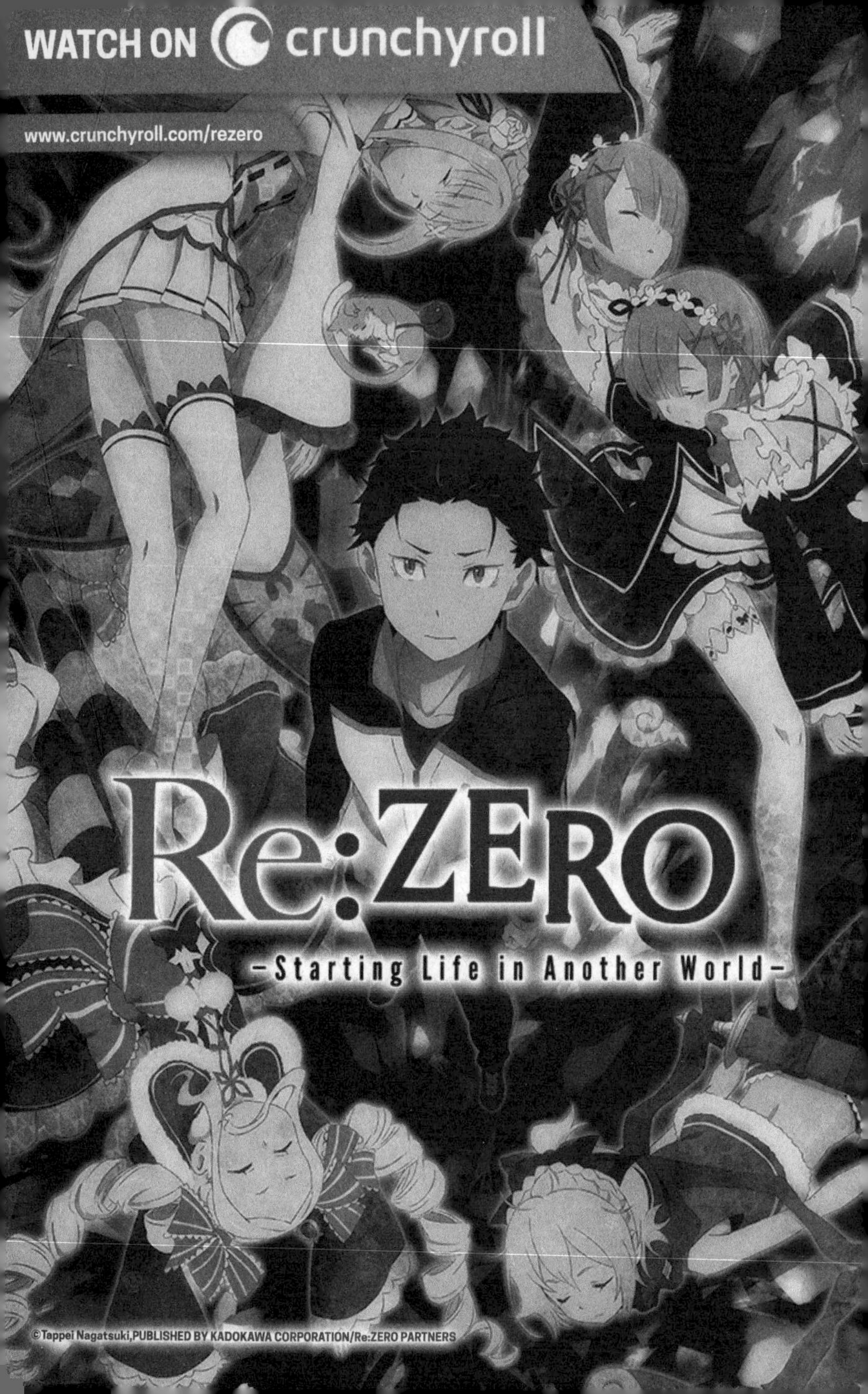
WATCH ON crunchyroll
www.crunchyroll.com/rezero
Re:ZERO
-Starting Life in Another World-
©Tappei Nagatsuki,PUBLISHED BY KADOKAWA CORPORATION/Re:ZERO PARTNERS

RE:ZERO -STARTING LIFE IN ANOTHER WORLD- ①
Chapter 1: A Day in the Capital

Daichi Matsuse
Original Story: **Tappei Nagatsuki**
Character Design: **Shinichirou Otsuka**

Translation: ZephyrRZ
Lettering: Bianca Pistillo

RE:ZERO KARA HAJIMERU ISEKAI SEIKATSU
© Daichi Matsuse / Tappei Nagatsuki 2014
First published in Japan in 2014 by KADOKAWA CORPORATION, Tokyo.
English translation rights arranged with KADOKAWA CORPORATION, Tokyo.
through TUTTLE-MORI AGENCY, Inc., Tokyo.

English translation © 2016 by Yen Press, LLC

Yen Press
1290 Avenue of the Americas
New York, NY 10104

Visit us at yenpress.com
facebook.com/yenpress
twitter.com/yenpress
yenpress.tumblr.com

First Yen Press Edition: July 2016

Yen Press is an imprint of Yen Press, LLC.
The Yen Press name and logo are trademarks of Yen Press, LLC.

Library of Congress Control Number: 2016936537

ISBNs: 978-0-316-31531-9 (paperback)
978-0-316-39851-0 (ebook)
978-0-316-39852-7 (app)

10 9 8 7 6 5 4 3 2 1

BVG

Printed in the United States of America